Hind Swaraj is Mahatma Gandhi's fundamental work. It is key to understanding not only his life and thoughts, but also the politics of South Asia in the first half of the twentieth century. Celebrating 100 years since *Hind Swaraj* was first published in a newspaper, this centenary edition includes a new Preface and Editor's Introduction, as well as a new chapter on 'Gandhi and the "Four Canonical Aims of Life"'. The volume presents a critical edition of the 1910 text of *Hind Swaraj*, fully annotated and including Gandhi's own Preface and Foreword (not found in other editions). Anthony J. Parel sets the work in its historical and political contexts and analyses the significance of Gandhi's experiences in England and South Africa. The second part of the volume contains some of Gandhi's other writings, including his correspondence with Tolstoy and Nehru.

CAMBRIDGE TEXTS IN MODERN POLITICS

EDITORS

John Dunn
King' s College, Cambridge

Geoffrey Hawthorn
Faculty of Social and Political Science, University of Cambridge

Political aspirations in the twentieth century are usually expressed in the political languages of Western Europe and North America. In Latin America, Africa and Asia, however, in the movements of 'national liberation' from colonial rule, in the justification of new states, and in the opposition to such states, these aspirations have also drawn on other traditions, and invented new ones. Outside the West, the languages of modern politics and the ideas these languages embody are nowhere simple, and almost nowhere derivatively Western. But for students and scholars access to the relevant texts is not easy.

Cambridge Texts in Modern Politics are intended to remedy this by providing editions in English (often for the first time) of texts which have been important in the politics of Latin America, Africa and Asia in the later nineteenth century and twentieth century, and which will continue in importance into the twenty-first. The editions will be authoritative and accessible, and can be used with confidence by students and teachers as a source. Each text will be edited by a specialist in the history and politics of the area concerned, whose introduction will explain its context, provenance and significance. Readers will also be provided with a chronology of events, brief biographies of relevant individuals and guides to further reading.

CAMBRIDGE TEXTS IN MODERN POLITICS

M. K. GANDHI

Hind Swaraj and other writings

Portrait of Mahatma Gandhi in London, 1909
© Dinodia Images / Alamy.

M.K. GANDHI

*

Hind Swaraj

and other writings

Centenary Edition

edited by

ANTHONY J. PAREL

University of Calgary, Canada

CAMBRIDGE
UNIVERSITY PRESS

CAMBRIDGE UNIVERSITY PRESS

Cambridge, New York, Melbourne, Madrid, Cape Town, Singapore, São Paulo,
Delhi, Dubai, Tokyo, Mexico City

Cambridge University Press
The Edinburgh Building, Cambridge CB2 8RU, UK

Published in the United States of America by Cambridge University Press, New York

www.cambridge.org
Information on this title: www.cambridge.org/9780521146029

First published 1997
Centenary edition 2009
Reprinted 2010

Printed in the United Kingdom at the University Press, Cambridge

A catalogue record for this publication is available from the British Library

ISBN 978-0-521-19703-8 Hardback
ISBN 978-0-521-14602-9 Paperback

To Rolande

✳

Contents

*

Preface to the centenary edition
*

The centenary of *Hind Swaraj* and recent developments in Gandhi scholarship have prompted the issuing of a revised centenary edition. The discovery that Gandhi had made the theory of the 'canonical aims of life' (*purusharthas*) the framework of his thought is the most significant of these developments (Parel 2006, 2008). The Introduction to this edition takes due note of this. Supporting evidence from Gandhi's writings has been added. They include the Introduction and 'Farewell' to his *Autobiography*, the Introduction to his translation of the *Bhagavad Gita* and his 'Foreword' to *Gokhale's Speeches*. The Gandhi–Nehru dialogue has been updated in view of the new materials that have come to light. Finally, new footnotes on such key topics as 'civilisation', 'technology' and the place of the English language in India have been added. On the debit side, in the interest of keeping this edition within reasonable length, the Gandhi–Wyberg letters and materials relating to Gandhi's 'Quit India' speech have been dropped.

Anthony J. Parel
Calgary
16 March 2009

Acknowledgements

*

In preparing this work for publication I have been very fortunate in receiving generous help from a number of colleagues from different parts of the world – Canada, India, Great Britain, the United States and South Africa – and it gives me great pleasure to express my gratitude to each of them. T. K. N. Unnithan first encouraged me to undertake this project; Christopher A. Bayly, Philip Charrier, Margaret Chatterjee, Dennis Dalton, James Hunt, Bhikhu Parekh and Anil Sethi read various versions of my introduction and notes and suggested ways of improving them. Jayshree Joshi, Nathubhai Joshi, Ramanbhai Modi and C. N. Patel spent many hours with me going over the Gujarati background of Gandhi and *Hind Swaraj*. Umesh Vyas very generously checked the references to the Gujarati text. Richard Bingle, Martin Moir and Edward Moulton helped me find valuable bibliographical data. Irene Joshi of the University of Washington Library found for me the Tolstoy–Taraknath Das material. Hasim Seedat of Durban put at my disposal his private Gandhi library.

I am most grateful to the Shastri Indo-Canadian Institute for a Senior Research Fellowship for the 1990 fall term and to the University of Calgary for a Killam Resident Fellowship for the 1992 winter term. A Visiting Fellowship at Clare Hall, Cambridge, for the 1994 Lent and Easter terms helped me greatly in the final stages of this work. Carolyn Andres of the Department of Political Science, University of Calgary, has been very diligent in getting the typescript ready.

My special thanks go to John Dunn and Geoffrey Hawthorn for inviting me to contribute to their series and for their editorial advice.

John Haslam and Anne Dunbar-Nobes of Cambridge University Press have exercised mahatma-like patience and skill in getting this volume ready for publication. To them my sincere thanks.

It is with great pleasure that I thank the Navajivan Trust and the Nehru Trust for their permission to use materials under their control.

Finally I thank my long-suffering wife Rolande, who, Kasturba-like, endured cheerfully my absences from home on visits to India, South Africa and Cambridge. This work is dedicated to her in partial fulfilment of my family obligations and abiding love.

Editor's introduction to the centenary edition

*

The framing of its argument makes *Hind Swaraj* an original work of modern Indian political philosophy. The argument is that India is in need of a systemic transformation – political, economic, ethical, aesthetic and spiritual. Being systemic in nature and affecting key aspects of national life, these transformations, if they are to succeed, should take place more or less simultaneously. Politics, economics, ethics, aesthetics and spirituality, according to Gandhi, should operate interactively and not in isolation from one another.

The argument for this is made in light of the theory of the 'canonical aims of life' (*purusharthas*) (see below). The use of this Indian intellectual framework makes *Hind Swaraj* the first text of modern Indian political philosophy. As such, it marks the beginning of the emancipation of the modern Indian political mind from dependency on Western frameworks for understanding India and its problems.

The argument hinges on four major themes – nationalism, civilisation, satyagraha and swaraj (the themes of 'machinery' or technology and education being subsumed under civilisation). Before we examine the way they are analysed, we need to mention briefly the book's dialogue form, and the historical identity of those engaged in the dialogue.

GANDHI'S INTERLOCUTORS

The dialogue form is integral to Gandhi's argument, especially since he was seeking to bring about the above-mentioned transformations peacefully, through persuasion, not coercion. He was making his case for dialogue and persuasion at a time when the key thinkers everywhere

xiv

else in the world were advocating transformation through violence, whether revolutionary, terrorist, anarchist or nihilist.

Gandhi's interlocutors in *Hind Swaraj* belong to two camps – those opposed to his philosophy and those in favour of it. Among those opposed, are, first, V. D. Savarkar and Shyamji Krishna Varma, the celebrated Indian Spencerian. They want to transform India into a Hindu ethnic state by the use of violence, including terrorist violence. The second group wants to transform India into a Marxist state through revolutionary violence, Virendranath Chattopadhyaya (a brother of Sarojini Naidu) being its chief proponent. Then there are the Muslim separatists (as opposed to the Muslim nationalists) who want to define India along religious lines. Gandhi does not mention by name any specific member of this group, but its position is duly recognised (*HS*, 50). Finally, among those who are open to Gandhi's ideas are Pranjivan Mehta (Mehta 1911) and the *later* Tarak Nath Das (thanks to whom we have Tolstoy's *Letter to a Hindoo*). Anyone who reads *Hind Swaraj* today would do well to keep in mind the arguments of these interlocutors.

INDIA: A CIVIC NATION

Any sensible project seeking the transformation of India should have a clear idea of what India is and who an Indian is. In other words, it should start with a definition of 'Hind' in *Hind Swaraj*. What is 'Hind'? Is it an inchoate collection of castes and tribes professing different religions and speaking a multitude of languages? Or, is it a civic nation or at least one capable of becoming such? Gandhi opts for the latter. A civic nation, a *praja* as he calls it, is a political community whose basic unit is the individual considered as a bearer of fundamental rights and a subject capable of swaraj – i.e., self-determination and self-development. However, in order for India to become such a nation, a transformation in India's consciousness would be needed.

This puts in question the status of the existing religious conscious-ness. A civic transformation of India can occur only if a transformation in the existing religious consciousness also occurs. Otherwise, there would be unresolved tension between the old religious consciousness and the new civic consciousness. It can be resolved, however, only if a change occurs in religious consciousness. Such a change is precisely what Gandhi advocates – a change from the closed concept of religion to a pluralist concept of the same. The following is its basic premise: 'there is a religion that underlies all religions' (HS, 41).

That is to say, there is religion in the singular and there are religions in the plural. The first represents the essence of religion, viz., the quest for transcendence and the movement of the individual towards the ultimate source of all that is, however one names it, whether Brahman, God, Allah or Truth. The second represents historical religions, such as Hinduism, Christianity, Islam, etc. They are the subspecies of religion in the singular and paths that converge to the same point (HS, 51). They therefore have equal validity and deserve equal respect. From this arises the new Gandhian ethic: *sarva dharma sama bhav* (equal respect for all historical religions).

Gandhi believed that his theory of religious pluralism could reconcile the religious consciousness of every religious group in India with the new all-India civic or secular consciousness. Such reconciliation would permit religious consciousness to yield to civic consciousness in the limited sphere of politics, without undermining the integrity of religion. If such reconciliation were to take place, it would permit every Indian to transcend his or her particular religious consciousness and develop a common all-India secular national consciousness. *Hind Swaraj* advocates precisely the evolution of such a national consciousness: 'those who are conscious of the spirit of nationality do not interfere with one another's religion. If they do, they are not fit to be considered a nation … The Hindus, the Mahomedans, the Parsees and the Christians who have made India their country are fellow countrymen' (HS, 50–1).

Thus, Gandhi emerges as the promoter of an all-India secular national consciousness that is capable of protecting the integrity of the religious consciousness of the followers of every religion. The ethic of his religious pluralism has the resources to accommodate the needs of both religion and civic nationalism. Whereas his concept of

India broadens the vision of humanity in every Indian, Savarkar's concept of India definitely narrows the same. In defining India and Indians in *Hind Swaraj* the way he does, he is responding *in advance* both to Savarkar's *Hindutva: Who is a Hindu?* and to the separatists' theory of India as two nations.

A NEW INDIAN CIVILISATION

Hind Swaraj's next concern is with the transformation of Indian civilisation. The object of Gandhi's famous attack on modern civilisation (more broadly, modernity) is to warn Indians against it. He is not exalting Indian civilisation in its present state of decline (*HS*, 68–9); he is defending only its foundations (*HS*, 64).

To get Gandhi right here, we have to know what he means by civilisation. He means two things by it. First, civilisation is a mode of life that points to the path of duty (*HS*, 65). Secondly, civilisation is a mode of life that pursues what it regards as 'object of life' (*HS*, 34). The original Gujarati term for 'object of life' is the philosophically loaded term *purushartha*. To understand any civilisation whatsoever, then, we have to understand the 'object of life' that it pursues or does not pursue.

The defect of modern civilisation is that it pursues 'bodily-welfare' (*HS*, 34) at the expense of spiritual welfare. In the language of the theory of 'the canonical aims of life', it pursues artha and kama, and neglects dharma and the pursuit of moksha. There is, in other words, a fatal structural imbalance in modernity.

We are reminded here of the body–soul split that occurred in the modern West. Introduced by Descartes, and systematised by Hobbes, this split ultimately presented 'man' as essentially body – an organism moved by voluntary motions, the senses, speech, imagination, science and instrumental reason. Modern science and technology help conquer nature in the interest of 'bodily welfare'. 'He that is to govern a whole nation must see in himself not this man or that particular man but mankind', Hobbes had written (Hobbes 10). By 'mankind' he meant mankind minus the spiritual soul.

Gandhi joins what Hobbes had cut asunder, and restores the soul and its welfare to their rightful place. He wants civilisation – every civilisation – to pay equal attention to the welfare of body and soul.

What is defective in current Indian civilisation is its overemphasis on other-worldliness and asceticism (on moksha) and underemphasis on this worldliness and engagement with the world (on artha). What Indian civilisation needs is a realignment of 'the canonical aims of life', and an end to the predominance of the ascetic tradition over culture.

Here Gandhi has a surprise for us. The new civilisation that India needs has to be mediated by the modern type of political and economic institutions and practices, and Western values such as rights, civil liberty, gender equality, economic development, rule of law, civic nationalism, etc. It would also need a major aesthetic facelift of India affecting public health, hygiene, sanitation, the arts, architecture, and village and urban renewal. He watched with horror modern Indian cities becoming 'the real plague spots' of India (*CW* 9: 479). His concern for aesthetics – should anyone doubt it – is the reason why he asks the readers of *Hind Swaraj* to read Tolstoy's *What is Art?* and Ruskin's *The Political Economy of Art* (*HS*, 118).

What is remarkable in all this is the way Gandhi detaches the Western elements that he takes from their Hobbsean–Benthamite framework and integrates them within the Indian framework of 'the canonical aims of life'.

SATYAGRAHA

Arguably, there is hardly a better example of modern creative Indian political thinking than the thinking that produced satyagraha. Gandhi transforms an existing political practice – civil disobedience – into something new and Indian. He does so in two co-ordinated ways. First, he makes the moral transformation of the civil disobedient a condition for the practice of satyagraha. The four moral virtues – truthfulness, detachment from possessiveness, celibacy and courage – are the means of bringing about the required transformation. Secondly, he makes the

Indian virtue of non-violence (*ahimsa*) a characteristic feature of satyagraha.

Satyagraha established Gandhi's reputation as a political philosopher. What we need to keep in mind, however, is that satyagraha's intellectual framework is Indian, not Western. Its effectiveness depends both on its rational techniques and on the moral transformation of the civil disobedient. Moral praxis and political praxis have to interact with each other.

SWARAJ

The establishment of the truth about swaraj was the real reason for writing *Hind Swaraj* (*HS*, 117). His interlocutors – Savarkar, the Marxists and the separatists – had their own notions of swaraj. By swaraj they meant political swaraj, viz., the replacement of British rule by Indian rule. Gandhi feared this would only result in the continuation of 'English rule without the Englishman' (*HS*, 27). The swaraj that he wanted required not only the political swaraj of the nation but also the spiritual swaraj of the citizen.

Gandhi's swaraj included political swaraj and economic swaraj (*CW* 39: 389), and, as noted, aesthetic renewal as well. However, even this would not be enough to have complete swaraj. To have complete swaraj the citizen would need the enjoyment of spiritual swaraj – inward freedom – achieved through spiritual transformation.

Spiritual swaraj has two component elements: self-discipline and self-transcendence. Self-discipline is praxis that contributes to the management of one's antisocial passions such as greed, covetousness, possessive individualism, the desire to dominate others, untruthfulness and egocentrism. Gandhi's ideal of a self-disciplined person is the *sthithaprajna* of *Gita* (II: 54–72). Self-discipline is difficult to achieve: the best one can do is to move towards it through praxis. The underlying assumption is that humans are morally fragile beings, requiring constant self-correction. Gandhi was fully aware of his own moral fragility, which was the reason why from about 1889 till the end of life he recited the famous

Gita verses mentioned above, daily, morning and evening, in the form of meditative prayer. Self-discipline as self-correction for Gandhi did not mean the asceticism of the old type. The pursuit of self-discipline was consistent with – indeed, it required – the life-affirming pursuit of the 'canonical aims of life'.

Self-transcendence is the pursuit of *spiritual* enlightenment or *tattva jnana* – deep experience of the truth of things. Spiritual exercise such as prayer and meditation prepares one for this. The goal here is the orientation of the acting person towards Truth and freedom from egoism. The spiritual capital accumulated in this experience is invested in action in the fields of politics, economics and social reform. Thus, the pursuit of spiritual transcendence promotes the disinterested service (*seva*) of fellow citizens without regard to their gender, religion, caste or class. The pursuit of self-transcendence too is consistent with the life-affirming pursuit of the 'canonical aims of life'.

The most striking aspect of spiritual swaraj is its *experiential* character. If Indians – especially those aspiring to power – can have an experience of spiritual swaraj, India as a civic nation would be the better for it. Spiritual swaraj is also socially dynamic. Gandhi writes:

> And in this you have a definition of Swaraj. It is Swaraj when we learn to rule ourselves. It is, therefore, in the palm of our hands. Do not consider this Swaraj to be a dream. Here there is no idea of sitting still. The Swaraj that I wish to picture before you and me is such that, after we have once realised it, we will endeavor to the end our lifetime to persuade others to do likewise. But such Swaraj has to be experienced by each one for himself. (*HS*, 71)

He returns to the idea of experience later in the text: only those who have experienced 'the force of the soul within themselves' would be able to enjoy full swaraj, and liberate themselves completely from the impact of colonialism and modernity (*HS*, 114).

To repeat, the combination of political swaraj and spiritual swaraj should be sought in action. That being the case, swaraj should mean not only the enjoyment of one's rights but also respect for the rights of others. Above all, it should mean national reconciliation of religions, castes, tribes and classes, and the adoption of civic nationalism in place of ethnic nationalism, the Marxist state and the separatist religious state. Gandhi does not present his case for swaraj as an option among many – among the notions of swaraj that his interlocutors propose. He presents his swaraj alone as true swaraj, and rejects the other three as untruthful. There is no ducking or weaving in his response to his interlocutors. He believes he has truth on his side.

This is also Gandhi's response to the followers of modern Western political philosophy, which traces its origin to Machiavelli and Hobbes. Those who rely *only* on this philosophy tend to believe that the split between body and soul is necessary and final, that the pursuit of spiritual transcendence is anti-human and anti-modern, and that the modern state can justify virtually any end that its pursues. *Hind Swaraj* questions the philosophical foundations of all this.

GANDHI'S THEORY OF THE 'CANONICAL AIMS OF LIFE' (*PURUSHARTHAS*)

What gives coherence and originality to the analysis of the four themes discussed above is the updated theory of the 'canonical aims of life' (*purusharthas*). *Purushartha*, as we have seen, means 'aim of life'. Humans are life-affirming, world-accepting, goal-setting and goal-pursuing beings. They pursue ethical integrity (dharma), wealth and political power (artha), pleasure (kama) and spiritual transcendence (moksha). The co-ordinated pursuit of these goals is indispensable for a well-lived life. Each goal has its validity and relative autonomy. At the same time, they, taken together, constitute a system of goals. This means, among other things, that a balance should be maintained in their pursuit. No one goal should be allowed to dominate the system. Their pursuit in unison constitutes the good life.

According to *Hind Swaraj*, the pursuit of 'the canonical aims of life' should inform the lives of individuals, nations and civilisations. Gandhi is being an innovator here: Indian philosophy for centuries had overemphasised the goal of moksha and underemphasised that of artha. He seeks to bring about a realignment of the 'canonical aims' and restore politics and economics (artha) to their legitimate and honourable place in the system of goals.

The depth of the philosophy of *Hind Swaraj* can be seen only when studied within the framework of his theory of the 'canonical aims of life'. Let us review briefly how it handles the four major themes mentioned above. To take civic nationalism first: it is a secular force. It belongs to the sphere of artha. Yet it is supposed to operate in collaboration with the ethic of religious pluralism, which belongs to the sphere of dharma. Similarly, civilisation, the second theme: it seeks bodily welfare, which belongs to the sphere of artha and kama. At the same time, it should do so in conjunction with the pursuit of the welfare of the soul, which belongs to the spheres of dharma and moksha. Satyagraha is a secular praxis and, as such, it belongs to the sphere of artha. Yet in Gandhi's theory, it relies for its success on the ethics of certain moral virtues, which belong to the sphere of dharma. Finally, swaraj: it comprises political, economic, aesthetic, ethical, and spiritual elements. That is to say, swaraj requires the interactive pursuit of all the great goals of life.

Hind Swaraj presents a comprehensive vision of human existence. Critics sometimes tend to emphasise one or other of the component parts of Gandhi's philosophy. This is true especially in the cases of his philosophy of non-violence, philosophy of religion and philosophy of politics. Such approaches are legitimate so long as they do not obscure his overall vision of life, with its emphasis on balance between the spiritual and the secular. His philosophy represents something that is greater than the sum of its parts. Readers of *Hind Swaraj* should aim to capture that 'something'.

GANDHI'S CURRENT 'INTERLOCUTORS'

A century on, the intellectual descendents of the original interlocutors of *Hind Swaraj* still challenge its philosophy. The ideological heirs of

Savarkar – the Rashtriya Swayam Sevak Sangh, the Vishva Hindu Parishad and the Bajrang Dal – want to turn India into an ethnic state. To this end, they are ready to use open violence against Indian Muslims, Christians, the Tribals and Scheduled Castes. Secondly, there are the Indian Marxists, Maoists and followers of Gramsci, who now dream of transforming India into a pale copy of China. They feel neither embarrassment nor compunction in adding insult to injury to Gandhi. Finally, there are the jihadists, who, in a bid to outflank nationalist Muslims, want to bring India into the orbit of what they call the new universal caliphate. In this, they rely on the teachings of such figures as Abul Ala Maududi (1903–79) and even Abul Hasan Ali Nadwi (1913–99).

Today's readers of *Hind Swaraj*, emulating Gandhi, have an obligation, I believe, to engage their interlocutors in serious intellectual dialogue. It is not enough to say that Gandhi, unlike them, interprets India from within a Gandhian framework. It is necessary to demonstrate that a Gandhian framework is better suited to bring about India's transformation than are their frameworks. And the demonstration has to be both theoretical and practical. It is not enough to know Gandhi's philosophy; it is necessary to put that knowledge to work for the actual transformation of society.

HOW TO READ *HIND SWARAJ* TODAY

V. S. Naipaul, the Nobel laureate, makes the startling claim that Indians love to talk about *Hind Swaraj* but not to read it. 'The book would not be read in India not even by scholars (and still hasn't been), but its name would often be taken as a milestone in the independence struggle, and it would be cherished as a holy object' (Naipaul 2008, 166–7). Whether Naipaul is right or not, his observation raises the question of how to read this text today. There are different ways of reading it. First, it should be read in its context and in our context, taking into account the arguments of both his original and current interlocutors. Secondly, it should be read in its Gujarati and English versions. For it is a bilingual and bicultural text that connects Indian thought and Western thought in a very original way. Thirdly, it should be read the way Gandhi read worthwhile books. He tells us in his *Autobiography* that his active life left him little time for reading. That only made him read all the more thoroughly what he did read. Thorough reading meant taking notes, and making even a paraphrase of what he read. We have records of such paraphrases, including those of Plato's *Apology* and Thoreau's *On the Duty of Civil Disobedience*. The most famous of these is of course *Sarvodaya*, his paraphrase of Ruskin's *Unto This Last*. And as the *Autobiography* tells us, he read this last work transformatively. It made him change his life.

Perhaps there is no better way of paying tribute to Gandhi in the centenary year of *Hind Swaraj* than reading it transformatively. If Indians can read it the way he read *Unto This Last*, India's transformation, to which this text is dedicated, is likely to come about peacefully and quickly.

Editor's introduction to the 1997 edition
*

Hind Swaraj is Gandhi's seminal work. It is also a work which he himself translated from Gujarati into English: no other work of his, not even the *Autobiography* (translated by his secretary), enjoys this distinction. As such, the English text of this work, which is being presented here, possesses an authority all of its own. It was this text that Tolstoy and Romain Rolland, Nehru and Rajaji read and commented upon. It was through this, not the Gujarati text, that he hoped, as he put it, 'to use the British race' for transmitting his 'mighty message of *ahimsa*' to the rest of the world (Watson 1969, 176). And it was to this text that he returned throughout his career as if to the source of his inspiration.

Hind Swaraj is the seed from which the tree of Gandhian thought has grown to its full stature. For those interested in Gandhi's thought in a general way, it is the right place to start, for it is here that he presents his basic ideas in their proper relationship to one another. And for those who wish to study his thought more methodically, it remains the norm by which to assess the theoretical significance of his other writings, including the *Autobiography*. It can also save them from the danger of otherwise getting drowned in the vast sea of Gandhian anthologies. No wonder that it has been called 'a very basic document for the study of Gandhi's thought' (M. Chatterjee 1983, 89), his 'confession of faith' (Nanda 1974, 66), 'a rather incendiary manifesto' (Erikson 1969, 217), 'a proclamation of ideological independence' (Dalton 1993, 16) and 'the nearest he came to producing a sustained work of political theory' (Brown 1989, 65). It has been compared to such diverse works as Rousseau's *Social Contract* (Heard 1938, 450), the *Spiritual Exercises* of St Ignatius Loyola (Catlin 1950, 215) and chapter IV of St Matthew or St Luke (*The Collected Works of Mahatma Gandhi* (hereafter cited as *CW*)

10: viii). This last comparison, though its allusion to Jesus would have embarrassed Gandhi, still merits attention. Just as it is in these Gospel chapters that we find Jesus first announcing his messianic mission, so it is in *Hind Swaraj* that we find Gandhi first announcing his own life-mission. This is nothing other than showing the way for the moral regeneration of Indians and the political emancipation of India.

The very composition of *Hind Swaraj* has something of the heroic about it. It was written in ten days, between 13 and 22 November 1909, on board the ship *Kildonan Castle* on the author's return trip from England to South Africa, after what proved to be an abortive lobbying mission to London. The whole manuscript was written on the ship's stationery, and the writing went on at such a furious pace that when the right hand got tired, Gandhi continued with the left: forty of the 275 manuscript pages were written by the left hand. And he wrote as if under inspiration. In the entire autograph, only sixteen lines have been scratched out and only a few words changed here and there (Prabhudas Gandhi 1957, 87–8). Critics speak of Gandhi's 'profound experience of illumination' on board the *Kildonan Castle* and compare it to Rousseau's on the road to Vincennes (Murry 1949, 424). At any event, Gandhi himself felt that he had produced 'an original work', for that was how he described it in a letter to his friend Hermann Kallenbach, the first to know about the book's completion (Gandhi 1909–46, 1, 94).

GANDHI'S INTENTIONS

The book is addressed to a mixed audience: the expatriate Indians greatly attracted to terrorism and political violence, the Extremists and Moderates of the Indian National Congress, the Indian nation and 'the English' (ch. xx). By the Indian nation Gandhi means ordinary Indians, irrespective of their religious, linguistic, regional or caste differences, as well as the new emerging middle class, referred to in the text as 'doctors', 'lawyers' and 'the wealthy'. And by 'the English' he means both the British ruling class living in India and Britons living in Great Britain.

As to why he wrote the book, there was first of all the question of an inner illumination and the consequent urge to communicate. 'The thing was brewing in my mind', he wrote to his friend Henry Polak a month before the actual writing. 'I, therefore feel that I should no longer withhold from you what I call the progressive step I have taken mentally ... After all they [the ideas] are not new but they have only now assumed such a concrete form and taken a violent possession of me.' The Foreword reflected the same sense of urgency: 'I have written because I could not restrain myself.' Years later he recalled the experience: 'Just as one cannot help speaking out when one's heart is full, so also I had been unable to restrain myself from writing the book since my heart was full' (*CW* 32: 489).

Secondly, he wanted to clarify the meaning of swaraj, the concept that provides the theoretical framework of the book. This is done by introducing a distinction between swaraj as self-government or the quest for home rule or the good state, and swaraj as self-rule or the quest for self-improvement.

Thirdly, he felt it necessary to respond specifically to the ideology of political terrorism adopted by the expatriates. The book was written in order to show that they were following 'a suicidal policy'. He recalled in 1921 how on his 1909 visit to London he had come into contact with 'every known Indian anarchist' there, and how he had wanted to write a book 'in answer to the Indian school of violence'. 'I felt that violence was no remedy for India's ills, and that her civilisation required the use of a different and higher weapon for self-protection' (*CW* 19: 277).

Fourthly, Gandhi was anxious to teach the Indians that 'modern civilisation' posed a greater threat to them than did colonialism. They appeared to him to take it for granted that modern civilisation was an unmixed blessing, and colonialism an unmixed evil, forgetting that colonialism itself was a product of modern civilisation. 'My countrymen, therefore, think', states the Preface, 'that they should adopt modern civilisation and modern methods of violence to drive out the English.' This point is further elaborated in the Preface to the second Gujarati edition of 1914: 'it is not the British that are responsible for the

misfortunes of India but we who have succumbed to modern civilisation ... The key to an understanding of *Hind Swaraj* lies in the idea that
worldly pursuits should give way to ethical living. This way of life has no
room for violence in any form against any human being, black or white'
(*CW* 12: 412). And in 1929 he came back to the same idea: 'The Western
civilisation which passes for civilisation is disgusting to me. I have given
a rough picture of it in *Hind Swaraj*. Time has brought no change in it'
(*CW* 40: 300). And in 1939: 'The key to understand that incredibly simple
(so simple as to be regarded foolish) booklet is to realise that it is not an
attempt to go back to the so-called ignorant, dark ages. But it is an
attempt to see beauty in voluntary simplicity, [voluntary] poverty and
slowness. I have pictured that as my ideal' (*CW* 70: 242). 'I would ask you
to read *Hind Swaraj* with my eyes', he exhorts the reader, 'and see therein
the chapter on how to make India non-violent. You cannot build non-
violence on a factory civilisation, but it can be built on self-contained
villages' (*CW* 70: 296).

Fifthly, he wanted to contribute towards the reconciliation of Indians
and Britons. This is evident from the 'exhortation' to 'the English' in
chapter xx. Modern civilisation posed as much a problem for them as it
did for the Indians. 'At heart you belong to a religious nation', he tells
them. And the desire for reconciliation can come about 'only when the
root of our relationship is sunk in a religious soil' (ch. xx).

Finally, Gandhi believed that through *Hind Swaraj* he would be able to
give Indians a practical philosophy, an updated conception of dharma,
that would fit them for life in the modern world. In the past dharma was
tied to a hierarchical system of duties and obligations and to the pres-
ervation of status. It gave little or no attention to the idea of democratic
citizenship. Gandhi felt that the time had come to redefine the scope of
dharma to include notions of citizenship, equality, liberty, fraternity
and mutual assistance. And in *Hind Swaraj* he presents in simple language his notion of such a redefined dharma, the vision of a new Indian
or Gandhian civic humanism, one that the *Gita* and the *Ramayana* had
always contained *in potentia*, but something which Indian civilisation
had not actualised fully in practice. In *Hind Swaraj* a conscious attempt is

being made to actualise that potential. 'This is not a mere political book', he writes. 'I have used the language of politics, but I have really tried to offer a glimpse of dharma. What is the meaning of *Hind Swaraj*? It means rule of dharma or *Ramarajya*' (*CW* 32: 489). 'We may read the *Gita* or the *Ramayana* or *Hind Swaraj*. But what we have to learn from them is desire for the welfare of others' (*CW* 32: 496).

These are the exalted aims of the book. Yet on a casual reading the book may strike the reader as being a rather simple one. This would not be an unwarranted reaction, since Gandhi sought simplicity in all things, including the way he presented his ideas. But first impressions in this case can be, and are, deceptive, for the book contains in compressed form the author's conception of what modern India ought to become and how politics may be made into the highest form of the active life. It is therefore a book that needs to be read reflectively, the way one would read, for example, a dialogue of Plato. Such a reading can be made easier if the reader keeps in view the historical and intellectual contexts within which the book was written.

HISTORICAL CONTEXT: MODERN CIVILISATION

Modern civilisation forms the broad historical context of *Hind Swaraj*. Its critique of that civilisation is one of its main contributions to modern political thought. In historical terms, it is Gandhi's apprehensions about certain tendencies in modern civilisation that made him the thinker and the political innovator that he is. The tone of his criticism is sometimes harsh and intemperate and is likely to mislead the reader. It is all the more necessary therefore to say at once that his attitude towards modern civilisation, though critical, is not wholly negative. Being critical implies the desire to improve the object criticised. So it is with Gandhi and modern civilisation. Thus he welcomes a number of its contributions – civil liberty, equality, rights, prospects for improving the economic conditions of life, liberation of women from tradition and religious toleration. At the same time, the welcome is conditional in that liberty has to harmonise with swaraj, rights with duties, empirical knowledge with moral insight, economic development with spiritual progress, religious toleration with religious belief and women's liberation with the demands of a broader conception of humanity.

Gandhi's admiration for the British constitution helps to put his attitude towards colonialism in its right perspective. In his *Autobiography* he speaks of the two passions of his life: the passion for loyalty to the British constitution and the passion for nursing (*CW* 39: 140–3). 'The history of British rule is the history of constitutional evolution. Under the British flag, respect for the law has become a part of the nature of the people' (*CW* 4: 322). Specifically, Queen Victoria's proclamation of 1858 was for him 'the Magna Carta of British Indians', 'a document of freedom for the people of India' giving them the 'full privileges and rights of British subjects' (*CW* 3: 357–8). The British constitution remained the standard by which to measure the quality of colonial administration: policies in conformity with it were thought to be good, and those contrary to it, evil. This was true even in the context of his doctrines of satyagraha. As he saw it, there was no inconsistency between these and loyalty to the constitution, for, as he said, a 'love of truth' lay at the root of both (*CW* 39: 140).

Gandhi has his own definition of civilisation: civilisation is 'that mode of conduct which points out to man the path of duty' (*sudharo*, ch. XIII). Barbarism (*kudharo*) is the absence of civilisation. By modern or Western civilisation (he often used these terms interchangeably) he meant that 'mode of conduct' which emerged from the Enlightenment, and more exactly, from the Industrial Revolution. 'Let it be remembered', he wrote in 1908, 'that western civilisation is only a hundred years old, or to be more precise, fifty' (*CW* 8: 374). The Industrial Revolution for him was much more than a mere change in the mode of production. As he interprets it, it brought into being a new mode of life, embracing a people's outlook on nature and human nature, religion, ethics, science, knowledge, technology, politics and economics. According to this outlook, nature was taken to be an autonomous entity operating according to its own laws, something to be mastered and possessed at will for the satisfaction of human needs, desires and political ambitions. This outlook brought about an epistemological revolution which in turn paved the way for the secularisation of political theory. The satisfaction of the desire for economic prosperity came to be identified as the main object of politics. Religion, when it was not dismissed as mere superstition, was valued only for its social and psychological use. The Industrial Revolution altered the concept of labour, now accepted mainly for its ability to produce profit, power and capital. Manual labour was looked upon as fit only for the unlettered and the backward. With the technological revolution that followed the industrial revolution, machines, hitherto allies of humans, seemed to assert their autonomy.

Modern political theory provided the general ethical framework within which the changes occurring in the scientific, technological and economic fields were to be integrated. Two types of political theory emerged, one for the industrialised societies and the other for the rest of the world. Liberalism and liberal institutions were thought appropriate for industrialised societies; imperialism and colonialism for the non-industrialised societies such as India. By the third quarter of the nineteenth century, the world for all practical purposes was divided into the industrialised and the non-industrialised, or the 'civilised' and the 'non-civilised', parts. Even the saint of liberalism, J. S. Mill, accepted this civilisational partition of the world. He would in all sincerity use the very doctrine of liberty to justify imperial rule over India.

It was perhaps James Fitzjames Stephen (1829–94), law member of the Viceroy's council, who most candidly articulated the meaning of imperialism in terms of modern civilisation. In his famous essay 'Foundations of the government of India' (1883), Stephen argued that every political theory whatever is a doctrine of or about force. The foundations of the government of India rest on conquest not consent. Such a government must therefore proceed upon principles different from and in some respects opposed to those which prevail in England. Representative government is a requirement of European civilisation, while absolute government is that of Indian civilisation. Only by such a government can any real benefit accrue to Indians. If *suttee*, other human sacrifices, infanticide, disability to marry on account of widowhood or change of religion were to be abolished, as indeed they were to be, only an absolute imperial government could have done it. Though, generally speaking, absolute government must be a temporary expedient for the purpose of superseding itself, in the case of India 'the permanent existence' of such a government would not in itself be a bad thing. For, as Stephen saw it, India in the last quarter of the nineteenth century gave little sign of producing the material and moral conditions necessary for self-government. How then was India to be governed? – by introducing 'the essential parts of European civilisation'. According to Stephen, the latter included 'peace, order, the supremacy of law, the prevention of crime, the redress of wrong, the enforcement of contracts, the development and concentration of the military force of the state, the construction of public works, the collection and expenditure of the revenue required for these objects in such a way as to promote the utmost public interest'. Modern European morality, modern European political economy and modern European conceptions of security of property and person – these, in Stephen's view, were what India needed. And if European civilisation, 'in the sense explained', is to be introduced into India, certain consequences followed – the most important, which included all the rest, being 'an absolute government, composed in all its most important parts of Europeans'. An Indian parliament or collection of Indian parliaments would produce unqualified anarchy: 'the English in India are the representative of a belligerent civilisation. The phrase is epigrammatic, but it is strictly true. The English in India are the representatives of peace compelled by force.' Only a belligerent civilisation can suppress by force the internal hostilities between Indians and teach them 'to live in peace with, and tolerate each other'. The introduction of such a civilisation into India, the *Pax Britannica*, was 'the great and characteristic task' of Britain in India.

It is in the context of arguments such as Stephen's that Gandhi develops his critique of modern civilisation.

HISTORICAL CONTEXT: THE POLITICS OF SOUTH AFRICA

The actual development of Gandhi's critique of modern civilisation takes an indirect route, for Gandhi entered the world historical stage not in India but in South Africa. A grasp of the significance of this fact is absolutely essential for a full understanding of the teachings of *Hind Swaraj*. In the first place, it was in South Africa, not in India, that he first acquired his vision of Indian nationalism, a fact which differentiates his nationalism from that of the other Indian nationalists. His idea of nationalism does not start with the locality and then gradually extend itself to the province and finally to the nation. Quite the reverse. He was first an Indian, then a Gujarati, and only then a Kathiavadi. And South Africa has a lot to do with this. Secondly, it is in the politics of the Transvaal, not Champaran or Bardoli, that he first developed his unique political philosophy and political techniques.

The account of his South African experiences – his leadership role in the Natal Indian Congress and the Transvaal British Indian Association, his campaigns against discriminatory legislation against indentured Indian labourers, traders and settlers, the discovery of the techniques of satyagraha, his career as a lawyer and as a journalist running the weekly journal *Indian Opinion*, his ventures into the field of education, and the establishment of the Phoenix Settlement for the formation of the new Gandhian personality, his incarcerations, his tussle with General J. C. Smuts – these and other pertinent matters are treated well in the available secondary literature (Huttenback 1971; Swann 1985; Brown 1989), so they do not require anything more than a mention here.

However, three issues associated with South Africa need highlighting. The first is that it was in South Africa that Gandhi for the first time became aware that modern civilisation was at the root of the colonial problem. If Lenin connected colonialism to capitalism, Gandhi went one step further and connected colonialism to modernity itself. The good that colonialism secured for the colonised – and there is no doubt that it did secure that – was not intrinsic to it. What was intrinsic to it was commercial expansion, the lust for domination and the glory resulting therefrom. When the two forces – good of the colonised and the glory of empire – clashed, there was no doubt which would prevail. The first recorded expression of these insights are found in his after-dinner speech on Christmas Day 1896. These are given in some detail in the

Autobiography: how he and his fellow passengers were quarantined in the Durban harbour, how the white settlers ashore wanted them to be returned to Bombay, how the captain of the ship invited Gandhi to Christmas dinner and to make a speech. The topic he chose was Western civilisation. 'I knew that this was not an occasion for a serious speech. But mine could not be otherwise ... I therefore deplored the civilisation of which the Natal whites were the fruit, and which they represented and championed. This civilisation had all along been on my mind ... I had in my speech described Western civilisation as being, unlike the Eastern, predominantly based on force' (*CW* 39: 153–4).

In 1908 Gandhi came back to the theme of modern civilisation in a lecture to the Johannesburg YMCA. He took this occasion to make the crucial distinction between Christian civilisation and modern Western civilisation: 'I do not mix up or confuse Western civilisation with Christian progress ... I refuse to believe that all this [industrial and technological] activity connotes Christian progress, but it does connote Western civilisation' (*CW* 8: 244). The latter, he averred, rested on two fallacious maxims: might is right and the survival of the fittest. Moreover, it lacked, he claimed, a 'goal', a *telos*, being 'centrifugal' and merely 'dynamic'. Indian civilisation, on the other hand, had a goal; it was 'centripetal', 'adaptive' and 'contemplative'. 'A civilisation or a condition in which all the forces fly away from the centre must necessarily be without a goal, whereas those who converge to a point have always a goal' (ibid.).

In the 1920s Gandhi returned to the problem of modern civilisation. In a remarkable passage in *Satyagraha in South Africa* (*CW* 29: 76–7) he wrote that it was neither vulgar racism nor crass trade jealousy that motivated the thoughtful opponents of Indians in South Africa: what motivated them, in his view, was their concern for modern civilisation, of which they considered themselves the respresentatives, and which they wanted to protect and promote at all costs. They believed that 'the nations which do not increase their material wants are doomed to destruction. It is in pursuance of these principles that Western nations have settled in South Africa and subdued the numerically overwhelmingly superior races of Africa.' The colonial community in South Africa believed that they were the 'representative' of Western civilisation, and India, that of Oriental civilisation. If peoples belonging to such rival civilisations met, they thought, the result would be an explosion. It is not the business of the statesman to adjudicate between the relative merits of these civilisations. His business is to try to preserve his own. Indians are disliked not for their vices but for their virtues – simplicity, perseverance, patience, frugality and other-worldliness. Westerners are enterprising, impatient, engrossed in multiplying their material wants and in satisfying them. They are afraid that allowing Indians to settle as immigrants in South Africa is tantamount to endorsing cultural suicide (*CW* 29: 77).

Gandhi naturally refused to recognise any validity for this argument. On the contrary, he felt that contact between civilisations would be healthy and beneficial to the civilisations concerned. In particular, he was of the opinion that Indian civilisation would benefit greatly from its contact with Western civilisation.

The second issue associated with South Africa that needs highlighting is the relative social freedom that it offered to Gandhi to conduct his social and political experiments for India. He found himself 'free from certain restrictions', as he put it, 'from which our people suffer in India' (*CW* 5: 290). As Judith Brown has pointed out, South Africa enabled him to play the role of a 'critical outsider' in India. The Phoenix Settlement which he established in 1904 just outside Durban (and where *Hind Swaraj* was first printed) would not have met with the success it did had it not been for this social freedom. It was here that he conducted his first experiments in developing a sense of all-India consciousness free from the harmful effects of modern civilisation, undue regionalism and the worst manifestations of the caste-mentality.

It was here too that Indian women were able to find liberation from a number of social taboos to which their counterparts in India were still subject. 'Phoenix is intended to be a nursery for producing the right men (and women) and right Indians,' he wrote; ' … whatever energy is put forth in Phoenix is not so much taken away from India, but it is so much given to India ... Phoenix is a more suitable place for making experiments and gaining proper training. Whereas in India there may be undesirable restraints, there are no such undesirable restraints in Phoenix. For instance, Indian ladies would never have come out so boldly as they are doing at Phoenix. The rest of the social customs would have been too much for them' (*CW* 9: 382).

How painful and radical these experiments were in those days may be gathered from one or two examples. There is the well-known case of his quarrel with his wife for refusing to clean the chamber-pot of a low-caste Indian Christian staying with the Gandhis. Prabhudas Gandhi recounts how difficult it was for his father, Chhaganlal Gandhi, the Mahatma's right-hand man in Phoenix and the Gujarati editor of *Indian Opinion*, to dine with Muslims. 'But since he had surrendered himself to Gandhiji he did his best to follow Gandhiji's ideas without protest.' However that might have been with Chhaganlal, his wife would still 'cleanse' the dinner utensils used by her Muslim friends by 'purifying' them (the utensils) in fire (P. Gandhi 1957, 58).

The third point that needs highlighting is the importance of his lobbying missions of 1906 and 1909 to London. And it was on these missions that Gandhi first acquired the diplomatic skills necessary for dealing with the British political establishment in London. More importantly, it was on these visits that he came into contact with a very important segment of the newly emerging Indian middle class, the expatriate Indians living abroad. These were the new converts to modern civilisation, and it is their uncritical acceptance of their newly found secular faith that really bothered Gandhi. Modern civilisation was bad enough for Britain, but when imported into India and propagated there by Indians themselves, its potential for mischief became incalculable.

HISTORICAL CONTEXT: THE POLITICS OF EXPATRIATE INDIANS

Expatriate Indians at the turn of the twentieth century were a motley crowd of university students, recent graduates and budding intellectuals who had gone abroad – to England mostly, but also to the United States, Canada, the Continent, and even Japan – to prepare themselves for modern careers in science, technology, law, medicine and the like. A significant number of them were drawn together by their nationalist fervour and by their disenchantment with the Indian National Congress. They were attracted to various European revolutionary movements and ideas – terrorism, Russian nihilism, Marxism, the ideologies of the Irish home rule movement and the Italian *risorgimento*. Some of them were active supporters of such Indian secret societies as the *Abhinav Bharat* of the Bombay Presidency and the *Anusilan Samiti* of Bengal. While abroad they continued their support of these societies by engaging in gun-running and by sending to India manuals for making bombs and other weapons of destruction. To Gandhi they appeared to be misguided Indians fully committed to 'modern civilisation' who wished to fashion India on the model of Great Britain, Italy or Japan. Even a superficial glance at *Hind Swaraj* will be enough to make the reader realise that Gandhi had this group very much in mind when he wrote *Hind Swaraj*. It is directed as much against them as against the practitioners of imperialism who in his view were violating the norms of the British constitution.

A key figure among these expatriates was undoubtedly Shyamji Krishnavarma (1857–1930). A Gujarati like Gandhi himself, he was a gifted linguist brought to England to be an assistant to the Oxford Sanskritist, Sir Monier Monier-Williams. Graduating from Balliol College, Oxford, in 1882, he qualified for the Bar from the Inner Temple. After a brief career in India serving under various maharajas, he returned to England to work full-time for the Indian nationalist cause. As befits a 'modern', he came completely under the spell of Herbet Spencer, in whose honour he endowed an annual lectureship at Oxford in 1905 (which continued until 1910, when the money was returned because of Krishnavarma's involvement in terrorist activities). In addition, he endowed five Herbert Spencer Indian fellowships, each valued at Rs. 2,000, and a Swami Dayanand fellowship as well. Six other fellowships, each valued at Rs. 1,000, named after Edmund Burke and

Ganesh Vasudev Joshi of Poona (the founder of the swadeshi movement there) were also established. In 1909, when Gandhi was still in London, four 'Martyr Dhingra scholarships' were established to honour the memory of the assassin of Sir William Curzon-Wyllie. The object of these educational endeavours was to bring bright Indian youths to Europe and America for training in the theory and practice of violent revolution.

Krishnavarma was also the founder of India House (1905) at Highgate in London to offer residential facilities for these young men. Gandhi himself stayed there for a few days on his 1906 visit to London and had long conversations with him on Indian politics and on the philosophy of swaraj. Even more significant was the founding of a revolutionary penny monthly, *The Indian Sociologist* (1905), which Krishnavarma edited and published from London. It was dedicated to propagating Spencer's ideas as being absolutely essential for the modernisation of India. As if to remind everyone of this, the monthly carried on its masthead two quotations from Spencer: 'Every man is free to do that which he wills, provided he infringes not the equal freedom of any other man' (Spencer 1893, 46); and 'Resistance to aggression is not simply justifiable but imperative. Non resistance hurts both altruism and egoism' (Spencer 1878, 168).

The activities of the extremists at India House became a matter of public concern and questions were raised in parliament. Suspecting danger, Krishnavarma left London for Paris in 1907 taking the monthly journal with him. Towards the end of 1909, following the assassination of Curzon-Wyllie by Madan Lal Dhingra, India House was closed down permanently.

Though the relationship between Gandhi and Krishnavarma was friendly – even respectful – in 1906, it had deteriorated beyond repair by 1909. A leading article in *The Indian Sociologist* of October 1913 denounced Gandhi's philosophy of non-violence as being 'utterly subversive of all ethical, political and social ideals'.

While Krishnavarma was the organising genius of the Indian expatriates, V. D. Savarkar (1883–1966) was the brain of the group. Recipient of a Shivaji scholarship (one of several established by Krishnavarma), Savarkar, on Tilak's recommendation, was brought to London in 1906, where he lived in India House for a period. His stay in London ended in early 1910, when he was arrested for revolutionary activities and deported to the Andamans. However, while in London, he produced two works, one a translation of Mazzini's *Life* from English into Marathi, and the other, the highly imaginative *The Indian War of Independence of 1857*, a militaristic interpretation of the events of 1857. Originally written in Marathi, it was translated into English by 'diverse hands' and published in London in May 1909, only two months before Gandhi's arrival there. Chapters of this book were read and discussed by the residents of India House. The most prominent among the revolutionaries to be influenced by Savarkar was Madan Lal Dhingra (c. 1887–1909), an engineering student from Imperial College, London, turned revolutionary (mentioned in ch. XVI). His assassination of Sir William Curzon-Wyllie, the ADC to the Secretary of State for India, on 1 July 1909, a few days before Gandhi's arrival in London, shook London, the Indian community in England and Gandhi himself. It was a *modern* political act par excellence – terrorism legitimised by nationalism. 'Every Indian should reflect thoroughly on this murder', Gandhi wrote to his friend Polak. 'Mr. Dhingra's defence (by Indian revolutionaries) was inadmissible ... He was egged on to do this act by ill-digested reading of worthless writings ... It is those who incited him to this that deserve to be punished' (*CW* 9: 302).

It was well known among Indian expatriates living in London that Savarkar was the man who 'incited' Dhingra to commit the murder. Gandhi had met Savarkar in the autumn of 1909 and shared a platform with him. On this occasion, they agreed to disagree on the question of whether the *Ramayana* taught *ahimsa* or not. 'When I was in London', Gandhi recalled later, 'Shyamji Krishnavarma and Savarkar and others used to tell me that the *Gita* and the *Ramayana* taught quite the opposite of what I said they did' (*CW* 32: 102). It is difficult to estimate the extent of Savarkar's role in the formulation of the philosophy of *Hind Swaraj*: D. Keer, the biographer of both Gandhi and Savarkar, goes so far as to claim that it was written in response to Savarkar. This is clearly an exaggeration, but there is definitely some truth in it. However that may be, during the later decades the ideological gap between the two only widened. Savarkar, who in his London days was a supporter of Hindu–Muslim unity, later changed his attitude towards the Muslims and propounded the intensely anti-Muslim ideology of *hindutva*. Not surprisingly, it was one of Savarkar's militant supporters who turned out to be Gandhi's assassin.

There are two other leading 'modern' expatriate Indian revolution-aries, both Gandhi's contemporaries, whose activities are worthy of note here. The first is the remarkable Parsee revolutionary, Madame Bhikaji Rustom Cama (1861–1936), a pioneer among Indian women in politics. Her base of operations was Paris, and for a while she and Har Dayal edited *Bande Mataram*, a penny monthly named after the now banned Calcutta *Bande Mataram* (once edited by the fiery Aurobindo Ghose). In 1907 she attended the Stuttgart International Congress of Socialists and moved a resolution demanding swaraj for India (seconded by 'Comrade' H. M. Hyndman, the British Marxist). The other was V. Chattopadhyaya (1880–1937?), a brother of the dis-tinguished Congress leader, Mrs Sarojini Naidu, and a colleague of Savarkar and Krishnavarma. He also attended the Stuttgart Interna-tional Congress of Socialists. Between 1909 and 1914 he edited yet another penny monthly, the *Talwar* (Sword), appearing from Rotterdam and Berlin. After joining the Communist party in Europe, he spent the rest of his life in Germany and the Soviet Union promoting various nationalist and communist causes, before facing his tragic fate at the hands of a Soviet firing squad sometime between 1937 and 1940. Cama and Chattopadhyaya were typical of the new generation of Indian intellectuals who were captivated by whatever was fashionable in Europe and who embraced one of modernity's major ideological expressions, Marxism. It goes without saying that it is with such mod-erns as these in mind that Gandhi wrote *Hind Swaraj*.

Indian expatriate activities were not limited to Great Britain and the Continent; they were being organised in Canada and the United States as well. The key figure here is Taraknath Das (1884–1958). A member of the Bengal secret society, the *Anusilan Samiti*, Das left India for Canada and the United States via Tokyo, reaching San Francisco in 1906. In 1908 he moved to Vancouver and founded a penny monthly, the *Free Hindusthan*, modelled on *The Indian Sociologist* of London and Paris, and carrying the same two quotations from Herbert Spencer on its masthead. As British and American intelligence were on his tracks, Das had to move his journal from Vancouver to Seattle, and later to New York, being assisted in this by George Freeman of the *Gaelic American* of New York and Edward Holton James, a Seattle attorney (and a nephew of Henry James and William James).

Das and *Free Hindusthan* are important in tracing the historical link between Gandhi and Tolstoy, and the development of some of the arguments in *Hind Swaraj*. It was in response to a letter from Das, as editor of *Free Hindusthan*, that Tolstoy wrote his famous *Letter to a Hindoo* (1908), listed in Appendix I to *Hind Swaraj*. A typescript of this work was circulating in Indian revolutionary circles in Paris in 1909, and it fell into Gandhi's hands while he was still in London, sent to him from Paris by his friend Dr Pranjivan Mehta. To verify its authorship Gandhi wrote directly to Tolstoy who not only verified its authenticity but also granted permission to publish it in both English and Gujarati. The translation and the editing took place on board the *Kildonan Castle*, during the same week that he wrote *Hind Swaraj*. Gandhi published both the English and the Gujarati versions of the *Letter* in *Indian Opinion* between December 1909 and January 1910. Almost simultaneously, unbeknown to Gandhi, Das also published the *Letter* in the Boston monthly, *The Twentieth Century*, together with a searing refutation of Tolstoy's thesis. V. Chattopadhyaya wrote his own refutation of Tolstoy in *Bande Mataram*, which was serialised in April 1910 in *The African Chronicle*, a Durban weekly run by Gandhi's Indian rivals in Natal. At the centre of these debates was the question of how India may attain swaraj: Tolstoy argued that nonviolence is the only legitimate means available to the morally upright conscience. Gandhi, in *Hind Swaraj*, supported this view, while expatriate moderns such as Das and Chattopadhyaya opposed it.

HISTORICAL CONTEXT: THE INDIAN NATIONALIST MOVEMENT

The Raj, among other things, made one historic contribution to India's development: it occasioned the fundamental debate on the nature of her national identity, which in some ways continues to this day. Gandhi states his case in *Hind Swaraj*. It is that Indians have a common identity, that they constitute a *praja* (nation), a term newly introduced by *Hind Swaraj*, and that Indian nationalism should never legitimise violence as a means of national liberation.

Hind Swaraj opens with an analysis of the Indian National Congress and ends with an exhortation to its two internal factions – the Moderates and the Extremists. As a lawyer, a political activist and, above all, as a journalist in South Africa, Gandhi was quite well informed of what was going on in the subcontinent. Increasing numbers of the rising generation of the politically conscious Indian middle class were being strongly attracted to modern civilisation and political violence. The split between the Moderates and the Extremists, which occurred in 1907, did not hide this fact. There is little doubt where Gandhi's sympathies lay. The Moderates stood for swaraj defined as self-government within the empire, achieved through the constitutional means of gradual reform 'granted' by the imperial parliament. This was the attitude taken by the early leaders of the Congress – Allan Octavian Hume, Sir William Wedderburn, Dadabhai Naoroji, Gopal Krishna Gokhale and Baddrudin Tyabji – all mentioned in the book and treated critically but respectfully. Mere constitutionalism, Gandhi knew from his South African experience, did not get anywhere nor did it raise the fundamental moral issue of the reform of the soul, which for Gandhi was a precondition for sound politics. Swaraj of the type he had envisaged could not be attained without the reform of the soul and this separated him from the Moderates as a group.

The Extremists stood for swaraj defined as complete sovereignty achieved through constitutional means if possible, but through other means if necessary. In contrast to the Moderates, no Extremist is mentioned by name in *Hind Swaraj* – an indication of Gandhi's distance from them. In other words, Tilak and Aurobindo Ghose, their distinguished leaders, are passed over in silence. Gandhi was aware of what they were writing in their newspapers, the *Kesari* and the *Mahratta*, and the *Bande Mataram*. Tilak's revival of the Ganapathi festival and the memory of Shivaji (1627–80), the hammer of the Moghuls, did not help the cause of a composite Indian nationalism that Gandhi was trying to promote. Neither would Aurobindo Ghose's appeal to *shakti* – power in its creative but violent forms, mythologised by Durga, Bhavani and Kali – have been more reassuring to the Mahatma.

While no work by the Extremists is included in the Appendix, two works by the Moderates, *Poverty and Un-British Rule in India* by Naoroji and *The Economic History of India* by R. C. Dutt do appear in it. These works, as far as Gandhi is concerned, set the tone of the argument against the evils of colonial rule. The colonial economic policies, they had argued, served primarily the interests of alien investors, and only secondarily those of the average Indian. But that in itself did not make the case of the Indian investors any stronger. For they too were as much under the spell of modern civilisation as were the British investors. In short, the Moderates have begun well, with good intentions, but it is time that they rethought their goals, methods and priorities. For there is an alternative to both uncreative constitutionalism and violent extremism, and the premonitions of what that alternative would entail can already be seen in chapters XVII and XX of Gandhi's new book.

Not forgotten in all this is the case of Indian Muslims. Gandhi's South African experience had given him a deep insight into the peculiar problems that Indian Muslims faced in a pluralist society such as India. He had worked in close harmony with Muslim leaders in all his South African campaigns. The famous burning of the objectionable registration cards took place in the premises of a Johannesburg mosque. On both his London trips he was accompanied by Muslim leaders of the Indian community. Given this background, Gandhi had no reason to think that Indian Muslims would turn away from the general direction that Indian nationalism was taking. That is why he is sympathetic to and supportive of the Minto-Morley recommendation for special electoral status for Indian Muslims. His conceptions of nationalism and swaraj, he believed, were neutral as far as religion as *sect* was concerned. His vision of politics as it emerges in 1909 saw Indians as primarily members of a single nation (*praja*) and only secondarily as members of a sect or a caste or a region, Indians whose humanity would be strong enough to enable them to tolerate difference within the context of a deeper national identity.

But the politics of the Congress and the Muslim League were not the only thing that concerned Gandhi on the eve of writing *Hind Swaraj*. The question of modern civilisation was also worrying him. On the one hand the colonial administrators behave as if they represent a superior civilisation – the modern civilisation. On the other hand, the new Indian middle class was behaving as if the colonial administrators were right. Both parties, in Gandhi's view, were profoundly mistaken. In defending the modern state merely as an efficient system of coercive power and nothing more than that, the colonial administrators were doing India a disservice. And in attempting to modernise India on the pattern of England and Japan, the modern middle class was wreaking economic havoc on India's poor and the rural population. In two very remarkable documents, one a letter to Henry Polak, the other a letter to Lord Ampthill, Gandhi unburdens his soul (for the text of these letters, see below, pp. 127–34). What India needed, he stated bluntly, was to unlearn what it had learnt in the last fifty years. And what Britain needed to do, he told Lord Ampthill, is to return to its Christian roots and discard modern civilisation. Both India and Britain had to reintegrate whatever was humane in modern civilisation within the framework of their own respective traditional religions. At such a time as they could accomplish this, and only then, could they do good to their own peoples and to the rest of the world. Colonialism was the fruit of modern civilisation, and only when this truth was grasped could the colonial problem find its 'final' solution.

The historical context of *Hind Swaraj*, then, comprised several rich and diverse elements. It brought into the open certain underlying ethical issues that concerned both the coloniser and the colonised. All this makes the book not only a tract for the times but also a treatise on modern politics.

THE INTELLECTUAL CONTEXT: WESTERN SOURCES

The intellectual context of *Hind Swaraj* is even more diversified than its historical context. To begin with, it comprehends both Eastern and Western sources, and within the latter, such diverse fields as jurisprudence, vegetarianism, theosophy, Christian theology, art criticism, criticism of the new industrial civilisation, and civil disobedience in its Socratic and New England forms. The Foreword informs the reader that the author had 'read much' and 'pondered much'. And the Preface acknowledges the author's special debt to 'Tolstoy, Ruskin, Thoreau, Emerson and other writers, besides the masters of Indian philosophy'. Appendix I lists twenty books which remain the ideal starting points for any serious discussion of Gandhi's own thought. In addition, there are other authors mentioned in the *Autobiography* and elsewhere in Gandhi's writings.

Gandhi's introduction to Western thought began in 1888 with his legal studies in London. The curriculum in the London Inns of Court then comprised Common Law and Roman Law. As the *Autobiography* records, he took an 'unflagging interest' in these. Nine months were spent on the Common Law of England – on Broom's *Common Law*, Snell's *Equity*, White and Tudor's *Leading Cases*, William and Edward's *Real Property*, Goodeve's *Personal Property*. He even managed to learn enough Latin to go through Justinian in the original. The impact of the legal training on Gandhi's political thought cannot be exaggerated. It deepened in him the idea of a higher law morally superior to any constitution and positive law, a notion very much present in chapter XVII of *Hind Swaraj*. Similarly his great practical skill in preparing petitions to governments, in drafting constitutions and resolutions for the various political bodies on which he served both in South Africa and India, is unimaginable without an appreciation of his training in Western jurisprudence. His approach to politics was as much jurisprudential as ethical.

Vegetarianism with him was more than a fad. He was a careful reader of books on the philosophy of vegetarianism which by the end of the nineteenth century had claimed its allegiance to 'true civilisation'. He read *The Perfect Way in Diet* (1881) by Anna Kingsford MD, Vice-president of the London Vegetarian Society. Originally her doctoral dissertation for the University of Paris, it advocated a return to the 'natural and ancient food of our race', and connected vegetarianism with 'the principles of true civilisation'. *The Ethics of Diet* (1881) by Howard Williams, a Cambridge scholar, advanced a similar point of view. Vegetarians, it claimed, were the pioneers of a 'truer civilisation'. A 'humaner and juster civilisation' would be impossible without vegetarianism. Williams also exploded the myth that vegetarianism was the 'cause' of the defeat of Hindus at the hands of beef-eating foreigners. Only prejudice, ignorance or sophistry will argue this way, Williams countered. Tolstoy's *First Step*, listed in Appendix 1 to *Hind Swaraj*, was his introduction to the Russian edition of Williams' work. Gandhi's life-long interest in the subject had a deep philosophical root and it was linked to his concept of true civilisation. His critique of modern medicine and modern doctors in chapter XII becomes intelligible in this context.

Gandhi's interest in theosophy was temporary but it played an important role in his intellectual development. For it made him aware of the richness of Indian religious literature; it was also instrumental in bringing him into contact with his life-long friends, Henry Polak and Hermann Kallenbach. But already in South Africa he had become highly critical of the 'humbug' associated with official theosophy (*CW* 11: 64–5).

His interest in Christianity, after his disappointment with the preachers in rural Gujarat, became deep and intense in South Africa. There it led him to undertake a serious study, not only of Christianity, but also of Hinduism and other religions. His attitude towards missionaries always remained ambivalent: he did not approve of high pressure evangelism. At the same time he was appreciative of their effort to make religion socially practical. He learnt from them the art of applying the principle of disinterested service to the disadvantaged. To begin with, his first biographer, Joseph Doke, was a Baptist missionary, whose disinterested work he greatly admired. And it was from another missionary, Lancelot Booth, an Anglican, that he learnt his much loved art of nursing: for a whole year, two hours daily, he received training as a nurse and com-pounder at Booth's hospital. His contact with the Catholic monks and nuns of Mariannhill, outside Durban, was no less beneficial. In 1895 he visited the monastery and wrote a very moving article for the London *Vegetarian*, praising the monks and nuns for combining prayer and work, for treating the Blacks as equals and for training them in useful arts such as farming, carpentry, shoe-making, book-binding, printing and baking. He himself sent Kallenbach to the monastery to learn the art of shoe-making. As Pyarelal, his secretary, wrote later, the pattern of life Gandhi saw in Mariannhill 'became an inspiring model for his various Ashrams. He kept harking back to it again and again' (Pyarelal 1965, 546). Back in India he would hold out Mariannhill as a model for insti-tutions devoted to Harijan service: 'My idea is to have a training institu-tion of this type' (*CW* 58: 261).

Gandhi's acquaintance with Hellenic thought, like that with Roman jurisprudence, was, as far as we know, limited to one book, Plato's *Apology*, listed in the Appendix. He found in it, as he put it, 'the qualities of an elixir' (*CW* 8: 174). In 1908 a paraphrase of it was published in a six-part series in *Indian Opinion*, and later as a pamphlet under the title *Story of a Soldier of Truth*. The major lesson he learnt from this book, a lesson which was to find its way to *Hind Swaraj*, was that there was an irrefra-gable moral link between the order in the soul and order in society. Of equal importance was the doctrine of the ultimacy of the inner con-science and the option to suffer harm rather than to inflict it.

Typically, Gandhi read Plato with Indian eyes: Socrates was 'a great *satyagrahi*' who practised satyagraha against his own people. The Gandhi of *Hind Swaraj* is no doubt the Socrates of modern India. It is not enough to find fault with the imperialists, he argues. Indians must become self-critical and examine their own shortcomings. For India's body politic is being afflicted by both the external virus of foreign rule and the internal virus of domestic corruption. It is necessary to make the right diagnosis and to let the result be known in public. Only then would the body politic be 'cured and cleansed both within and without'. If India destroys only one kind of germ, and not the other kind, the body politic will still be ruined. The leaders of the Congress are focusing only on the external malady. They should turn their attention to India's internal weaknesses as well. 'If, through cowardice or fear of dishonour or death, we fail to realise or examine our shortcomings and fail to draw the people's attention to them, we shall do no good to India's cause, notwithstanding the number of external remedies we may adopt, notwithstanding the Congress sessions (we may hold), not even by becoming extremists' (*CW* 8: 173).

The influence of Tolstoy on Gandhi is widely recognised. For example, Martin Green alone has devoted three books to this subject (Green 1978, 1983 and 1986). Gandhi himself directs the readers of *Hind Swaraj* to read six of Tolstoy's works, listed in the Appendix. Between them, they cover four broad topics: Christianity as an ethical religion, aesthetics and political action, critique of the new industrial civilisation, and the colonial question in India.

The Kingdom of God Is Within You, which Gandhi read for the first time in 1894, as the *Autobiography* records, had 'overwhelmed' him. In this work Tolstoy presents Christianity, not as a dogmatic, revealed religion, but as an ethical system. At the heart of its teaching is the ethic of the Sermon on the Mount, which, according to Tolstoy, teaches the doctrine of non-violence and the ultimacy of the conscience. This admittedly facile view of the New Testament disregards many troubling questions that the New Testament raises – questions regarding daily temptations, doubt, agony, death and resurrection, and, above all, Pilate's troubling question 'What is Truth?' But Tolstoy thought that he had found in the New Testament an answer to at least one question – the question of violence in the world, namely 'how to settle the conflict between people who now consider a thing evil that others consider good, and vice versa' – and a workable solution for it. Either one must find 'an absolute and indubitable criterion of evil', or one must not 'resist evil by violence'. The first solution had been tried but was found wanting; the second solution, taught by Christ, is the only viable one (Tolstoy 1935, 58).

But two major obstacles stood in the way. The first was posed by institutional Christianity, which justified the state, endorsed the theory of just war, and condoned military service. This, in Tolstoy's view, was due to the corruption of Christianity, for 'Christianity in the true sense puts an end to the state' (ibid., 281). The second obstacle was posed by modern social scientists. They tended to reject the primacy of the conscience, inner illumination and inner change in favour of external or institutional changes. According to Tolstoy, however, religion is 'the faculty of seeing prophetically the true meaning of life'; as such it is an indispensable source of all sound political theory. But moderns such as Renan, Strauss, Comte, Spencer and Marx either reject religion as superstition or value it only for its social or psychological uses. They insist that human betterment is effected 'not by moral efforts of individual men towards recognition, elucidation, and profession of truth, but by a gradual alteration of the general external conditions of life'. They believe that 'the chief activity of man who wishes to serve society and improve the condition of mankind should be directed not to the elucidation and profession of truth, but to the amelioration of external political, social, and, above all, economic conditions' (ibid., 401–2). 'Let all those external conditions be realised', responds Tolstoy, 'the position of humanity will not be bettered' (ibid., 411). It can and will be bettered, contends Tolstoy, if both internal and external changes occur, when humans learn to listen to their true Christian conscience in which alone is revealed the Kingdom of God, which is a kingdom of love and non-violence.

The Kingdom of God Is Within You was mandatory reading for members of the Phoenix Settlement, and later Gandhi had it translated into Gujarati.

With Tolstoy's *What is Art?*, which he also arranged to be translated into Gujarati, we enter into what was for Gandhi an unsuspected new intellectual terrain. For contrary to popular belief Gandhi had a deep understanding of the connection between aesthetics, symbols, ethics and political action; he derived his basic ideas on this point from Tolstoy and, as we shall see shortly, from Ruskin as well.

To begin with, Tolstoy rejects the doctrine of an autonomous art – of art for art's sake. According to him art is a very important form of human activity; but it is an activity connected to other forms of human activity. It does not enjoy a privileged position in respect to goodness and truth. The separation of the claims of aesthetics from those of goodness, for which he blames Nietzsche, the French Decadents and the early Oscar Wilde, is contributing greatly to the corruption of life in modern times. What passes for art today tends to pander to the hedonistic instincts of the people, especially the wealthy. All authentic art for Tolstoy springs from an inner experience of the 'religious' perception of the meaning of life. 'Art is a human activity consisting in this, that one man consciously, by means of certain external signs, hands to others feelings he has lived through, and that others are infected by these feelings and also experience them ... To evoke in oneself a feeling one has once experienced and, having evoked it in oneself, then by means of movements, lines, colours, sounds, or forms expressed in words, so to transmit that feeling that others experience the same feeling – this is the activity of art' (Tolstoy 1924, 173). Thus he distinguishes between the internal criterion of art and the subject matter of art. The internal criterion, by which all art must be judged in the first instance, is the ability to evoke feelings. But art has an external criterion as to its subject matter: the external criterion by which art is judged in the second instance is art's ability or the lack thereof of promoting feelings of love and human solidarity. According to Tolstoy art has an indispensable role to play in the great task of counteracting the hedonistic tendencies of modern culture. Its task today, as to its external criterion, 'is to make that feeling of brotherhood and love of one's neighbour now attained by only the best members of society, the customary feeling and instinct of all men' (ibid., 332).

Tolstoy's emphasis on experience and feeling, on the religious origins of great art, on the need to communicate feeling through appropriate symbols, evoked a deep response in Gandhi. *Hind Swaraj* (ch. xiv) underlines the importance of the need to have an *inner experience* of what swaraj means; only then would one be able to communicate to others one's concern for them with credibility and authenticity. Moreover, the invention, or perhaps more accurately, the reinvention, by Gandhi of the symbol of the spinning-wheel (ch. xx) was an artistic invention of the first order. Through that symbol alone – there were many others that he used with great effect – he communicated values of solidarity between the rich and the poor, of manual labour, and what we would now describe as appropriate technology.

Three other of Tolstoy's works listed in the Appendix – *How Shall We Escape?*, *The Slavery of Our Times* and *The First Step* – are essentially criticisms of the various aspects of the new industrial civilisation. They deal with the evils of exploitation of the workers, the degradation of the peasants, the absence of the virtue of moderation and the rampant consumerism characteristic of modern life.

Finally there is the controversial *Letter to a Hindoo*, referred to above. At the heart of the *Letter* lies Tolstoy's explanation of colonialism in India. Indians are as much responsible for it as are the British, if not more: 'it is not the English who have enslaved the Indians, but the Indians who have enslaved themselves'. If the English have enslaved Indians it is because the latter 'recognised, and still recognise, force as the fundamental principle of social order'. In accord with this principle 'they submitted to their little rajahs', and on their behalf struggled against one another, fought the Europeans and the English. For the Indians to complain about the English is like the alcoholic complaining about the wine merchants. If Indians renounce the law of violence, Tolstoy concludes, 'not only will hundreds not enslave millions, but even millions will be unable to enslave one individual' (Tolstoy 1987, 55–6). What India needed was not revivalism ('by your Vivekanandas, Baba Bharatis, and others', ibid., 60), but a practical commitment to non-violence. In 1909/1910 Gandhi published both the English and the Gujarati versions of the *Letter* introducing them with two significant prefaces. These share with *Hind Swaraj* a common ideological outlook.

In addition, Gandhi read a large number of nineteenth-century British critics of the new industrial civilisation, among them Carlyle, Ruskin and others mentioned in the Appendix. It is from Ruskin that

Gandhi derives the basic principles of his economic philosophy. The first of two books by Ruskin which affected Gandhi – *A Joy for Ever and Its Price in the Market* – was originally the text of two lectures delivered at the famous Art Treasures Exhibition held in Manchester in 1857, and published in the same year under the title *The Political Economy of Art*. It was reissued under its new title in 1880, and the inspiration for the change came from Keats' famous line 'A thing of beauty is a joy for ever', the motto of the Manchester Exhibition. This work marks the beginning of Ruskin's critique of the industrial civilisation. One of the defects of the latter, he pointed out, was its disregard for aesthetics. True political economy, unlike the one accepted by modernity, is the proper management of the nation's labour. Now the proper management of the nation's labour ought, Ruskin urged, to provide for both 'utility and splendour'. In other words, it should provide for the basic needs for food, shelter and clothing, pleasant objects of minimum luxury, healthful rest and serviceable leisure – and in that order. When labour is well managed, it would be able to provide for all these. However, while the new political economy provides for the luxury of the few, it does not seem capable of satisfying the basic needs of the many. Ruskin's view is that 'blankets' must come before 'silk laces': 'as long as there are cold and nakedness in the land around you, so long there can be no question at all that splendour in dress is a crime ... as long as there are any who have no blankets for their beds, and no rags for their bodies, so long it is blanket-making and tailoring we must set people to work at – not lace' (Ruskin 1911, 59). There can be little doubt that Gandhi adapts Ruskin's dictum to India in the form of his doctrine of appropriate technology.

But it was the second book of Ruskin's, *Unto This Last* (1860), that had the more profound impact on Gandhi. The *Autobiography* speaks of 'the magic spell' of this book which he read in 1904 on a night journey from Johannesburg to Durban. It produced an almost instantaneous change in him. The following is the account of what he learnt from that book: '(1) That the good of the individual is contained in the good of all. (2) That a lawyer's work has the same value as the barber's, inasmuch as all have the same right of earning their livelihood from their work. (3) That a life of labour, i.e., the life of the tiller of the soil and the handicraftsman, is the life worth living. The first of these I knew. The second I had dimly realised. The third had never occurred to me … I rose with the dawn, ready to reduce these principles into practice' (*CW* 39: 239).

The reading of *Unto This Last* produced two immediate results. The first was Gandhi's decision to establish the Phoenix Settlement, a community of friends who shared in his newly discovered convictions. It remained the prototype of the three other communities, or *ashrams*, he founded later in his life, the Tolstoy Farm outside Johannesburg, the Sabarmati Ashram outside Ahmedabad and Sevagram outside Wardha. And the second was to serialise a nine-part paraphrase of Ruskin's book in *Indian Opinion*, and later to publish it as a pamphlet under the title *Sarvodaya*, a name which he also gave to his newly formulated economic philosophy. The title *Unto This Last* came from St Matthew 20: 14. Gandhi gave it the title of *Sarvodaya* for the sake of 'Indians who do not know English'. Other adaptations also followed. Ruskin had postulated 'social affection' as the basic principle of a humane economy, in place of 'self-interest' and 'competition' postulated by modern political economy. Gandhi understood 'social affection' in terms of the Hindu concept of *daya* (compassion). Ruskin wanted to moderate the forces of the market by the principle of honour: if the clergyman or the soldier could work for honour, not profit, why not the businessman or the industrialist? And Gandhi understood honour in terms not of obligations of status, but of equality and of *satya* (truth). Finally, Ruskin saw the value of handicrafts even in an industrial society; Gandhi saw the value of the spinning-wheel and handicrafts for the whole of India.

The last chapter of *Sarvodaya* reads like a prelude to *Hind Swaraj*. As Gandhi recognised, the Indian middle class was clamouring for swaraj, which it identified with political power – to be gained by driving out the British by force – and with economic prosperity – to be brought about by rapid industrialisation. Gandhi found such a notion of swaraj totally unacceptable. He felt that even if the British were expelled violently and economic development achieved, it would still not bring any real swaraj to India. Real swaraj required not only political power and economic prosperity but also, and above all, a certain moral development among the people, especially the middle class. 'Real swaraj consists in restraint. He alone is capable of this who leads a moral life, does not cheat anyone, does not forsake truth and does his duty.' And the new Indian middle class, in his opinion, had not yet reached that level of moral development. 'We must have industry', he agreed, 'but of the right kind.' The kind of industry that emerged in the nineteenth century had levied a heavy toll on everyone in terms of civilisation. Ruskin had convinced him of that. He therefore wondered whether India could think of a different pattern of political and economic development, one hospitable to its civilisation, and one that would preserve and promote, rather than destroy, its traditional values. 'India was once looked upon as a golden land', he wrote, 'because Indians then were people of sterling worth. The land is still the same but the people have changed and that is why it has become arid. To transform it into a golden land again', he concluded, 'we must transmute ourselves into gold by leading a life of virtue. The philosopher's stone which can bring this about consists of two syllables: *satya* [truth]. If therefore, every Indian makes it a point to follow truth always, India will achieve swaraj as a matter of course' (*CW* 8: 373–5).

Gandhi's concern for modern civilisation and swaraj expressed itself in his deep interest in the revitalisation of India's villages. This explains the inclusion of Henry Sumner Maine's classic, *Village Communities in the East and West* (1871), in the Appendix. Here again *Hind Swaraj* breaks new ground. No Indian thinker had a better grasp of the truth that swaraj would mean little for India if the lives of the poor in the villages saw no significant improvement. He viewed with alarm the rapid rise of new urban centres – 'the real plague spots' of India, as he called them. In a country so overpopulated and so heavily dependent on agriculture, the villages held the key to economic and political development.

It was Maine's contention that villages in traditional India were representative institutions, and that the ancient village council had enjoyed both quasi-judicial and quasi-legislative powers. The introduction of the new utilitarian state, with its new adversarial court system, led to the ruin of the villages as the ultimate unit of national life, shifting their economic power to the new urban centres and their quasi-judicial and quasi-legislative powers to the new breed of lawyers condemned in chapter xı of *Hind Swaraj*. As far as Gandhi was concerned, this was one of the worst consequences of the introduction of modern civilisation into India. The life of the Indian peasant had become a veritable hell. He had become prey for the greedy urban middle class.

Gandhi used Maine's thesis for two purposes. First, he used it to support his argument that Indians in South Africa should be allowed to vote, since, as Maine had shown, they were inheritors of a civilisation that had representative institutions (*CW* 1: 93, 152, 154; *CW* 3: 332, 341). And back in India he used Maine's thesis in his life-long campaign on behalf of the Indian village (*CW* 28: 108; *CW* 48: 197; *CW* 85: 79).

A good deal of *Hind Swaraj's* scepticism regarding the new industrial civilisation comes from the authors he had been reading in South Africa and London – Edward Carpenter, Max Nordau, Godfrey Blount, Thomas Taylor and Robert Harborough Sherard – not household names today, but names (listed in the Appendix) that carried some weight at the turn of the century. Carpenter's *Civilisation: Its Cause and Cure*, originally a lecture delivered in 1889 to the Fabian Society, is mentioned in chapter vi. Carpenter viewed civilisation in historicist terms (something which Gandhi does not): civilisation is a stage through which every society passes, just as having measles is a stage through which every individual passes. Hence Carpenter's use of the metaphor of 'disease' for civilisation. Gandhi retains the metaphor but modifies its use – modern civilisation is a *curable* disease, and Gandhi presumably its doctor, at least as far as India is concerned.

Blount's pamphlet, *A New Crusade* (which was also the name of an organisation he founded to counteract the ill effects of modern civilisation), was summarised in *Indian Opinion* in 1905. Its motto, 'simplicity, art, aspiration', appealed to Gandhi greatly. Its principles did so even more: the betterment of society begins with the betterment of the individual; country life is the best form of the good life; handicrafts and agriculture are conducive to human well-being; machinery is 'the

Devil's instrument'; politics can only seal, never initiate, social reform; life without work is guilt, while work without art is brutality; work is a form of liturgy, etc. Blount anticipates, as it were, Gandhi's crusade for the homespun *khadi*: members of the 'new crusade' were to wear homespuns and use only hand-made boots, crockery, furniture and so on (Blount 1903).

Taylor's *Fallacy of Speed* was also summarised in *Indian Opinion* (*CW* 10: 379). Divided into three short chapters – 'Speed and population', 'Speed and profit' and 'Speed and pleasure' – the book challenges the prevailing assumption that 'faster is better'. He had in mind the railways (see *Hind Swaraj*, ch. IX), the shift of population from rural areas to new, ugly urban centres, the dwindling of opportunities for leisure and relaxation. Life is being lived 'on a high-speed basis' regardless of whether 'the results in their sum total are beneficial'. Taylor reaches the pessimistic conclusion that 'on the whole' healthy conditions are less readily available under the reign of speed than they were under the reign of a slower pace: 'there is something about the age in which we live which militates against leisure in considerable sections of the community ... Does quick locomotion finally tend more to give leisure or to destroy it?' (Taylor 1909, 63).

Max Nordau is included in the Appendix as being the author of 'Paradoxes of civilisation'. This obviously is an error, since there is no such work in any Nordau bibliography. But Nordau did write *Conventional Lies of Civilisation* (1895) and *Paradoxes* (1906). Gandhi may have read both; there is sufficient internal evidence in *Hind Swaraj* to suggest that *Conventional Lies of Civilisation* is the book that is relevant here. *Hind Swaraj*'s pessimism about modern civilisation is attributable to a large extent to Nordau. Pessimism, Nordau held, was the keynote of nineteenth-century European civilisation, as piety was that of the civilisation of the Middle Ages – pessimism in art, literature, religion, economics and politics (Nordau 1895, 6). The reason is the opposition between thought and action, and 'the lack of truth in our lives'. The contrast Gandhi draws in *Hind Swaraj* between modes of modern life and the earlier modes of life with respect to clothing, food, dwellings and so forth is reminiscent of what Nordau writes in his chapter 'The economic lie'. In earlier civilisations clothing was coarser, dwelling-places less comfortable, the food more primitive, the utensils fewer in number. Today the cities grow at the expense of the farming population, and the attitude of the moderns towards manual labour is reprehensible (Nordau 1895, 186ff.). The modern liberal professions, especially those of modern lawyers and doctors, are parasitic since they draw on both the rich and the poor (ibid., 206–14).

Pessimism is also the dominant note of *White Slaves of England: Being a True Picture of Certain Social Conditions in the Kingdom of England in the Year 1897*, written by Robert Harborough Sherard (1861–1943), son of an Anglican clergyman and a great-grandson of William Wordsworth, and biographer of Oscar Wilde. The book contains a harrowing account of the life of the average industrial worker in England at the turn of the century – the alkali workers, the nail-makers, the slipper-makers and tailors, the wool-combers, the white-lead workers, and the chain-makers. They share a common 'horrible slavery', the landlord's tyranny, poor wages and poor health care. The condition of women in the new factories is unimaginably appalling – a fact noted by Gandhi in chapter VI.

Sherard's point is that the affluence which the industrial civilisation has produced has not improved the lot of the vast majority of human-kind, nor is it likely to do so unless there is a moral change on the part of the rich and the powerful. And there is little sign of such change occur-ring, since affluence has not lessened the extent and intensity of want among the rich and the powerful, and since science and technology *per se* seem incapable of doing anything about it. Sherard invokes in support of this pessimistic view T. H. Huxley's testimony. 'I do not hesitate to express the opinion', wrote the great scientist, 'that there is no hope of a large improvement of the condition of the greater part of the human family; if it is true that the increase of knowledge, the winning of a greater dominion over nature, which is its consequence, and the wealth which follows upon that dominion, are to make no difference in the extent and intensity of want, with its concomitant physical and moral degradation amongst the masses of the people, I would hail the advent of some kindly comet which would sweep the whole affair away as a desirable consummation' (cited by Sherard 1897, 241). Gandhi would have agreed with Huxley's analysis though not with his pessimism. Pessimism is never normative to *Hind Swaraj*; on the contrary, the book is hopeful that the advent of a moral revolution in the hearts and minds of the rich and the powerful, i.e., the advent of real swaraj, would still be a possibility.

Hind Swaraj has its American, or rather New England, sources as well. Henry David Thoreau is mentioned in the Appendix, and Ralph Waldo Emerson in the Preface. Also worthy of mention is William MacIntyre Salter, whose *Ethical Religion* Gandhi had paraphrased and published in an eight-part series in 1907 in *Indian Opinion*. The authors mentioned or discussed in this book included John D. Rockefeller, Jeremy Bentham, Wendel Phillipps, Daniel Webster, Matthew Arnold, Ralph Waldo Emerson, St Francis Xavier, St Theresa and Charles Darwin (to whom Gandhi devoted a chapter). Thoreau remained a source of life-long inspiration for him, though the genesis of satyagraha had occurred independently of him. Gandhi did find in him ample confirmation for his new philosophy. His *Principles of Civil Disobedience* was paraphrased and published in 1907 in *Indian Opinion*. He was heartened to read that conscience, not majorities, should have the ultimate say in judging what is politically right and wrong, that while it is not one's duty to eradicate evil, it is certainly one's first duty not to give support to it, that even one person's action counts although the multitude may be opposed to it, that in an unjust political regime the prison is the right place for the just person, that only that state is worthy of obedience which recognises the just individual 'as a higher and independent power' from which the state's own power is ultimately derived. As for *Life Without Principle*, also listed in the Appendix, it too confirmed many ideas germinating in Gandhi's mind. He would have agreed with Thoreau's dicta that politics without virtue is 'a kind of vegetation', that good manners cannot be a substitute for civic virtue. What modern politics lacks and what it needs most is 'a high and earnest purpose', and an appreciation for 'culture more than for potatoes'.

He read Emerson's *Essays*, and read it very carefully; how carefully may be gathered from the instructions he gave to Maganlal Gandhi, his deputy at Phoenix: the latter was to read Emerson by marking important passages first, and later by copying them out in a notebook (*CW* 9: 209). This gives us a clue to Gandhi's own reading habits. He read Emerson in early 1909, in the Pretoria jail (*CW* 9: 240), but unfortunately we are not told which essays or in which edition. The 1903 edition, first series, available in South Africa, contained such essays as 'History', 'Self-reliance', 'Spiritual laws', 'Heroism', 'The over-soul', and 'Art'. In any case, Gandhi saw in Emerson's essays, as he put it, 'the teaching of Indian wisdom in a Western garb' (ibid.).

Readers of *Hind Swaraj* may wonder what nineteenth-century Italy has to do with colonial India and why Italy deserves a chapter (ch. xv) in Gandhi's book, and why Giuseppe Mazzini should appear in the Appendix. The reason is that Italy's struggle against Austria and the history of its unification had an almost normative standing in late nineteenth- and early twentieth-century Indian consciousness. Already in the 1870s the Bengali intelligentsia were reading Mazzini, and Savarkar, as noted earlier, had translated one of Mazzini's works into Marathi. Besides, Sir John Seeley's influential *Expansion of England* (1883), which Gandhi had read before 1903 (*CW* 3: 462), deliberately compared the way Italy achieved its unification with the way India was trying to achieve its own. By listing Mazzini's *Duties of Man* in the Appendix, Gandhi was sending a signal to the Indian nationalists that he was to be interpreted in strictly ethical and non-violent terms, and not in militaristic terms, as the Indian revolutionaries had done.

A glimpse into Gandhi's Western intellectual sources should go a long way towards correcting the view held by some that the Mahatma was opposed to Western civilisation as such. Such a view is so simple as to be false. As Sir Ernest Barker puts it, he was 'a bridge and reconciler' (Barker 1949, 58). The breadth and depth of his knowledge of Western intellectual sources suggest that his attack was limited to certain unhealthy tendencies in modern Western civilisation and that the attack was not motivated by any consideration of narrow nationalism or anti-colonialism. On the contrary, in *Hind Swaraj* he joins forces with many concerned Western thinkers in the defence of true civilisational values everywhere, East and West. He hoped for the day when England would reintegrate modernity within the framework of traditional British culture (ch. xx).

THE INTELLECTUAL CONTEXT: INDIAN SOURCES

It is Indian philosophical thought that enables Gandhi to integrate the ideas he gathered from the West into a coherent whole. The process of the discovery of his Indian philosophical identity begins in a conscious, technical way in London in 1888 and reaches its critical stage in South Africa. We have already referred to the philosophical roots of nineteenth-century vegetarianism, and the religious aspects of theosophy. Gandhi began reading texts of Indian philosophy in London with *The Song Celestial* – Sir Edwin Arnold's translation of the *Gita*. This was followed with books relevant to religions associated with India: *The Light of Asia*, the biography of the Buddha, also by Sir Edwin Arnold, *Life of Mahomet and His Successors* by Washington Irving, Carlyle's life of the Prophet in *Heroes and Hero Worship*, and a book of the Parsee religion, *The Sayings of Zarathustra*.

But the thinker who was most influential in guiding him in the development of his thought in Indian philosophy was Rajchandra Ravjibhai Mehta (1868–1901), a Gujarati Jain, mystic and diamond merchant. In 1894, Gandhi underwent what may be described as a major intellectual crisis. He expressed the chief elements of this crisis in his now famous 27-point letter to Rajchandra (*CW* 1: 90–1). What is the nature of the soul (*atma*), God (*Ishwar*), liberation (moksha), the *Vedas*, the *Gita*, animal sacrifice, the religion of the Aryans, Christianity, the Bible, theistic devotion (*bhakti*), the doctrines of transmigration, incarnation and trinity (Brahma, Vishnu, Shiva)? Rajchandra's response (*CW* 32: 593–602; Hay 1970, 29–38) was lengthy, and drew heavily on Jain philosophy. The soul is the indestructible, non-material, eternal substance whose essence is consciousness, knowledge, bliss and freedom.

God is but the soul in its absolute perfection. Humans, being caught in their bodily existence, are in need of liberation from passions, which is attainable only through rigorous asceticism, self-purification and withdrawal from the world. And since this is not easily achieved, humans have to pass through a countless series of births and rebirths.

As regards the other religions, Rajchandra expounded the Jaina doctrine of 'the many-sidedness' of religious truth (*anekantavada*). The human mind can only acquire fleeting and fragmentary understanding of truth, and therefore it is presumptuous for any human group to claim to have possession of absolute truth.

Rajchandra also explained the meaning of that elusive notion, dharma. 'Dharma does not mean any particular creed or dogma. Nor does it mean reading or learning by rote books known as *Shastras* (sacred texts) or even believing all that they say' (*CW* 32: 11). Rather, dharma is 'a quality of the soul' present in every human being. 'Through it we know our duty in human life and our true relation with other souls … dharma is the means [*sadhana*] by which we can know ourselves' (ibid.). No organised religion is a special repository of dharma. 'We may accept this means [*sadhana*] from wherever we get it, whether from India or Europe or Arabia' (ibid.). Rajchandra recommended several books for further reading: among them *Panchikaran*, *Maniratnamala*, *Mumukshu Prakaran* of Yogavasishta and *Mokshamala*. Gandhi followed this up by a study of the classics of Indian thought – the *Upanishads*, Patanjali's *Yogasutra*, the *Code of Manu*, the Tulsidas *Ramayana* and the *Gita*.

Although Gandhi never accepted Rajchandra as his spiritual guru (nor anyone else for that matter), there is hardly any doubt that his notion of the many-sidedness of truth had a lasting influence on the Mahatma. His idea of a 'religion which underlies all religions' (ch. VIII) also has its source in Rajchandra.

However deep Rajchandra's influence might have been in the 1890s, Gandhi went beyond the intellectual horizons that Rajchandra had opened up for him: already by the first decade of the century his spiritual life was focusing more and more on the *Gita* and the Tulsidas *Ramayana*. These classics, in contrast to the Jain classics, were theistic in orientation. Tulsidas is quoted in chapters xiv and xvii, and the technical definition of swaraj as self-rule, understood as the rule of the mind over itself and the passions, is derived from the *Gita*. The *sthithap-rajna*, 'the man of steady mind or steady wisdom' (*Gita* ii, 54–72), is Gandhi's ideal of the person who strives to attain inner swaraj. The notion of the self underlying Gandhi's political philosophy is derived from the *Gita*. The latter draws a fundamental distinction between self as *atman* (the imperishable, eternal, spiritual substratum of the being of every individual) and self as *dehin* (the embodied spatio-temporal self, composed of body, senses, mind and soul). The self that is directly involved in politics – in the pursuit of swaraj – is the *dehin*. Though the *dehin's* ultimate end is self-realisation or *atmadarshan*, it is the intermediate ends of the *dehin*, comprehensively summed up under the headings of artha (power, property and security) and kama (pleasure and the avoidance of pain) that are the proper objects of the active life. But the proper pursuit of these ends requires that they be pursued within the framework of dharma. But the *dehin* can do so only if the mind maintains its freedom and exercises control over itself and the senses. Thus the mind emerges as the key faculty in Gandhi's political philosophy, swaraj being the rule of the mind over itself and the passions (ch. xx). The possession of a disciplined mind – free from an *inordinate* desire for property, pleasure and power – is the prerequisite for the proper practice of satyagraha, the non-violent way of achieving home rule. But, as Gandhi argued, the ideal of swaraj can be achieved in modern times only in a united Indian nation, or *praja*. Swaraj and home rule must meet in a newly constituted Indian *praja*.

Thus by 1909 Gandhi had integrated all the essential ingredients of his political philosophy into a coherent whole, ingredients that were derived from the East and the West. He had by then acquired a definite philosophical vision which enabled him to assess the relative significance of things that concerned him – the problem of the self and of the Indian *praja*, the nature of Indian nationalism, the modern industrial civilisation, colonialism, the extreme selfishness of the Indian middle class, racialism, the spectre of rising violence in India and the legitimation of terroristic violence by extreme nationalists. It is from that vision that the basic argument of *Hind Swaraj* emerges.

THE LITERARY GENRE, THE STRUCTURE AND THE ARGUMENT OF *HIND SWARAJ*

Hind Swaraj is written in the literary genre of dialogue: a dialogue between a newspaper Editor and a Reader. It is significant that Gandhi chose for himself the role of a newspaper editor – a very *modern* figure – not that of a traditional figure, the guru. The Reader is a composite of 'modern' Indians including the expatriates he had met in London in 1906 and 1909. According to the Foreword, this particular genre was chosen to make the reading 'easy'; and according to the Preface, it was chosen because 'the Gujarati language readily lends itself to such treatment' and because it was considered 'the best method of treating difficult subjects'. It may be noted in passing, however, that the dialogue form common to traditional Indian philosophical discourse is not mentioned at all as a reason for the choice.

The dialogue form gives the careful reader certain general guidelines of interpretation. A dialogue does not contain a blueprint; as such, *Hind Swaraj* may not be looked upon as a blueprint (Sethi 1979, 5–27). Dialogues, especially those on 'difficult subjects', remain open-ended affairs, requiring an attitude of give and take from the participants. There is little room for dogmatism, and this should be kept in mind when interpreting the controversial issues in the book, including the topic of modern civilisation. Even when the argument seems conclusive, it is open to further discussion by other people at other times. Being open to each other's point of view is of course the hallmark of a true *satyagrahi*.

The book is divided into twenty short chapters. Eleven of these deal with historical reflections, while the rest deal with philosophical ones. The historical reflections begin with an assessment of the contributions of the Indian National Congress towards the rise of Indian nationalism (ch. 1). The Congress has made a good start, but its conceptions of swaraj need rethinking. The partition of Bengal has caused much excitement which requires to be directed in non-violent channels (chs. II and III). There follows an analysis of the causes and the consequences of British rule in India (chs. VII–XII). The causes, briefly, are on the one hand the commercial and power interests of the British, and on the other, the political and moral decay of Indian society: 'it is truer to say that we gave India to the English than that India was lost'. The consequences are an uncritical attitude towards modern civilisation and the rise of an uncaring middle class – the 'doctors' and the 'lawyers'. India must get out of the quagmire in which she finds herself, but she can best do so with the help of the moral and intellectual resources available to her in her own traditions. The examples of Britain, Japan and Italy are considered but rejected as being unsuitable for India's condition (chs. V and XV).

Philosophical reflections begin with a preliminary statement on the nature of swaraj (ch. IV), followed by a revised statement (ch. XIV). A similar two-step examination of the nature of civilisation follows (chs. VI and XIII). With chapters XVI and XVII we reach the high point of the book – the futility of violent revolutions and the need to use ethically sound means (satyagraha) to attain independence. Additional means of attaining independence – educational reforms (ch. XVIII) and a technology appropriate to India's needs (ch. XIX) – are discussed. Chapter XX makes a series of practical proposals to the Moderates, the Extremists, the new middle class and the English.

The argument of *Hind Swaraj* may be outlined briefly as follows. Political life has the potential of becoming the highest form of the active life. However, it can become such *only* when it is practised within the framework of an updated dharma – i.e., a dharma suited for life in the modern world of liberty, equality and prosperity. If, and only if, Indians can develop and implement such a dharma will they be able to integrate within their own culture whatever is good in colonialism and modern civilisation.

Civilisation can be a help or a hindrance in this process of personal and national reintegration, depending on its ethical orientation. Indian civilisation in its present unrenovated condition is as much a hindrance as is the modern civilisation that has emerged from the industrial revolution. Only an innovated Indian civilisation can help India attain swaraj. Such a civilisation, Gandhi believes, would contribute towards the reduction of political violence, the moderation of greed, the increase of compassion, the advent of economic prosperity and the spiritual integration of the individual.

The attainment of swaraj is the immediate task facing colonial India. But here Gandhi draws a subtle distinction between swaraj as self-rule and swaraj as self-government or home rule. Swaraj as self-rule is the rule of the self by the self. More precisely, it is the rule of the *mind* over itself and the passions – the passions of greed and aggression, in particular. Self-rule enables one to pursue artha and kama within the bounds of dharma.

Swaraj as self-government or home rule is the rule of the nation (*praja*) by the nation. It is the founding and maintaining of the good state (*surajya*). The good state or good self-government is possible only if Indians acquire the capacity for self-rule; but self-rule itself can flourish only within an appropriate political community. That community in modern times is the nation-state. In *Hind Swaraj* Gandhi defends the view that India is a nation deserving self-government. That India is a nation was a contested issue at the time Gandhi was writing *Hind Swaraj*. He enters into the debate by claiming that India is a *praja*, the word he uses for nation. India was a *praja* already in the pre-Islamic period; the ancient *acharyas* (teachers of Indian philosophy) contributed immensely towards the consolidation of the idea of *praja*. The places of pilgrimage they established in the South and the North, the East and the West, of India were important *praja*-building centres. Moreover, pre-Islamic Indian Culture was characterised by its openness to outside values and by its assimilative capacity. It therefore was able to assimilate the assimilable values of Islam and other religions. The recent Hindu–Muslim hostilities are therefore resolvable within the context of the notion of *praja*. In other words, the traditional notion of *praja* offers a basis upon which the new edifice of a modern, composite Indian nation-state could be built.

The Gujarati text uses the same word, swaraj, for self-rule and self-government. The English text, by contrast, uses two different words to convey these two different meanings – 'swaraj' (now used as an English word) for self-rule; and 'home rule', for self-government. It is axiomatic in *Hind Swaraj* that the good of self-government or true home rule that India achieves will be in proportion to the good of self-rule that Indians achieve. In other words, true self-government requires persons who rule themselves. That is why Britain cannot *give* self-government to Indians; they must fit themselves for it by undergoing a suitable degree of self-transformation. Once Indians have undergone such self-transformation, they will refuse to use violent means to obtain self-government or home rule. Satyagraha will appear to be a legitimate means available to those who enjoy self-rule. The Reader in *Hind Swaraj* mistakenly believes that the end of the Raj will automatically bring swaraj. The Editor replies that this is not so: it may bring mere home rule (the rule of the modern coercive state) but not true home rule (the rule of the just, limited state); in any case it will not bring about self-rule. The dispute between the Editor and the Reader (and all future readers of *Hind Swaraj*) centres on the crucial question of whether there can be true home rule or self-government without self-rule.

It becomes clear by now that self-rule cannot be acquired without the acquistion of a stable character, which can be acquired in turn only by the practice of certain virtues. The chief among them are (1) temperance/chastity (*brahmacharya*), (2) truth or truthfulness (*satya*), (3) justice or freedom from possessiveness and greed and (4) courage or the capacity to overcome fear, including the fear of death. Moreover, swaraj as self-rule is something that is capable of being experienced within oneself. Such inner experience of self-rule enables the citizens to reinforce their political ethics by their aesthetic feelings, their political action by political symbols. Gandhi invented and used with great effect the symbol of the spinning-wheel. Its invention, which occurs just prior to the writing of *Hind Swaraj*, was owed in great measure to his *experience* of self-rule at the aesthetic level. The spinning-wheel remained for him a symbol of many things – of spiritual dynamism, of the importance of manual labour, of solidarity between the rich and the poor, of the protest against the tyranny of modern 'machinery' (technology) and the economic exploitation of the poor by the rich.

According to *Hind Swaraj*, a major obstacle to Indian self-government is the sectarian nationalism fostered by certain sections of both Muslims and Hindus. The solution to this evil lies in the development of a moderate, liberal nationalism, based on the concept of *praja*, reintroduced into the political vocabulary by *Hind Swaraj*. In an effort to free religion of the evil of sectarianism, Gandhi introduces his famous distinction between religion as organisation and religion as ethics and spirituality. Underlying all organised religions there is a universal ethic and spirituality (ch. VIII) which teaches the unconditional love of God and the neighbour. At the same time religion as organisation serves as a convenient means of maintaining a certain type of pre-political identity, and as a means of reaching certain, much yearned for spiritual ends. As such, every organised religion has legitimacy. It follows that organised religions ought to practise toleration towards each other. *Hind Swaraj* teaches that there are good *religious* reasons for practising toleration.

If colonial rule in India is to be brought to an end, what Indians need is the right means to bring it about. The constitutional approach of the Moderates is politically ineffective and the violent approach of the Extremists is morally repugnant. That leaves satyagraha as the only morally acceptable alternative.

The Reader believes that the adoption of the modern state is sufficient for achieving self-government. Gandhi disputes this. He believes that the modern state without swaraj as self-rule would only replace the British Raj with an Indian Raj. In *Hind Swaraj*'s striking phrase, such a rule would produce *Englistan,* not Hindustan, 'English rule without the Englishman', 'the tiger's nature, but not the tiger' (ch. IV). The tiger is Gandhi's metaphor for the modern state: all tigers seek their prey, and it makes no difference whether the tiger is British or Indian. *Hind Swaraj* offers a greater challenge to the Indian elite aspiring to be the new rulers of India than it does to the old British elite actually ruling India. The point of this greater challenge is one of the lasting lessons of the book.

Gandhi's teaching on non-violence is another of the book's lasting lessons. Though it has its roots in Indian metaphysics, it is used in *Hind Swaraj* as a political, not metaphysical, doctrine. Its exercise has to be guided by prudence, not metaphysics. Circumstances modify the way in which the principle is applied. Casuistry, in the good sense of that term, is part and parcel of Gandhian moral reasoning on non-violence. Moreover, the theory of non-violence forms part of Gandhi's general theory of ends and means in politics. Means have to be morally as defensible as the ends themselves. The analogies that he employs in chapter XVI to illustrate this point are worth close scrutiny.

Three strands of thought on non-violence are present in *Hind Swaraj*. The first is that involuntary violence is consistent with Gandhian non-violence. 'Going to the root of the matter', Gandhi writes, 'not one man really practises such a religion [of *ahimsa*] because we do destroy life. We are said to follow that religion [of *ahimsa*] because we want to obtain freedom from liability to kill any kind of life' (ch. X). In other words, what the ethic of non-violence seeks is the freedom from moral culpability for the sort of necessary involuntary violence that ordinary embodied life entails. The second strand concerns intention: for an act to be violent in the Gandhian sense, an intention to harm another living being has to be present. Thus, for example, the act of restraining a child rushing into a fire is only apparently violent. 'I hope you will not consider that it is still physical force, though of a low order, when you would forcibly prevent the child from rushing towards the fire if you could' (ch. XVI). The third strand has to do with legitimate self-defence: self-defence within the limits of natural justice is consistent with non-violence. Gandhian non-violence expects the *just* state to be the guarantor of internal peace and external security. What is inconsistent with non-violence is the principle of *raison d'état* that refuses to recognise the higher law of dharma, namely the behaviour of the modern state when it pursues policies on the basis of an allegedly autonomous 'national interest' (*prajano swarth*, ch. XVI).

What is being defended in *Hind Swaraj*, then, is the relative moral superiority of non-violence over violence: 'at least in the majority of cases, if not, indeed, in all, the force of love and pity is infinitely greater than the force of arms' (ch. xvɪ). Non-violence, according to Gandhi, has its source in soul-force (*atmabal*), and violence in body-force (*sharirbal*). He uses a number of terms to describe the qualities of soul-force: love-force (*prembal*), truth-force (*satyabal*), compassion-force (*dayabal*), suffering-force (*tapbal*) and justice-force (*nitibal*). The soul is able to exercise these forces natural to it only when the mind is able to exercise control over itself and the passions. Ultimately, then, the success of the ethic of non-violence depends on the state of the soul, the mind and the passions – in one word, on self-rule.

The success of a non-violent social order depends also on an appropriate system of education and an appropriate technology. Part of the fascination of Indians for modern civilisation arises from the uncritical attitude Indians have developed towards the existing educational system and towards 'machinery'. And it should come as no surprise that *Hind Swaraj* should repudiate Macaulay's 'Minute on education'.

The attitude that *Hind Swaraj* exhibits towards 'machinery' is controversial, to say the least. In the course of time, Gandhi moderated his stand. But even in *Hind Swaraj*, as a close study of the similes he uses for 'machinery' would suggest, his stand is not at all one-sided. True, similes such as 'Upas tree', 'snake-hole', 'whirlwind', 'drift-net' and 'craze' point to the harmful potential of modern technology. But these are not the decisive similes of the book: the decisive simile is 'curable disease'. 'Machinery' no doubt tends to produce cultural diseases; but such diseases need not be fatal, provided a competent doctor (Gandhi himself, presumably) can be found in good time.

Gandhi has no doubt that technology can make a positive contribution. But it can do so only if it is informed by a moral vision of the human good. For him that vision can be found in dharma – dharma not as a subjective legitimising device, but as something rooted in truth (*satya*) itself and discoverable by the natural power of the soul. That truth stipulates that the technology that is appropriate for India should meet the needs of the masses of India. Modern technology does not stipulate this; historically it has tended to reward the skilled and the powerful and to marginalise the poor and the weak. Gandhi wants to modify this trend. He wants a technology for India that would improve the material welfare of all, not just that of the rich and the highly educated, and improve it without undermining the process of self-rule. His debate is not on whether India needs technology; his debate is on the kind of technology that India needs. In any case, he sees very clearly the connection between truth, swaraj, the moral vision of the human good, technology and economic development.

In *Hind Swaraj*, he says, he 'took it as understood that anything that helped India to get rid of the grinding poverty of her masses would in the same process also establish swaraj' (*CW* 39: 389). That being the case, to give an ascetic interpretation to *Hind Swaraj*, and indeed to his political philosophy, as some critics tend to do, is to do a great injustice both to the book and its author. Gandhi wants Indians to be well fed, well housed, well clothed, well governed, well read, and cognisant of the place and function of aesthetics and art in life. It is therefore absolutely essential to separate the asceticism peculiar to Gandhi as an individual from the humanism that he promotes as a social and political philosopher. If there was one thing that pained him more than anything else, it was the poverty of the Indian masses. His asceticism is a penitential expression of that pain: he wanted to suffer voluntarily in his person what the multitude suffered involuntarily in their persons – so that their pain may be brought to a quicker end.

Finally, the political theory enunciated in *Hind Swaraj* is a theory of, and about, practice. Such a theory requires that the theoretician be simultaneously the practitioner. Whoever enjoys self-rule transforms himself or herself in some measure. Self-rule without self-transformation is not Gandhian. Hence swaraj is not, and is not intended to be, a Utopia. 'Do not consider this swaraj to be a dream. There is no idea of sitting still' (ch. xiv). Swaraj is not a dream in the sense that each individual must attempt to improve himself or herself. It is not a dream in a second sense in that it contributes towards the achievement of true home rule and the introduction of necessary institutional changes.

THE RECEPTION OF *HIND SWARAJ*

The initial reception of *Hind Swaraj*, except in the case of Tolstoy, was hostile. The sage of Yasnaya Polyana wrote to say that the question of passive resistance raised in the book was 'of the greatest importance not only for India but for the whole of humanity' (*CW* 10: 505). In March 1910 the Government of India reacted by banning the book for fear of sedition. Shyamji Krishnavarma wrote a blistering attack in his *The Indian Sociologist* (October 1913): Gandhi, 'an admirer of Jesus Christ', wrote the admirer of Herbert Spencer, was trying to put into practice 'the extreme Christian theory of suffering'. W. J. Wybergh, though more respectful, was no less critical. Even Gokhale thought that Gandhi had written in haste and that, upon reflection, he would revise the book's philosophy.

Only in 1919 did *Hind Swaraj* become widely known in India. It was then treated as the manifesto of the Gandhian revolution by most Indians. But there were critics from the right and from the left. The pioneers of Indian Marxism, such as S. Dange, in his *Gandhi vs Lenin* (1921), and M. N. Roy, in his *India in Transition* (1922), saw the significance of the book, only to dismiss it as representing 'Christian piety' and mere humanitarianism, and as being ignorant of the 'laws' of class struggle. Sir Sankaran Nair, one of India's outstanding legal minds and a former president of the Congress, castigated Gandhi in his *Gandhi and Anarchy* (1922) for the alleged anarchical tendencies inherent in satyagraha. From the 1930s onward B. R. Ambedkar became one of Gandhi's severe critics. But, strangely enough, he did not confront *Hind Swaraj* as such.

By contrast, the reception of Gandhi in the United States was warm and enthusiastic. An American edition of *Hind Swaraj* under the title *Sermon on the Sea* (1924) was edited by Haridas T. Mazumdar and introduced by John Haynes Holmes, the leading American Christian liberal of the day. Gandhi became a lively topic of debate on such issues as mass production and centralisation vs decentralisation (Pearson 1924, 948–9; Frank 1925, 568–72; Penty 1925, 79; Kapur 1992).

The first serious appraisal of *Hind Swaraj* by British writers took place in the September 1938 issue of *The Aryan Path*. The reaction ranged from enthusiasm to respectful criticism. Among the participants were G. D. H. Cole, John Middleton Murry, Frederick Soddy and Gerald Heard.

In 1945 Gandhi had his celebrated debate with Nehru on the social policy suitable for a free India. And *Hind Swaraj* was the point of departure of this historic encounter. (For the text of the debate, see below, pp. 149–56.) In October 1973 *Gandhi Marg*, the official journal of Gandhi Peace Foundation, published a scholarly symposium on the book. While most articles were favourable to Gandhi, R. C. Majumdar's was critical of his stand on modern civilisation and the Hindu–Muslim problem. In 1985 a substantial volume, *Hind Swaraj: A Fresh Look* (Prasad 1985), appeared. It reviewed the book's impact on modern Indian politics and proposed ways of increasing it in the future.

So much for works concerned specifically with *Hind Swaraj*. It remains to be added that all serious studies and biographies of Gandhi, whose number is now legion, unfailingly recognise that this book is the indispensable tool for the study of Gandhi.

HIND SWARAJ IN RELATION TO GANDHI'S CONTEMPORARY INFLUENCE

In the post-colonial era Gandhi's influence is being felt in a number of fields. In India it inspired Vinoba Bhave's land-gift movement and J. P. Narayan's resistance movement against Indira Gandhi's authoritarian regime of 1975–7. It also inspired, and continues to inspire, a host of voluntary organisations dedicated to the economic and social improvement of India's poor. For Indian intellectuals such as Bhikhu Parekh (1989a, 1989b) and Ashis Nandy (1987), Gandhi remains the model analyst of India's colonial experience. For a large number of Indian writers both in English and in Indian languages (R. K. Narayan, Mulk Raj Anand, Raja Rao, Prem Chand, to mention a few), he remained and still remains a source of artistic inspiration.

Outside India, Gandhi's ideas have given impetus to such sociopolitical movements as Lanza del Vasto's 'Community of the Ark' movement, (France, 1948), Martin Luther King Jr's civil rights movement, the peace movement of the 1960s and 1970s, and the contemporary green and environmental movements. In 'conflict resolution studies', thanks to such scholars as Joan Bondurant, Arne Naess and Gene Sharp, Gandhi occupies the status of a founding father. The same is the case with 'development studies' pioneered by such scholars as Fritz Schumacher. In studies related to the problem of religious pluralism Gandhi, according to Margaret Chatterjee, is now recognised as a pathfinder. Erik Erikson's *Gandhi's Truth* has contributed significantly to the sub-field of psycho-history. As if capping these influences is the opera *Satyagraha*, by Philip Glass, the American composer. Briefly, Gandhi's influence is not limited to what Indians sometimes call 'the anti-colonial discourse'; instead it extends along a much broader front. But no matter which aspect of his influence one wishes to explore, it will not be long before one will be led to *Hind Swaraj*.

Moving in another direction, one sees *Hind Swaraj* as a text that lends itself to the study of comparative political thought. As someone who attempted to integrate what is worth salvaging in modern civilisation within the framework of Hindu thought, Gandhi compares favourably with those in the West who have made a similar attempt to integrate modernity within the framework of Western classical political thought. In so far as this is the case, *Hind Swaraj* may profitably be read alongside the basic texts of such figures as Jacques Maritain, Eric Voegelin, Leo Strauss and Hannah Arendt, for part of Gandhi's enduring significance lies, as Susanne Rudolph and Lloyd Rudolph have well argued, in his effort to update the Indian tradition.

Hind Swaraj has also something to contribute to our understanding of the nature of freedom in general and liberal freedom in particular. Swaraj as self-rule means inner freedom or positive freedom. Gandhi's argument that without swaraj as self-rule swaraj as self-government could degenerate into state oppression even in the so-called liberal societies is worth pondering. In this context his definition of satyagraha in chapter XVII is of great value: satyagraha is 'a method of securing rights by personal suffering'. 'Rights' here has a liberal meaning, albeit a meaning according to Gandhi's concept of liberalism, which is that to every right there is a corresponding duty. And even though Gandhi's liberalism is not the same as contemporary Western liberalism, that by itself does not disqualify its being a kind of liberalism. For there may well be a liberalism with a Gandhian face, a liberalism suited to the Indian environment. In so far as this is the case, *Hind Swaraj* may be compared and contrasted with such Western texts as J.S. Mill's *On Liberty*.

Finally, there is one aspect of *Hind Swaraj* which past critics have underlined and which deserves underlining again today. That aspect refers to Gandhi's conception of the connection between self-realisation (*atmadarshan*) and politics (*rajyaprakaran*). According to Gandhi, the two may not be radically separated. Inner change within the individual ought to be the starting point of outer changes in society. Modern social science tends to ignore this principle. Gandhi reinstates it into political philosophy. George Catlin understood Gandhi correctly on this point when he drew a comparison between *Hind Swaraj* and the *Spiritual Exercises* (Catlin 1950, 215): both teach that the project of outer trans-formation ought to begin with the inner transformation of the moral agent. Gerald Heard also saw the same point when he drew a compar-ison between genuine *satyagrahis* and Jesuits trained in intelligence and deep will (Heard 1949, 88). In short, *Hind Swaraj*, besides being a dialogue on swaraj, is also an intensely 'spiritual' and intensely 'practical' book, one that teaches that there is a link between inner life and outer achievement, that individual regeneration and national regeneration constitute one continuum. However difficult the task of bringing about outer transformation may appear to be, there is always something that the concerned individual can do, and that is to try to bring about his or her inner transformation. That certainly was the point of some advice that Gandhi once gave to a colleague who felt somewhat discouraged the first time he read *Hind Swaraj*. This colleague had wondered: what can one individual do to emancipate India? 'Please do not carry unneces-sarily on your head the burden of emancipating India', Gandhi wrote back. 'Emancipate your own self. Even that burden is very great. Apply everything to yourself. Nobility of soul consists in realising that you are yourself India. In your emancipation is the emancipation of India. All else is make-believe' (*CW* 10: 206–7).

A corollary to the above point is that a single emancipated person can make a difference in the world. 'If there be only one such [emancipated] Indian', states chapter xx, 'the English will have to listen to him.' Gandhi undoubtedly was one such Indian. But the same may be said of any individual who implements the teachings of *Hind Swaraj*: when such a person speaks, the other will listen and the dialogue will continue.

A note on the history of the text
*

1909 *Hind Swarajya* was written in Gujarati between 13 and 22
November on board the *Kildonan Castle*, on Gandhi's return trip
from England to South Africa; it was published in two
instalments in the Gujarati section of *Indian Opinion* (11 and 19
December).

1910 Published in book form in January by Gandhi's own
International Printing Press, Phoenix, Natal, South Africa; the
Gujarati text was banned from India for security reasons, 24
March; the English translation by Gandhi, under the title *Indian
Home Rule*, with Preface and Foreword, was published by
International Printing Press, Phoenix, Natal, 20 March. On the
title page of the English translation Gandhi changes the
Gujarati title from *Hind Swarajya* to *Hind Swaraj*.

1914 The second Gujarati edition, with a new Preface, was published
by International Printing Press, Phoenix, Natal.

1919 The first Indian edition of *Indian Home Rule*, with a new Foreword
by Gandhi and a 'Note' by C. Rajagopalachari, was published in
Madras by Ganesh and Co. It dropped both the 1909 Foreword
and the 1910 Preface; adopted as the manifesto of the Gandhian
revolution.

1921 The first Hindi translation, with a new Preface and a 'Note'
endorsing the place of Indian-owned textile mills in India, was
published in Ahmedabad by Navajivan. In a *Young India* editorial
of 26 January Gandhi gave the English text the new title *Hind
Swaraj or Indian Home Rule*. All subsequent editions of the English
text are known under this combined title. Two other Madras

publishers, Natesan and Co. and Tagore and Co., brought out their own reprints of the 1919 Indian edition.

1924 An American edition under the title of *Sermon on the Sea*, edited by Haridas T. Mazumdar, and with an Introduction by John Haynes Holmes, was published by Universal Publishing Company, Chicago.

1938 Navajivan Karyalaya of Ahmedabad published a reprint of the 1919 Madras edition with a Preface dated 2 February by Mahadev Desai, Gandhi's secretary. Later in the same year Navajivan, Ahmedabad, published the Revised New Edition (RNE), with a 'Preface to the New Edition' dated 11 December by 'M. D.' (Mahadev Desai). The Navajivan Trust secured the copyright of *Hind Swaraj or Indian Home Rule*. The ban on *Hind Swaraj* was lifted on 21 December (Mss. no. 605, Nehru Museum).

1939 Navajivan, Ahmedabad, reissued the RNE. *The Collected Works of Mahatma Gandhi* 10 (1963) and the Oxford edition of *The Moral and Political Writings of Mahatma Gandhi* (1986, edited by Raghavan Iyer) have used the text of the RNE.

1997 The 1910 English text (with its Foreword and Preface), which the present editor believes to be the most authentic of all existing English texts, is reissued here for the first time since 1910 with the permission of the Navajivan Trust, Ahmedabad.

The present editor, following the Madras and Ahmedabad editors, has added a table of contents which the 1910 edition did not have. Where appropriate, spelling and punctuation have been brought up to date; other editorial changes to the 1910 text have been duly noted in the footnotes.

Principal events in the life of
Mohandas Karamchand Gandhi
*

1869 Born on 2 October at Probandar, Gujarat, into a Modh Bania family.

1883 Marries Kasturbai Makanji.

1888 Birth of Harilal, his eldest son; leaves for England to study law.

1890 Joins the London Vegetarian Society.

1891 Called to the Bar from the Inner Temple (debarred in 1922, reinstated in 1988); returns to India.

1893 Arrives in Durban, South Africa, to work for an Indian Muslim trading firm; experiences racial discrimination at the Pietermaritzburg railway station.

1894 Becomes the founder-secretary of Natal Indian Congress; enrolled as barrister in the High Court of Natal; starts campaign against anti-Indian racial laws.

1895 Visits the Mariannhill Trappist Monastery, outside Durban.

1896 Visits India, June-November.

1897 Returns to South Africa; at Durban harbour met by an angry mob of white settlers; escapes, with the assistance of local white police, in the guise of an Indian constable.

1899 Organises an Indian Ambulance Corps to assist the British in the Second Anglo-Boer War.

1901 Returns to India for a year.

1902 Returns to South Africa.

1903   Settles in Johannesburg; *Indian Opinion* commences
        publication; work against anti-Indian racial legislation
        continues.

1904   Reads Ruskin's *Unto This Last*; founds an experimental Phoenix
        Settlement outside Durban.

1906   Organises an Indian Ambulance Corps during the Zulu
        'Rebellion'; takes the vow of chastity; at a mass meeting
        moves the famous resolution IV proposing civil disobedience
        against anti-Indian racial legislation; visits London on a
        Transvaal Indian Deputation to lobby for Indian interests.

1908   The term 'satyagraha' formally adopted; the mass burning of
        registration certificates in Johannesburg; first imprisonment
        (10–30 January); second imprisonment (7 October–12 December).

1909   Third imprisonment (25 February–24 May); July–November in
        London to lobby for South African Indian interests; on the
        return voyage, 13–22 November, writes *Hind Swaraj* and
        translates Tolstoy's *Letter to a Hindoo*. [R. Shamasastry
        publishes the text of the newly discovered *Arthasastra* of
        Kautilya in *Bibliotheca Sanskrita*, Mysore.]

1910   Establishes the Tolstoy Farm, outside Johannesburg, on land
        donated by his friend Hermann Kallenbach.

1913   Leads the 'great march' of *satyagrahis* (2, 037 men, 127 women
        and 57 children) from Charlestown to Volksrust to protest
        against anti-Indian legislation; fourth imprisonment
        (11 November–18 December).

1914   The Gandhi–Smuts agreement reached; leaves South Africa
        for good; in London August–December; organises an
        Ambulance Corps of Indians living in England to help in
        World War I.

1915   Arrives in India in January; establishes the Sabarmati Ashram
        in Ahmedabad.

1917 Applies principles of satyagraha to settle the grievances of indigo workers in Champaran, Bihar.

1918 Applies principles of satyagraha to settle the Ahmedabad textile workers' strike and the Kheda peasants' grievances; actively recruits volunteers for the Indian army to fight in World War I.

1919 Leads the all-India satyagraha against the Rowlatt Act; *Hind Swaraj* printed and distributed as the manifesto of the Gandhian revolution; supports the Khilafat movement; becomes editor of the weeklies, *Navajivan* (Gujarati) and *Young India* (English); under arrest, 9–11 April, while on a train journey from Kosi to Bombay.

1920 The Indian National Congress adopts Gandhi's programme of non-cooperation.

1922 The Chauri Chaura massacre of 21 Indian policemen by unruly mob forces Gandhi to suspend satyagraha; fifth imprisonment (10 March 1922–5 February 1924).

1924 President of the Indian National Congress.

1927 Publishes *The Story of my Experiments with Truth* Vol. I.

1928 Publishes *Satyagraha in South Africa*; visits Kerala in support of Vykom satyagraha.

1929 Publishes *The Story of my Experiments with Truth* Vol. II.

1930 Leads the 200-mile Salt March, from Ahmedabad to Dandi, 12 March–5 April, and breaks the salt laws; sixth imprisonment (5 May 1930–26 January 1931).

1931 The Gandhi–Irwin Pact; attends the Round Table Conference in London.

1932 Seventh imprisonment (4 January–20 September); fasts to protest against the proposed separate electorate for the Untouchables.

1933 Eighth imprisonment (1–4 August); ninth imprisonment (4–23 August); founds the English weekly, *Harijan*; Sabarmati Ashram closed down permanently.

1934   Inaugurates all-India Village Industries Association; resigns formally from the Indian National Congress.

1936   Founds the Sevagram Ashram, near Wardha.

1937   Inaugurates New Educational Conference at Wardha.

1941   Publishes *Constructive Programme: Its Meaning and Place.*

1942   Launches the Quit India Movement; tenth imprisonment (9 August 1942–6 May 1944).

1944   Death of his wife in prison; Gandhi–Jinnah talks on Hindu–Muslim unity.

1946   Meets with the Cabinet Mission and attends the Simla Conference; tours the riot-ridden districts of Bengal.

1947   The partition of India and Indian independence; in Calcutta, begins a fast as a means to restore Hindu–Muslim peace.

1948   Begins a fast in New Delhi as a means to restore Hindu–Muslim–Sikh peace; 29 January writes a draft constitution for the Indian National Congress; 30 January assassinated in New Delhi by Nathuram Godse, a Hindu extremist.

Biographical synopses

*

LORD AMPTHILL (1869–1935). Governor of Madras, 1900–6; acting Viceroy, 1904; author of the Foreword to Doke's biography of Gandhi; president of South Africa British Indian Committee (London); corresponded with Gandhi during his 1909 London stay; received a 'preview' of *HS*.

ASQUITH, Herbert Henry (1852–1928). Liberal prime minister, 1908–16; mentioned in ch. v.

BALFOUR, Arthur James (1848–1930). Conservative prime minister, 1902–5; mentioned in ch. v.

CARLYLE, Thomas (1795–1881). Gandhi read his biographies of Burns, Johnson and Scott, *French Revolution* and *Of Heroes and Hero Worship and the Heroic in History*, during his two prison terms in 1908; mentioned in ch. v.

CARPENTER, Edward (1844–1929). English writer, vegetarian, teetotaller, Anglican priest, author of *Civilisation, its Cause and Cure*; mentioned in ch. vi and in Appendix 1 to *HS*.

CAVOUR, Conte Camillo Benso di (1810–61). Founder, with Count Cesare Bilbao of *Il Risorgimento*, the organ of the Italian nationalist movement; mentioned in ch. xv.

CHAMBERLAIN, Joseph (1836–1914). As Secretary of State for Colonies, he wanted to prosecute Gandhi's 1897 racial assailants; Gandhi addressed several important memorials to him on his 1902 South Africa visit; mentioned in ch. vii.

CURZON, George Nathaniel (1859–1925). Viceroy, 1899–1905; responsible for the partition of Bengal in 1905; mentioned in ch. ii.

DESAI, Mahadev Haribhai (1892–1942). Gandhi's secretary from 1917 to 1942; translated Gandhi's *Autobiography* into English, and edited the 1938 new revised edition of *HS*; died in prison.

DHINGRA, Madan Lal (*c.* 1887–1909). Born in Amritsar district he came to London in 1906 to study engineering at Imperial College; came under the spell of V. D. Savarkar; lived in India House (London) for two periods between 1908 and 1909; on 1 July 1909 assassinated Sir William Curzon-Wyllie, aide-de-camp to Lord Morley, the Secretary of State for India; tried, hanged and buried in London on 17 August 1909; remains were exhumed and brought back to India and cremated at Amritsar in 1976; mentioned in ch. xv.

DUTT, Romesh Chunder (1848–1909). Born in Calcutta, member of the Indian Civil Service; Revenue Minister of Baroda, lecturer in Indian history at the University of London, and the author of the *Economic History of India* (1901–2) listed in Appendix I to *HS*; mentioned in ch. xix.

GAEKWARD, Sayaji Rao III (1863–1939). Maharaja of Baroda; introduced compulsory free primary education in Baroda; patron of B. R. Ambedkar; in 1910 passed an order in council to admit *bhangis* (low castes) into state schools; mentioned in ch. xviii.

GARIBALDI, Giuseppe (1807–82). Italian patriot and military leader and one of the architects of Italian unification. Mentioned in chs. xiv and xv.

GHOSE, Manomohan (1844–96). Born in Krishnagar; educated at Presidency College, Calcutta; called to the bar from Lincoln's Inn in 1862; active member of Brahmo Samaj, British Indian Association, and Indian National Congress; a pioneer in women's education in India; mentioned in ch. xi.

GLADSTONE, William Ewart (1809–98). British prime minister, 1868–74, 1880–5, 1886, 1892–4; mentioned in ch. vii.

GOKHALE, Gopal Krishna (1866–1915). Born in Ratnagiri, Maharashtra; member of the Deccan Education Society, 1884; professor at Fergusson College, 1885–1902; secretary of the Poona

Sarvajanik Sabha, 1890; editor of its *Quarterly Journal*, 1887–96;
joint secretary of the Indian National Congress, 1897; president
in 1890; member of the Bombay Legislative Council, 1899; the
Imperial Legislative Council, 1902–12; founder of the Servants
of India Society, 1905; author of a Draft Constitution of India,
1915; leader of the Moderates; Gandhi's *rajya guru* (political
guru) whose death he mourned by walking barefoot for an
entire year; mentioned in ch. I.

GRAMSCI, Antonio (1891–1937). Founding member of the Communist
Party of Italy, author of *Prison Notebooks*; influenced the
development of Neo-Marxist thought in modern India.

HUME, Allan Octavian, CB (1829–1912). Son of Joseph Hume, the
Radical MP; born in London; joined the Bengal Civil Service
in 1849; appointed to the district of Etawah, Uttar Pradesh,
where he introduced free primary education and founded a
vernacular newspaper, *Lokmitra (People' s Friend)*; author of
Agricultural Reform of India, and the three-volume classic
The Game Birds of India; after retirement worked towards the
formation of the Indian National Congress in 1885, of which he
remained secretary until 1906; author of the famous 'Circular
letter to the graduates of the University of Calcutta', and of
various pamphlets, among them *The Rising Tide or the Progress
of Political Activity in India* (1886), *The Old Man' s Hope* (1886), *The
Star in the East* (1886), *A Conversation between Moulvi Farid-ud-din …
and Rambuksh* (1887); the first to recommend the Canadian
model of self-government as suitable for India; mentioned
in ch. I.

KALLENBACH, Hermann (1871–1945). Architect, theosophist, Tolstoyan,
one of Gandhi's closest Jewish friends in South Africa, and the
donor of the 1,100-acre Tolstoy Farm. Born in Lithuania, he
arrived in South Africa in 1896, and first met Gandhi in 1902;
Gandhi dictated the English translation of *HS* to him; in 1913
jailed with Gandhi; accompanied him to London in 1914; visited
him in India in 1937 and also 1939. A four-volume

correspondence between the two is preserved at Nehru Museum, New Delhi.

KRISHNA VARMA, Shyamji (1857–1930). Expatriate Indian nationalist living in London at the turn of the twentieth century; founder of 'India House', Highgate, London; founding editor of *The Indian Sociologist*; follower of the philosophy of Herbert Spencer. Conflict with the authorities forced him to flee London in 1907 for Paris; later settled in Geneva, where he died. His ashes were transferred to India in 2003.

KRUGER, Stephanus Johannes Paulus (1825–1904). Transvaal statesman, general and president of the Transvaal, 1883–1900. Gandhi wrote a generous obituary for him (*CW* 4: 225); mentioned in ch. VII.

LLOYD GEORGE, David (1863–1945). British prime minister, 1916–22; mentioned in ch. XVIII.

MACAULAY, Thomas Babington (1800–59). Law member of the Supreme Council of India, 1834–8; president of the commission to oversee the drafting of the penal code and the code of criminal procedure for India, 1837; author of the 'Minute on education' (1835); mentioned in ch. XVIII.

MAINE, Henry James Sumner (1822–88). Law member of the Supreme Council of India, 1863–9; member of Secretary of State's Council for India, 1871–88; Regius professor of civil law at Cambridge, 1847–54; professor of comparative jurisprudence at Oxford, 1869–78; professor of international law at Cambridge, 1887–8; author of *Village Communities*, listed in Appendix 1 to *HS*.

MAUDUDI, Sayyid Abul Ala (1903–1979). Major twentieth-century militant Islamist thinker; born in Aurangabad, India; founder of the Jamaat-e-Islami (1941); migrated to Pakistan after Partition; author of *Jihad in Islam* (1939) and *Political Theory of Islam* (1939); died in Buffalo, New York.

MAZZINI, Giuseppe (1805–72). Italian patriot, founder of Young Italy and collaborator with Garibaldi in the Italian nationalist movement. In 1905 Gandhi wrote an appreciative essay about him (*CW* 5: 27–8); mentioned in chs. XIV and XV.

MEHTA, Pranjivan (1858–1932). Medical doctor, lawyer, jeweller and one of Gandhi's closest friends and greatest benefactors; first met Gandhi in London in 1888; introduced him to Rajchandbhai Mehta in 1891; visited him in South Africa in 1897; spent two months (September–October 1909) with him in London; instrumental in getting a copy of Tolstoy's *Letter to a Hindoo* for Gandhi; donor of Rs. 250,000 to the Gujarath Vidyapith; author of *M. K. Gandhi and the South African Problem* (1911), one of the best analyses of Gandhi's life and thought up to 1910.

MEHTA, Rajchandbhai Ravjibhai (1868–1901), also Rajchandra and Rajchand. Jain mystic, poet and jeweller, and Gandhi's spiritual adviser but not guru. Gandhi wrote an Introduction to his *Life and Thought*.

MILL, John Stuart (1806–73). British philosopher and economist; clerk at India House, 1823–56; Chief Examiner of India Correspondence, 1856–8; mentioned in ch. IV.

MORLEY, John (1838–1923). Secretary of State for India 1905–10; author, with Lord Minto, of the Minto–Morley Reforms (1909); mentioned in chs. X and XV.

NAOROJI, Dadabhai (1825–1917). The Grand Old Man of India. A Parsee, he graduated from Elphinstone College, Bombay, in 1845; professor of Gujarati at the University of London, 1856–66; founded the London India Society, 1865, East India Association, 1866; dewan of Baroda, 1874; member of the Bombay Legislative Council, 1885; president of the Indian National Congress, 1886, 1893 and 1906; liberal member of the House of Commons elected from Central Finsbury, London, 1902; leader of the Congress Moderates; author of *Poverty and Un-British Rule in India*, 1901, listed in Appendix I to *HS*; mentioned in ch. I.

NADWI, Abul Hasan Ali (Ali Miyan) 1913–1999. A major Islamic thinker of the twentieth-century, Rector of Darul Uloom, Nadwatul Ulama, Lucknow, India; author of the very influential *Islam and the World* (1951), with an Introduction by Saiyyid Qutub of Cairo, and translated from the Urdu by Mohammad Asif Kidwai, published by the Academy of Islamic Research and Publications, Lucknow.

NEHRU, Jawaharlal (1889–1964). The first prime minister of India, 1947–64; friend and confidant of Gandhi.

POLAK, Henry Solomon Leon (1882–1959). Lawyer, journalist and one of Gandhi's close friends. Born in London, he emigrated to South Africa where he first met Gandhi in 1904; instrumental in introducing Gandhi to Ruskin; third editor of *Indian Opinion*; articled with Gandhi at Johannesburg; Gandhi was the 'sponsor' at his wedding; in 1909 sent to India as an emissary of South African Indians; recipient of the 'preview' of *HS*; imprisoned with Gandhi in 1913.

RANADE, Mahadev Govind (1842–1901). Eminent jurist, pioneer social reformer, economist, historian and one of the founders of the Indian National Congress; was educated at Elphinstone College, Bombay, graduating in history, economics and law, 1864; editor of the Anglo-Marathi daily, *Induprakash*, 1864–71; the founder of the *Quarterly Journal of the Sarvajanik Sabha*; law member of the Bombay Legislative Council, 1885; a Judge of the Bombay High Court, 1893–1901; and author of *Essays in Indian Economics* (1899) and *Rise of the Maratha Power* (1901); mentioned in ch. XVI.

RUSKIN, John (1819–1900). Slade professor of art at Oxford, and social critic; his *Unto This Last* (1860) is one of the major formative influences on Gandhi.

SAVARKAR, Vinayak Damodar (1883–1966). Author of *Hindutva: Who is a Hindu?* (1923); president of Hindu Maha Sabha, 1937–43; Gandhi's interlocutor in *Hind Swaraj*, and the first proponent of the extreme ethnocentric Hindutva nationalist ideology.

SPENCER, Herbert (1820–1903). English political philosopher; political guru of Shyamji Krishnavarma; mentioned in ch. IV.

SMUTS, Jan Christian (1870–1950). South African statesman and Gandhi's
political opponent; the Gandhi–Smuts agreement of 1914
brought the South African phase of Gandhi's life to a close.

THOREAU, Henry David (1817–62). American political thinker. In two of
his essays, *On the Duty of Civil Disobedience* (1849) and *Life Without
Principle* (1863), Gandhi found confirmation of his own ideas of
civil disobedience.

TOLSTOY, Count Leo Nikolaevich (1828–1910). One of the major
influences on Gandhi's philosophy of non-violence and his
philosophy of religion; six of his works listed in Appendix I to
HS; translated his *Letter to a Hindoo* and had his *The Kingdom of God
is Within You* and *What is Art?* translated into Gujarati. Tolstoy
personally endorsed the philosophy of *HS*.

TULSIDAS (1532–1623). The greatest Hindi poet, and author of
Ramcharitmanas; mentioned in chs. xiv and xvii.

TYEBJI, Badruddin (1844–1906). Muslim statesman from Bombay; called
to the Bar from the Middle Temple, 1867; president of the Indian
National Congress, 1887; prosperous lawyer with an annual
income from legal practice of about Rs. 100,000 (*CW* 5: 142);
mentioned in ch. I.

VICTOR EMANUEL II (1820–78). Took part in the war against Austria,
1848–9; king of Italy, 1861–78; mentioned in ch. xv.

WEDDERBURN, Sir William (1838–1918). Joined the Indian Civil Service in
1859 and retired in 1887 as chief secretary to the Government of
Bombay; after retirement worked for the Indian National
Congress becoming its president twice (1889 and 1910); MP for
Banff, 1892–1900; Gandhi maintained an extensive
correspondence with him and spoke warmly of him in ch. I.

Guide to further reading

*

Bondurant, Joan, 1965. *Conquest of Violence*, Berkeley, CA.

Brown, Judith M., 1989. *Gandhi: Prisoner of Hope*, New Haven, CT.

Chatterjee, Margaret, 1983. *Gandhi's Religious Thought*, London.

Dalton, Dennis, 1993. *Mahatma Gandhi: Non-Violent Power in Action*, New York.

Erikson, Erik H., 1969. *Gandhi's Truth*, New York.

Gandhi, M. K., 1927. *The Story of my Experiments with Truth*, Ahmedabad.

    1928. *Satyagraha in South Africa*, Ahmedabad.

Gandhi, Rajmohan, 1995. *The Good Boatman*, New Delhi.

Green, Martin, 1983. *Tolstoy and Gandhi: Men of Peace*, New York.

Lanza del Vasto, Joseph Jean, 1972. *Return to the Sources*, New York.

Merton, Thomas (ed.), 1965. *Gandhi on Non-Violence*, New York.

Nanda, B. R., 1985. *Gandhi and His Critics*, Delhi.

Parekh, Bhikhu, 1989. *Gandhi's Political Philosophy*, London.

Parel, Anthony, 2006. *Gandhi's Philosophy and the Quest for Harmony*, Cambridge.

Glossary and abbreviations

*

GLOSSARY

ahimsa	non-violence
anasakti	non-attachment
artha	wealth/power, one of the four ends of human existence
atman	the permanent self underlying human personality
atma	soul
bahadur	courageous, honourable, an honorific title
Bania	third highest caste in social hierarchy – Gandhi's caste
Bapu	'Father'
bhakti	devotion to God, one of the three paths to moksha
brahmacharya	celibacy
brahmachari	one who practises celibacy
Brahman	the ultimate reality
brahmin	highest caste in social hierarchy
charkha	spinning-wheel
crore	the sum of 10,000,000
dastur	spiritual leader of Parsees
daya	mercy, compassion
dehin	the embodied self
dharma	duty, natural moral law; religion as ethics and religion as sect
dhurna	a traditional form of 'sit-down strike'
Jain or Jaina	a follower of the Jain religion
kali-yug	an 'era' of corruption

kama	pleasure, one of the four ends of human existence
khadi	home-spun cloth, made famous by Gandhi
khaddar	another name for khadi
Khuda-Ishwar	God
kudharo	uncivilised way of life (opposite of sudharo)
Kshatriya	second highest caste in the social hierarchy
lakh	the sum of 100,000
maulvi	a Muslim teacher-scholar
mullah	spiritual leader of Muslims
muni	a recluse
moksha	salvation or the ultimate end of life
panchayat	village council
pice	the basic unit of the rupee in Gandhi's time
praja	Gandhi's term for 'nation' in *Hind Swaraj*
purushartha	aim of life
purusharthas	the four canonical aims of life – dharma, artha, kama and moksha
rishi	sage
the Raj	the British regime in India
sannyasa	the last stage in the Hindu life cycle
sannyasi	one in the last stage of the Hindu life cycle, an ascetic
shastras	traditional, often considered sacred, texts
satya	truth
satyagraha	firmness in adhering to truth
satyagrahi	one who practises satyagraha
shastri	learned in Hindu scriptures
swadeshi	pertaining to one's own country
swaraj	self-rule, self-government
Upas tree	*Antiaris toxicaria*, whose poisonous latex is used as arrow poison; symbol of any life-destroying entity
vaid	name for 'medical doctors' in pre-modern India
varna	the ideal unit of a functionally divided Hindu society
varnashrama	the four-fold hierarchical division of Hindu society
Vaishnava	a member of the sect who worships Vishnu, a Hindu God
yagna	sacrificial offering

ABBREVIATIONS

HS   *Hind Swaraj or Indian Home Rule*
CW   *The Collected Works of Mahatma Gandhi*
AICC   All-India Congress Committee
AISA   All-India Spinners' Association
AIVIA   All-India Village Industries Association

Indian Home Rule

[or Hind Swaraj]

*

by

M. K. Gandhi

Being a Translation of '*Hind Swaraj*'
(Indian Home Rule), published in the
Gujarati columns of *Indian Opinion*,
11th and 18th Dec., 1909

Contents

Preface to the English translation

It is not without hesitation that the translation of 'Hind Swaraj' is submitted to the public. A European friend[1] with whom I discussed the contents, wanted to see a translation of it and, during our spare moments, I hurriedly dictated and he took it down. It is not a literal translation but it is a faithful rendering of the original. Several English friends have read it, and whilst opinions were being invited as to the advisability of publishing the work, news was received that the original was seized in India.[2] This information hastened the decision to publish the translation without a moment's delay. My fellow-workers at the

---

1 Hermann Kallenbach, Gandhi's close friend and donor of the Tolstoy Farm.
2 On 10 March 1910 *Hind Swaraj* (*HS*) was intercepted at Bombay and placed in the hands of the Gujarati interpreter of Madras High Court. On 15 March he submitted a 21-page typed resume of the book to Sir H. A. Stuart, Secretary of the Home Department. 'I have given sufficient matter to form an opinion whether it is seditious or not', wrote the interpreter. 'Nowhere the author of the book advocates revolt or the use of physical force against the British Government in India. But he openly advocates passive resistance to subvert British supremacy. He advises all people not to cooperate with Government. If this idea takes hold of the mind of young inexperienced men, it might lead to systematic strikes among Government servants of various classes, as well as Public Works such as Railway, Post, Telegraph, etc. Surely a very dangerous thought to the safety of Government. The sooner it is suppressed the better.' On the basis of this recommendation, on 24 March 1910 the Governments of India, Bombay, Madras and Bengal banned the book. For the full text of the report, see Parel (1993, 240–54).

5

International Printing Press shared my view and, by working overtime – a labour of love – they have enabled me to place the translation before the public in an unexpectedly short time. The work is being given to the public at what is practically cost-price. But, without the financial assistance of the many Indians who promised to buy copies for themselves and for distribution, it might never have seen the light of day.

I am quite aware of the many imperfections in the original. The English rendering, besides sharing these, must naturally exaggerate them, owing to my inability to convey the exact meaning of the original. Some of the friends who have read the translation have objected that the subject matter has been dealt with in the form of a dialogue. I have no answer to offer to this objection except that the Gujarati language readily lends itself to such treatment and that it is considered the best method of treating difficult subjects. Had I written for English readers in the first instance, the subject would have been handled in a different manner. Moreover, the dialogue, as it has been given, actually took place between several friends,[3] mostly readers of *Indian Opinion*, and myself.

Whilst the views expressed in 'Hind Swaraj' are held by me, I have but endeavoured humbly to follow Tolstoy, Ruskin, Thoreau, Emerson and other writers, besides the masters of Indian philosophy.[4] Tolstoy has been one of my teachers for a number of years. Those who want to see a

---

3 These include Dr Pranjivan Mehta (*CW* 71: 238), Shyamji Krishnavarma (*CW* 6: 28, 40, 73, 83-4) and V. D. Savarkar (*CW* 32: 102).

4 'the masters of Indian philosophy': during his first jail term in South Africa (January 1908) Gandhi read Manilal Nabhubhai Dwivedi's *Rajayoga, Commentary on the Gita* (Dwivedi attended the 1893 World Parliament of Religions, held at Chicago; the other to attend was Swami Vivekananda). During his second incarceration (October–December 1908) he read the *Bhagavad Gita* 'almost every day'; and during the third term (February–May 1909), the *Gita, Veda-Shabda-Sangana, the Upanishads, Manusmriti, Ramayana, Patanjal-Yoga-Darshan, Ahnika-Prakasha* and Rajchand's *Sandhya-ni Gutika* ('I memorised a portion of his [Rajchand's] writings and of the book on *Sandhya*. I would repeat them over and over again in my mind whenever I happened to wake up at night, and every morning I spent half an hour meditating on them' (*CW* 9: 241-2)).

corroboration of the views submitted in the following chapters, will find it in the works of the above named masters. For ready reference, some of the books are mentioned in the Appendices.

I do not know why 'Hind Swaraj' has been seized in India. To me, the seizure constitutes further condemnation of the civilisation represented by the British Government. There is in the book not a trace of approval of violence in any shape or form. The methods of the British Government are, undoubtedly, severely condemned. To do otherwise would be for me to be a traitor to Truth, to India, and to the Empire to which I own allegiance. My notion of loyalty does not involve acceptance of current rule or government irrespective of its righteousness or otherwise. Such notion is based upon the belief – not in its present justice or morality but – in a future acceptance by governments of that standard of morality in practice which it at present vaguely and hypocritically believes in, in theory. But I must frankly confess that I am not so much concerned about the stability of the Empire as I am about that of the ancient civilisation of India which, in my opinion, represents the best that the world has ever seen. The British Government in India constitutes a struggle between the Modern Civilisation, which is the Kingdom of Satan, and the Ancient Civilisation, which is the Kingdom of God. The one is the God of War, the other is the God of Love. My countrymen impute the evils of modern civilisation to the English people and, therefore, believe that the English people are bad, and not the civilisation they represent. My countrymen, therefore, believe that they should adopt modern civilisation and modern methods of violence to drive out the English. 'Hind Swaraj' has been written in order to show that they are following a suicidal policy, and that, if they would but revert to their own glorious civilisation, either the English would adopt the latter and become Indianised or find their occupation in India gone.

It was at first intended to publish the translation as a part of *Indian Opinion*, but the seizure of the original rendered such a course inadvisable. *Indian Opinion* represents the Transvaal Passive Resistance struggle and ventilates the grievances of British Indians in South Africa generally. It was, therefore, thought desirable not to publish through a representative organ, views which are held by me personally and which may even be considered dangerous or disloyal. I am naturally anxious not to compromise a great struggle by any action of mine which has no connection with it. Had I not known that there was a danger of methods of violence becoming popular, even in South Africa, had I not been called upon by hundreds of my countrymen, and not a few English friends, to express my opinion on the Nationalist movement in India, I would even have refrained, for the sake of the struggle, from reducing my views to writing. But, occupying the position I do, it would have been cowardice on my part to postpone publication under the circumstances just referred to.

M. K. Gandhi

Johannesburg
March 20th, 1910

Foreword

I have written some chapters on the subject of Indian Home Rule which I venture to place before the readers of *Indian Opinion*. I have written because I could not restrain myself.[5] I have read much,[6] I have pondered much, during the stay, for four months in London of the Transvaal Indian deputation.[7] I discussed things with as many of my countrymen as I could. I met, too, as many Englishmen as it was possible for me to meet. I consider it my duty now to place before the readers of *Indian Opinion* the

5 'I could not restrain myself': an indication of the inner intensity that prompted Gandhi to write *HS*. Writing to Henry Polak a few weeks before the writing of *HS*, Gandhi confessed how certain ideas were 'brewing in my mind' and how they 'had taken a violent possession of me' (*CW* 9: 478, 481; see also *CW* 32: 489).

6 During his first prison term (January 1908), Gandhi read or re-read the Bible, the Koran, Thomas Huxley's lectures, Carlyle's biographies of Burns, Johnson and Scott, Bacon's essays on civil and moral counsel, and the writings of Tolstoy, Ruskin and Plato (*CW* 8: 159). During his second prison term (October–December 1908) he read or re-read 'two books by the great Ruskin, the essays of the great Thoreau, some portions of the *Bible*, the life of Garibaldi (in Gujarati), essays of Lord Bacon' (*CW* 9: 181–2). During his third prison term (February–May 1909) he read or reread Tolstoy, Emerson, Carlyle's *French Revolution*, Mazzini and portions of the Bible (*CW* 9: 208, 241); for a survey of Gandhi's readings after 1909, see Iyer (1986–7, 1, 66–198).

7 'The Transvaal Indian deputation': in the summer of 1909 the British Parliament was debating a draft bill for the creation of the Union of South Africa. To lobby for their interests, the Transvaal Asians sent a deputation consisting of Hajee Habib and Gandhi to London. The deputation spent four disappointing months (July–November 1909) in London, and returned empty-handed (*CW* 9: 288–301; Hunt 1978, 105–42).

conclusions, which appear to me to be final. The Gujarati subscribers of
Indian Opinion number about 800. 1 am aware that, for every subscriber,
there are at least ten persons who read the paper with zest. Those who
cannot read Gujarati have the paper read to them. Such persons have
often questioned me about the condition of India. Similar questions were
addressed to me in London. I felt, therefore, that it might not be improper
for me to ventilate publicly the views expressed by me in private.

These views are mine, and yet not mine. They are mine because I
hope to act according to them. They are almost a part of my being. But,
yet, they are not mine, because I lay no claim to originality. They have
been formed after reading several books. That which I dimly felt
received support[8] from these books.

The views I venture to place before the reader are, needless to say,
held by many Indians not touched by what is known as civilisation, but I
ask the reader to believe me when I tell him that they are also held by
thousands of Europeans.[9] Those who wish to dive deep, and have time,

8 A key to the interpretation of the influence of other thinkers on Gandhi.
According to George Woodcock, 'Even the influence of Tolstoy and Ruskin can
be exaggerated, and Gandhi himself was inclined to do so, partly from a principle
of humility that made him reluctant to accept all the credit for his achievements'
(Woodcock 1972, 25–6). Of the influences of the Buddha and Buddhism, Mahavira
and Jainism, and Christ and Christianity on Gandhi, K. G. Mashruwala, one of his
close associates, declared that, of the three, Buddha and Buddhism exerted
relatively little influence on Gandhi; as for Mahavira and Jainism, he was
attracted more to their doctrine of the many-sidedness of truth (*syadvada*) than
to their theory of non-violence; by contrast, Christ and Christianity exerted a
relatively strong influence on him. He recognised that there was a 'great difference between Christ's active non-violence coupled with humanitarian service
and the retiring, inactive non-violence of Jainism and Buddhism'. The latter two
religions did not have a concept of God, which presented him with a theoretical
problem in dealing with his Buddhist and Jain friends. According to Mashruwala,

Bapu [Gandhi] was often heckled about this. It led to Bapu's particular interpretation of the term God, by the proposition 'Truth is God' instead of such others
as 'God is Truth' or 'God is Love', etc. He thereby sought to make God acceptable
not only to Jains and Buddhists but also to Marxists. (Mashruwala 1983, 126–7)

9 An indication of the fact that Gandhi's criticism of modern Western civilisation is
not inspired by any Indocentric animus.

may read certain books themselves. If time permits me, I hope to translate portions of such books for the benefit of the readers of *Indian Opinion*.

If the readers of *Indian Opinion* and others who may see the following chapters will pass their criticism on to me, I shall feel obliged to them.

The only motive is to serve my country, to find out the Truth, and to follow it. If, therefore, my views are proved to be wrong, I shall have no hesitation in rejecting them. If they are proved to be right, I would naturally wish, for the sake of the Motherland, that others should adopt them.

To make it easy reading, the chapters are written in the form of a dialogue between the reader and the editor.

M. K. Gandhi
Kildonan Castle,
November 22nd, 1909

CHAPTER I

*

The Congress[10] and its officials

READER: Just at present there is a Home Rule wave[11] passing over India. All our countrymen appear to be pining for National Independence. A similar spirit pervades them even in South Africa. Indians seem to be eager after acquiring rights. Will you explain your views in this matter?

EDITOR: You have well put the question, but the answer is not easy. One of the objects of a newspaper is to understand the popular feeling and to give expression to it; another is to arouse among the people certain desirable sentiments; and the third is fearlessly to expose popular defects. The exercise of all these three functions is involved in answering your question.[12] To a certain extent, the people's will has to be expressed; certain sentiments will need to be fostered, and defects will have to be brought to light. But, as you have asked the question, it is my duty to answer it.

READER: Do you then consider that a desire for Home Rule has been created among us?

---

10 The Indian National Congress, a political 'party' founded in 1885, is referred to as 'the Congress' throughout *HS*.

11 'Home Rule wave': in the first decade of the twentieth century, home rule or swaraj had become the focus of Congress nationalism. *Indian Opinion* in 1906 had reported on the Home Rule Movement in India (*CW* 5: 314).

12 The three functions mentioned here are also the functions that he had proposed for his newspaper, *Indian Opinion* (*CW* 4: 320 and *CW* 5: 289–90).

EDITOR: That desire gave rise to the National Congress. The choice of the word 'National' implies it.

READER: That, surely, is not the case. Young India[13] seems to ignore the Congress. It is considered to be an instrument for perpetuating British Rule.

EDITOR: That opinion is not justified. Had not the Grand Old Man of India[14] prepared the soil, our young men could not have even spoken about Home Rule. How can we forget what Mr Hume has written, how he has lashed us into action, and with what effort he has awakened us, in order to achieve the objects of the Congress? Sir William Wedderburn has given his body, mind and money to the same cause. His writings are worthy of perusal to this day. Professor Gokhale, in order to prepare the Nation, embraced poverty and gave twenty years of his life. Even now, he is living in poverty. The late Justice Buddrudin Tyebji was also one of those who, through the Congress, sowed the seed of Home Rule. Similarly, in Bengal, Madras, the Punjab and other places, there have been lovers of India and members of the Congress, both Indian and English.

READER: Stay, stay, you are going too far, you are straying away from my question. I have asked you about Home or Self-Rule; you are discussing foreign rule. I do not desire to hear English names, and you are giving me such names. In these circumstances, I do not think we can ever meet. I shall be pleased if you will confine yourself to Home Rule. All other wise talk will not satisfy me.

EDITOR: You are impatient. I cannot afford to be likewise. If you will bear with me for a while, I think you will find that you will obtain what you want. Remember the old proverb that the tree does not grow in one day.[15] The fact that you have checked me, and that you do not want to

---

13 'Young India': the Indian revolutionaries associated with India House (1905–9), London, referred to themselves as the 'Young India Party'. The name had its origin in Mazzini's concept of Young Italy. *Young India* was also the name of the weekly newspaper Gandhi edited in India from 1919 to 1931.

14 An honorific title given to Dadabhai Naoroji.

15 A Gujarati proverb: 'mangoes do not ripen in a hurry'.

hear about the well-wishers of India, shows that, for you at any rate, Home Rule is yet far away. If we had many like you, we would never make any advance. This thought is worthy of your attention.

READER: It seems to me that you simply want to put me off by talking round and round. Those whom you consider to be well-wishers of India are not such in my estimation. Why, then, should I listen to your discourse on such people? What has he whom you consider to be the father of the nation done for it? He says that the English Governors will do justice, and that we should co-operate with them.

EDITOR: I must tell you, with all gentleness, that it must be a matter of shame for us that you should speak about that great man in terms of disrespect. Just look at his work. He has dedicated his life to the service of India. We have learned what we know from him. It was the respected Dadabhai who taught us that the English had sucked our life-blood.[16] What does it matter that, today, his trust is still in the English nation? Is Dadabhai less to be honoured because, in the exuberance of youth, we are prepared to go a step further? Are we, on that account, wiser than he? It is a mark of wisdom not to kick against the very step from which we have risen higher. The removal of a step from a staircase brings down the whole of it. When, out of infancy, we grow into youth, we do not despise infancy, but, on the contrary, we recall with affection the days of our childhood. If, after many years of study, a teacher were to teach me some thing, and if I were to build a little more on the foundation laid by that teacher, I would not, on that account, be considered wiser than the teacher. He would always command my respect. Such is the case with the Grand Old Man of India. We must admit that he is the author of Nationalism.[17]

READER: You have spoken well. I can now understand that we must look upon Mr Dadabhai with respect. Without him and men like him,

---

16 A reference to the 'drain theory' made popular by Naoroji's *Poverty and Un-British Rule in India*.

17 'the author of Nationalism': the Gujarati text reads, 'We must say that the Indian nation (*praja*) is behind him.'

we would probably not have the spirit that fires us. How can the same be said of Professor Gokhale? He has constituted himself a great friend of the English; he says that we have to learn a great deal from them, that we have to learn their political wisdom, before we can talk of Home Rule. I am tired of reading his speeches.[18]

EDITOR: If you are tired, it only betrays your impatience. We believe that those who are discontented with the slowness of their parents, and are angry because the parents would not run with their children, are considered disrespectful to their parents. Professor Gokhale occupies the place of a parent. What does it matter if he cannot run with us? A nation that is desirous of securing Home Rule cannot afford to despise its ancestors. We shall become useless, if we lack respect for our elders. Only men with mature thoughts are capable of ruling themselves, and not the hasty-tempered. Moreover, how many Indians were there like Professor Gokhale, when he gave himself to Indian education? I verily believe that whatever Professor Gokhale does he does with pure motives and with a view to serving India. His devotion to the Motherland is so great, that he would give his life for it, if necessary. Whatever he says is said not to flatter anyone but because he believes it to be true. We are bound, therefore, to entertain the highest regard for him.

READER: Are we, then, to follow him in every respect?

EDITOR: I never said any such thing. If we conscientiously differed from him,[19] the learned Professor himself would advise us to follow the dictates of our conscience rather than him. Our chief purpose is not to cry down his work, but to believe that he is infinitely greater than we, and to feel assured that compared with his work for India, ours is

---

18 See Gokhale 1908, *passim*.

19 Despite Gandhi's deep respect for Gokhale, the two differed on the questions relating to modern technology, Western education and industrialisation. Although Gokhale allowed for 'certain scope' for village industries, he maintained that 'our main reliance now – exposed as we are to the competition of the whole world – must be on production with the aid of steam and machinery' (Gokhale 1908, 816).

infinitesimal. Several newspapers[20] write disrespectfully of him. It is our duty to protest against such writings. We should consider men like Professor Gokhale to be the pillars of Home Rule. It is a bad habit to say that another man's thoughts are bad and ours only are good, and that those holding different views from ours are the enemies of the country.

READER: I now begin to understand somewhat your meaning. I shall have to think the matter over, but what you say about Mr Hume and Sir William Wedderburn is beyond comprehension.

EDITOR: The same rule holds good for the English as for the Indians. I can never subscribe to the statement that all Englishmen are bad. Many Englishmen desire Home Rule for India. That the English people are somewhat more selfish than others is true, but that does not prove that every Englishman is bad. We who seek justice will have to do justice to others. Sir William does not wish ill to India – that should be enough for us. As we proceed, you will see that, if we act justly, India will be sooner free. You will see, too, that, if we shun every Englishman as an enemy, Home Rule will be delayed. But if we are just to them, we shall receive their support in our progress towards the goal.

READER: All this seems to me at present to be simply nonsensical. English support and the obtaining of Home Rule are two contradictory things. How can the English people tolerate Home Rule for us? But I do not want you to decide this question for me just yet. To pass time over it is useless. When you have shown how we can have Home Rule, perhaps I shall understand your views. You have prejudiced me against you by discoursing on English help. I would, therefore, beseech you not to continue this subject.

EDITOR: I have no desire to do so. That you are prejudiced against me is not a matter for much anxiety. It is well that I should say unpleasant things at the commencement, it is my duty patiently to try to remove your prejudice.

---

20 *Kesari* and the *Mahratta*, both owned and edited by Tilak, were hostile to Gokhale: *The Indian Sociologist*, edited by Shyamji Krishnavarma (London and Paris), considered Gokhale and the Moderates as 'lackeys' of British imperialism.

READER: I like that last statement. It emboldens me to say what I like. One thing still puzzles me. I do not understand how the Congress laid the foundation of Home Rule.

EDITOR: Let us see. The Congress brought together Indians from different parts of India, and enthused us with the idea of Nationality. The Government used to look upon it with disfavour. The Congress has always insisted that the Nation should control revenue and expenditure. It has always desired self-government after the Canadian model.[21] Whether we can get it or not, whether we desire it or not, and whether there is not something more desirable, are different questions. All I have to show is that the Congress gave us a foretaste of Home Rule. To deprive it of the honour is not proper,[22] and for us to do so would not only be ungrateful, but retard the fulfilment of our object. To treat the Congress as an institution inimical to our growth as a Nation would disable us from using that body.

21 The position originally suggested by A. O. Hume and adopted by the Moderates.
22 The Gujarati text reads: 'It would be improper for others [the Indian revolutionaries] to claim that honour.'

CHAPTER II

*

The Partition of Bengal[23]

READER: Considering the matter as you put it, it seems proper to say that the foundation of Home Rule was laid by the Congress. But you will admit that it cannot be considered a real awakening. When and how did the real awakening take place?

EDITOR: The seed is never seen. It works underneath the ground, is itself destroyed, and the tree which rises above the ground is alone seen. Such is the case with the Congress. Yet, what you call the real awakening took place after the Partition of Bengal. For this we have to be thankful to Lord Curzon. At the time of the Partition, the people of Bengal reasoned with Lord Curzon, but, in the pride of power, he disregarded all their prayers – he took it for granted that Indians could only prattle, that they could never take any effective steps. He used insulting language, and, in the teeth of all opposition, partitioned Bengal. That day may be considered to be the day of the partition of the British Empire. The shock that the British power received through the Partition has never been equalled by any other act. This does not mean that the other injustices done to India are less glaring than that done by the Partition.

---

23 The Partition of Bengal (1905–11) was a political step taken by Lord Curzon, the Viceroy, by means of which the Province of Bengal was divided into two provinces: (1) West Bengal, Bihar and Orissa with a Hindu majority, and (2) East Bengal and Assam with a Muslim majority. Gandhi was well informed of developments in Bengal; see *CW* 5: 44, 'Will India Wake Up?'; *CW* 5: 114, 'Brave Bengal'; *CW* 5: 121–2, 'Divide and Rule').

The salt-tax[24] is not a small injustice. We shall see many such things later on. But the people were ready to resist the Partition. At that time, the feeling ran high. Many leading Bengalis were ready to lose their all. They knew their power; hence the conflagration. It is now well nigh unquenchable; it is not necessary to quench it either. Partition will go, Bengal will be re-united, but the rift in the English barque will remain; it must daily widen. India awakened is not likely to fall asleep. Demand for abrogation of Partition is tantamount to demand for Home Rule. Leaders in Bengal know this, British officials realise it. That is why Partition still remains. As time passes, the Nation is being forged. Nations are not formed in a day; the formation requires years.

READER: What, in your opinion, are the results of Partition?

EDITOR: Hitherto we have considered that, for redress of grievances, we must approach the Throne, and, if we get no redress, we must sit still,

---

24 Salt is mentioned again in ch. xx. In view of the famous salt march of 1930, the reference to a salt tax here is quite significant. As far back as 1905, the salt question had entered Gandhi's political consciousness (*CW* 5: 9). The duty on salt dated back to Moghul times. Clive in Bengal set up a monopoly of salt for his senior colleagues and himself. In 1780 Warren Hastings put the manufacture of salt in the hands of the government, the price being fixed by the Governor-General in Council. In 1878, a uniform tax policy was adopted throughout India, both British India and Princely India. The private manufacture of salt and the possession of salt not derived from government sources both became illegal. Bengal and Assam got its salt from England; Bombay, Madras and Central Provinces and the Southern Princely states from the sea; and North India from rock-salt mines. Before 1878 duty on salt per maund (82 lb) was Rs. 1–13 in Bombay, Madras, Central Provinces and the Southern Princely states, Rs. 3–4 in Bengal and Assam, and Rs. 3–0 in the North. After 1878, it was respectively Rs. 2–8, 2–14, and 2.8. Net revenue from salt in 1880 was £7 million from a population of 200 million. (See Moon 1989, 857–8, 1039–41; Balfour 1899, 463–75.)

On 6 April 1946, at Gandhi's personal request, Sir Archibald Rowlands, the Finance Member of the Viceroy's Executive Council, on his own initiative ordered the abolition of the salt tax. But the Viceroy, Lord Wavell, vetoed the initiative on the grounds that premature abolition of the tax would create a salt famine. He thought that 'vanity' was prompting Gandhi (Moon 1973, 236). Gandhi was greatly upset by this. The salt tax was finally abolished by Nehru's Interim Government in October 1946. For a lively account of the last days of the salt tax, see Ghosh 1967, 122–32.

except that we may still petition. After the Partition, people saw that petitions must be backed up by force, and that they must be capable of suffering. This new spirit must be considered to be the chief result of Partition. That spirit was seen in the outspoken writings in the press.[25] That which the people said tremblingly and in secret began to be said and to be written publicly. The Swadeshi movement[26] was inaugurated.

25 Among the prominent extremist papers of the day in Bengal were *The Bande Mataram* and *The Karmayogin* (both edited by Aurobindo Ghose), *The Jugantar*, edited by Barindra Kumar Ghose and Bhupendra Nath Dutta (the brother of Swami Vivekananda) and *The Sandhya*, edited by Brahmo Bandhap Upadhyaya; in Bombay, the extremist papers included *The Kesari* and *The Mahratta*, both edited by B. G. Tilak, and *The Kal*, edited by S. M. Paranjpe.

26 *Swadeshi*: things pertaining to one's own country. A many-faceted national movement which arose in reaction to the Partition of Bengal. At the *economic* level it involved the boycott of British imports. At the *educational* level, it introduced national educational institutions in Calcutta. In 1906 Aurobindo Ghose resigned his post at Baroda College to take up the post as professor of history and political science and principal of Bengal National College in Calcutta. At the *political* level, it led to resignations from legislative councils. (See Majumdar 1975, 33–64.) As early as 1905, Gandhi saw the revolutionary potential of the Swadeshi movement: 'The movement in Bengal for the use of *swadeshi* goods is much like the Russian movement' (*CW* 5: 132). In 1907 he compared the Swadeshi movement to *Sinn Fein*, which 'literally translated into Gujarati, means exactly our *Swadeshi* movement' (*CW* 7: 213).

No cause for unhappiness would remain if *swadeshi* were to replace everything foreign. We can easily attain happiness if we exert ourselves to that end during the year that has just commenced. *Swadeshi* carries a great and profound meaning. It does not mean merely the use of what is produced in one's own country. That meaning is certainly there in *swadeshi*. But there is another meaning implied in it which is far greater and much more important. Swadeshi means reliance on our own strength. We should also know what we mean by 'reliance on our own strength'. 'Our strength' means the strength of our body, our mind and our soul. From among these, on which should we depend? The answer is brief. The soul is supreme, and therefore soul-force is the foundation on which man must build. Passive resistance or satyagraha is a mode of fighting which depends on such force. That, then, is the only real key (to success) for the Indians. (*CW* 9: 118)

For Gandhi 'swadeshi' also meant love of one's own language. The love of the Boers for Dutch, and of the Jews for Yiddish, reflect their versions of swadeshi. 'We do not believe that those who are not proud of their own language, who are not proficient in it, can have the true spirit of *swadeshi*' (ibid., 177–8).

People, young and old, used to run away at the sight of an English face; it now no longer awed them. They did not fear even a row, or being imprisoned. Some of the best sons of India are at present in banishment.[27] This is something different from mere petitioning. Thus are the people moved. The spirit generated in Bengal has spread in the North to the Punjab, and, in the South, to Cape Comorin.

READER: Do you suggest any other striking result?

EDITOR: The Partition has not only made a rift in the English ship, but has made it in ours also. Great events always produce great results. Our leaders are divided into two parties: the moderates[28] and the extremists.[29] These may be considered as the slow party and the impatient party. Some call the moderates the timid party, and the extremists the bold party. All interpret the two words according to their preconceptions. This much is certain – that there has arisen an enmity between the two. The one distrusts the other, and imputes motives. At the time of the Surat Congress,[30] there was almost a fight. I think that this division is not a good thing for the country, but I think also that such divisions will not last long. It all depends upon the leaders how long they will last.

---

27 The most prominent of those banished at this time was B. G. Tilak, imprisoned in Mandalay from 1908 to 1914.

28 The Moderates: a faction of the Congress which stood for the constitutional method of attaining self-government similar to that enjoyed by Canada. Prominent among them were Dadabhai Naoroji, Dinshaw Wacha, Pherozeshah Mehta, G. K. Gokhale, Surendranath Bannerji and Madan Mohan Malaviya.

29 The Extremists: a faction of the Congress which believed that both constitutional and extra-constitutional methods were necessary for attaining swaraj. Prominent among them were B. G. Tilak, Aurobindo Ghose, Lajpat Rai and Bepin Chandra Pal.

30 The formal split between the Moderates and the Extremists occurred in December 1907 at the Surat session of the Congress which ended in pandemonium. The transition from words to blows did not take long: 'a flying missile, a shoe, hit Pherozesha Mehta and Surendranath Bannerjea, the Moderate leaders seated on the dais. This was followed by the brandishing of sticks and the unrolling of turbans, the breaking of chairs and bruising of heads; the crowning humiliation occurred when the police came and cleared the hall' (Nanda 1977, 287).

CHAPTER III

*

Discontent and unrest

READER: Then you consider Partition to be a cause of the awakening? Do you welcome the unrest which has resulted from it?

EDITOR: When a man rises from sleep, he twists his limbs and is restless. It takes some time before he is entirely awakened. Similarly, although the Partition has caused an awakening, the comatose state has not yet disappeared. We are still twisting our limbs and still restless, and just as the state between sleep and awakening must be considered to be necessary, so may the present unrest in India be considered a necessary and, therefore, a proper state. The knowledge that there is unrest will, it is highly probable, enable us to outgrow it. Rising from sleep, we do not continue in a comatose state, but, according to our ability, sooner or later, we are completely restored to our senses. So shall we be free from the present unrest which no one likes.

READER: What is the other form of unrest?

EDITOR: Unrest is, in reality, discontent. The latter is only now described as unrest.[31] During the Congress period it was labelled discontent; Mr Hume always said that the spread of discontent in India was necessary. This discontent is a very useful thing. So long as a man is contented with his present lot, so long is it difficult to persuade him to come out of it. Therefore it is that every reform must be preceded by discontent. We throw away things we have, only when we cease to like

31 During the 1906-9 period Gandhi was following closely the course of 'discontent and unrest' in India. See, for example, 'Indian unrest', *Indian Opinion*, 20 October 1906, and 'Unrest in India', *Indian Opinion*, 1 June 1907.

them. Such discontent has been produced among us after reading the great works of Indians and Englishmen.[32] Discontent has led to unrest, and the latter has brought about many deaths, many imprisonments, many banishments. Such a state of things will still continue. It must be so. All these may be considered good signs, but they may also lead to bad results.

32 'the great works of Indians and Englishmen': these included works of Dadabhai Naoroji and R. C. Dutt, and Allan Octavian Hume.

CHAPTER IV

*

What is Swaraj?[33]

READER: I have now learnt what the Congress has done to make India one nation, how the Partition has caused an awakening, and how discontent and unrest have spread through the land. I would now like to know your views on Swaraj. I fear that our interpretation is not the same.

EDITOR: It is quite possible that we do not attach the same meaning to the term. You and I and all Indians are impatient to obtain Swaraj, but we are certainly not decided as to what it is. To drive the English out of India is a thought heard from many mouths, but it does not seem that many have properly considered why it should be so. I must ask you a question. Do you think that it is necessary to drive away the English,[34] if we get all we want?

READER: I should ask of them only one thing, that is: 'Please leave our country.' If after they have complied with this request, their withdrawal from India means that they are still in India, I should have no objection. Then we would understand that, in our language, the word 'gone' is equivalent to 'remained'.

EDITOR: Well, then, let us suppose that the English have retired. What will you do then?

READER: That question cannot be answered at this stage. The state after withdrawal will depend largely upon the manner of it. If, as you

33 This chapter is a critique of the prevailing notions of swaraj.
34 Here Gandhi attacks the revolutionaries' view that physical expulsion of the British from India is the necessary and sufficient condition of swaraj.

assume, they retire, it seems to me we shall still keep their constitu-tion,[35] and shall carry on the government. If they simply retire for the asking, we should have an army, etc., ready at hand. We should, there-fore, have no difficulty in carrying on the government.

EDITOR: You may think so; I do not. But I will not discuss the matter just now. I have to answer the question, and that I can do well by asking you several questions. Why do we want to drive away the English?

READER: Because India has become impoverished by their Government. They take away our money from year to year. The most important posts are reserved for themselves. We are kept in a state of slavery. They behave insolently towards us, and disregard our feelings.

EDITOR: If they do not take our money away, become gentle, and give us responsible posts, would you still consider their presence to be harmful?

READER: That question is useless. It is similar to the question whether there is any harm in associating with a tiger,[36] if he changes his nature. Such a question is sheer waste of time. When a tiger changes his nature, Englishmen will change theirs. This is not possible, and to believe it to be possible is contrary to human experience.

EDITOR: Supposing we get self-government similar to what the Canadians and the South Africans have, will it be good enough?

READER: That question also is useless. We may get it when we have arms and ammunition even as they have. But, when we have the same powers, we shall hoist our own flag. As is Japan, so must India be.[37] We

35 Here Gandhi is attacking the meaning of swaraj held by the Extremists: expel the British but keep their political, military and economic institutions.

36 One of the striking metaphors of the book, comparable to the metaphor of the lion found in Machiavelli's *The Prince*.

37 Gandhi rejects the Japanese model of development, to which many Indians at the turn of the century were powerfully attracted. Gandhi's own attitude towards Japan underwent a gradual evolution in the period 1903–9. As a journalist he remained a keen observer of the rise of modern Japan. In 1905 he spoke of 'the epic heroism' exhibited by the Japanese in the 1905 naval victory over Russia, comparing the latter to the British victories over the Spanish Armada and over Napoleon. The secret of the Japanese victory was

must own our navy, our army, and we must have our own splendour, and then will India's voice ring through the world.

EDITOR: You have well drawn the picture. In effect it means this: that we want English rule without the Englishman. You want the tiger's nature, but not the tiger; that is to say, you would make India English, and, when it becomes English, it will be called not Hindustan but Englistan. This is not the Swaraj that I want.

READER: I have placed before you my idea of Swaraj as I think it should be. If the education we have received be of any use, if the works of Spencer, Mill[38] and others be of any importance, and if the English Parliament be the Mother of Parliaments, I certainly think that we

> unity, patriotism and the resolve to do or die. All the Japanese are animated by the same spirit. No one is considered greater than the other, and there is no rift of any kind between them. They think nothing else but service to the nation … This unity and patriotic spirit together with a heroic indifference to life (or death) have created an atmosphere in Japan the like of which is nowhere to be found in the world. (*CW* 4: 467)

> The explanation of the Japanese victory, he wrote, 'deserves to be inscribed in one's mind' (*CW* 5: 32). Writing in 1907, he traced a link between the Japanese sense of self-respect and their political independence; and contrasted the Japanese situation with India's state of bondage and the resulting lack of self-respect. 'When everyone in Japan, the rich as well as the poor, came to believe in self-respect, the country became free. In the same way we too need to feel the spirit of self-respect' (*CW* 6: 457). But in *HS* he has become sceptical of the desirability of taking Japan as a model for India.

38 'the works of Spencer, Mill': i.e., Herbert Spencer and J. S. Mill. From available data it is not possible to indicate which works of Spencer and Mill Gandhi might have read by 1909. But we do know that he disapproved of the position of S. Krishnavarma and his colleagues in India House (London) who acted as though what India needed was the philosophy of Spencer. To counteract them he used with approval a witty article by G. K. Chesterton:

> They talk about Herbert Spencer's philosophy and other similar matters. What is the good of Indian national spirit if they cannot protect themselves from Herbert Spencer? … One of their papers is called *The Indian Sociologist*. Do the Indian youths want to pollute their ancient villages and poison their kindly homes by introducing Spencer's philosophy into them? … But Herbert Spencer is not Indian; his philosophy is not Indian philosophy; all this clatter about the science of education and other things is not Indian. I often wish it were not English either. But this is our first difficulty, that the Indian nationalist is not national. (*CW* 9: 425-7)

should copy the English people, and this to such an extent, that, just as they do not allow others to obtain a footing in their country, so should we not allow them or others to obtain it in ours. What they have done in their own country has not been done in any other country. It is, therefore, proper for us to import their institutions. But now I want to know your views.

EDITOR: There is need for patience. My views will develop of themselves in the course of this discourse. It is as difficult for me to understand the true nature of Swaraj as it seems to you to be easy. I shall, therefore, for the time being, content myself with endeavouring to show that what you call Swaraj is not truly Swaraj.

As for J. S. Mill, Gandhi did mention *On Liberty* by name in the 1920s. He told a university audience:

I know that in the West there is a powerful trend towards licence. But I have no desire to see students in India take to such licence ... I want to tell you that the man who has not received education for freedom – and you may be sure this is not to be had by reading Mill on 'Liberty' – cannot be taken to be a free man. (*CW* 19: 26, 103)

CHAPTER V

✱

The condition of England

READER: Then from your statement I deduce that the Government of England is not desirable and not worth copying by us.

EDITOR: Your deduction is justified. The condition of England at present is pitiable. I pray to God that India may never be in that plight. That which you consider to be the Mother of Parliaments is like a sterile woman and a prostitute.[39] Both these are harsh terms, but exactly fit the case. That Parliament has not yet of its own accord done a single good thing, hence I have compared it to a sterile woman. The natural condition of that Parliament is such that, without outside pressure, it can do nothing. It is like a prostitute because it is under the control of ministers who change from time to time. Today it is under Mr Asquith, tomorrow it may be under Mr Balfour.

---

39 'a sterile woman and a prostitute': Gandhi was criticised by one of his English friends (Mrs Annie Beasant?) for using the metaphor of 'prostitute'; and he regretted using it (CW 15: 330); this was the only word he was prepared to drop from the book. The word 'prostitute' occurs again in ch. v, and the word 'prostitution' in chs. XI and XIII. Erikson (1969, 219) exaggerates the point when he writes that the word 'prostitution' is 'a word used rather often' in HS.

The criticism of parliament in this chapter and elsewhere may not be interpreted to mean that Gandhi was against the institution of parliament. For example, in 1920 he said that what he wanted for India was 'a parliament chosen by the people with the fullest power over the finance, the police, the military, the navy, the courts and the educational institutions' (CW 19: 80). In 1921 he advised the readers of HS that his corporate activity was devoted to 'the attainment of parliamentary swaraj in accordance with the wishes of the people of India' (CW 19: 277-8).

READER: You have said this sarcastically. The term 'sterile woman' is not applicable. The Parliament, being elected by the people, must work under public pressure. This is its quality.

EDITOR: You are mistaken. Let us examine it a little more closely. The best men are supposed to be elected by the people. The members serve without pay[40] and, therefore, it must be assumed, only for the public weal. The electors are considered to be educated, and, therefore, we should assume that they would not generally make mistakes in their choice. Such a Parliament should not need the spur of petitions or any other pressure. Its work should be so smooth that its effect would be more apparent day by day. But, as a matter of fact, it is generally acknowledged that the members are hypocritical and selfish. Each thinks of his own little interest. It is fear that is the guiding motive. What is done today may be undone tomorrow. It is not possible to recall a single instance in which finality can be predicated for its work. When the greatest questions are debated, its members have been seen to stretch themselves and to doze.[41] Sometimes the members talk away until the listeners are disgusted. Carlyle has called it the 'talking-shop of the world'.[42] Members vote for their party without a thought. Their so-called discipline binds them to it. If any member, by way of exception, gives an independent vote, he is considered a renegade. If the money and the time wasted by the Parliament were entrusted to a few good men, the English nation would be occupying today a much higher platform. The Parliament is simply a costly toy of the nation. These views are by no means peculiar to me. Some great English thinkers have

---

40 Remuneration for British MPs was introduced only in 1911.

41 'doze': given as 'dose' in original text.

42 'the talking-shop of the world': the Gujarati text does not mention Carlyle, referring instead to 'one of their great writers'. The source of this remark is Carlyle (1907, 319) where he is discussing the inability of the Rump Parliament to give a clear answer to Cromwell: 'For three years, Cromwell says, this question had been sounded in the ears of the Parliament. They would make no answer; nothing but talk, talk. Perhaps it lies in the nature of parliamentary bodies; perhaps no Parliament could in such case make any answer but even that of talk, talk.' Professor C. N. Patel of Ahmedabad drew my attention to this passage.

expressed them. One of the members of that Parliament recently said that a true Christian[43] could not become a member of it. Another said that it was a baby. And, if it has remained a baby after an existence of seven hundred years, when will it outgrow its babyhood?

READER: You have set me thinking; you do not expect me to accept at once all you say. You give me entirely novel views. I shall have to digest them. Will you now explain the epithet 'prostitute'?

EDITOR: That you cannot accept my views at once is only right. If you will read the literature on this subject, you will have some idea of it. The Parliament is without a real master. Under the Prime Minister, its movement is not steady, but it is buffeted about like a prostitute. The Prime Minister is more concerned about his power[44] than about the welfare of the Parliament. His energy is concentrated upon securing the success of his party.[45] His care is not always that the Parliament shall do right. Prime Ministers are known to have made the Parliament do things merely for party advantage. All this is worth thinking over.

READER: Then you are really attacking the very men whom we have hitherto considered to be patriotic and honest?

EDITOR: Yes, that is true; I can have nothing against Prime Ministers, but what I have seen leads me to think that they cannot be considered really patriotic. If they are to be considered honest because they do not take what is generally known as bribery, let them be so considered, but they are open to subtler influences. In order to gain their ends, they certainly bribe people with honours. I do not hesitate to say that they have neither real honesty nor a living conscience.

READER: As you express these views about the Parliament, I would like to hear you on the English people, so that I may have your view of their Government.

EDITOR: To the English voters their newspaper is their Bible. They take their cue from their newspapers, which latter are often dishonest. The same fact is differently interpreted by different newspapers,

---

43 'a true Christian': the Gujarati text has *dharmisht*, 'an ethical person'.
44 'power': *satta*.   45 'party': i.e., political party, *paksh*.

according to the party in whose interests they are edited.[46] One newspaper would consider a great Englishman to be a paragon of honesty, another would consider him dishonest. What must be the condition of the people whose newspapers are of this type?

READER: You shall describe it.

EDITOR: These people change their views frequently. It is said that they change them every seven years. These views swing like the pendulum of a clock and are never steadfast. The people would follow a powerful orator or a man who gives them parties, receptions, etc. As are the people, so is their Parliament. They have certainly one quality very strongly developed. They will never allow their country to be lost. If any person were to cast an evil eye on it, they would pluck out his eyes. But that does not mean that the nation possesses every other virtue or that it should be imitated. If India copies England, it is my firm conviction that she will be ruined.

READER: To what do you ascribe this state of England?

EDITOR: It is not due to any peculiar fault of the English people, but the condition is due to modern civilisation.[47] It is a civilisation only in name. Under it the nations of Europe are becoming degraded and ruined day by day.

---

46 The Gujarati text adds: 'One party magnifies its own importance while the other party minimises it.'

47 The distinction between 'British people', whom Gandhi admired, and 'modern' British civilisation, which Gandhi criticised, is crucial to his argument, which is that modern civilisation has corrupted a basically good people. The root of this corruption he traces back to the de-Christianisation of modern Britain.

CHAPTER VI

*

Civilisation

READER: NOW you will have to explain what you mean by civilisation.[48]

EDITOR: It is not a question of what I mean. Several English writers refuse to call that civilisation which passes under that name. Many books have been written upon that subject. Societies[49] have been formed to cure the nation of the evils of civilisation. A great English writer[50] has written a work called 'Civilization: its Cause and Cure'. Therein he has called it a disease.

48 The Gujarati text adds: 'According to you, [modern] civilisation [sudharo] is not civilisation, but barbarism [kudharo].' The sudharo/kudharo dichotomy adds colour to the Gujarati text.

49 In 1906 Gandhi made contacts with officials of the Union of Ethical Societies in London. It had then fourteen member societies in London, and nine elsewhere in England. Henry Polak and his wife Millie Graham were members of the South Place Ethical Society. Miss Florence Winterbottom, who helped Gandhi with his lobbying in London, was the Secretary of the Union of Ethical Societies (Hunt 1986, 8–10). On his 1909 visit to London Gandhi gave a lecture to the Union of Ethical Societies at the Emerson Club (CW 9: 473-4.475–6). On the same visit he also visited an ex-Tolstoyan Colony at Whiteway, near Stroud (ibid., 369). Gandhi was also familiar with the activities of 'New Crusade Society', a society based on the social teachings of John Ruskin, propagating the values of country life, agriculture, handicrafts, homespun clothes and opposing the 'increasing dependence on machinery' and 'competitive mechanical production'. The moving spirit behind this society was Godfrey Blount, author of A New Crusade: An Appeal (1903). This book is listed in the Appendix to HS. A brief summary of its activities was also published in Indian Opinion (1905).

50 Edward Carpenter.

READER: Why do we not know this generally?

EDITOR: The answer is very simple. We rarely find people arguing against themselves. Those who are intoxicated by modern civilisation are not likely to write against it. Their care will be to find out facts and arguments in support of it, and this they do unconsciously, believing it to be true. A man, whilst he is dreaming, believes in his dream; he is undeceived only when he is awakened from his sleep. A man labouring under the bane of civilisation is like a dreaming man. What we usually read are the works of defenders of modern civilisation, which undoubtedly claims among its votaries very brilliant and even some very good men. Their writings hypnotise us. And so, one by one, we are drawn into the vortex.

READER: This seems to be very plausible. Now will you tell me something of what you have read and thought of this civilisation?

EDITOR: Let us first consider what state of things is described by the word 'civilisation'.[51] Its true test lies in the fact that people living in it make bodily welfare the object of life.[52] We will take some examples. The people of Europe today live in better built houses than they did a hundred years ago. This is considered an emblem of civilisation, and this is also a matter to promote bodily happiness. Formerly, they wore skins, and used as their weapons spears. Now, they wear long trousers, and, for embellishing their bodies, they wear a variety of clothing, and, instead of spears, they carry with them revolvers containing five or more chambers. If people of a certain country, who have hitherto not been in the habit of wearing much clothing, boots, etc., adopt European clothing,

---

51 'Civilisation': what is meant here is the civilisation produced by the industrial revolution. 'Let it be remembered that Western civilisation is only a hundred years old, or to be more precise fifty. Within this short span the Western people appear to have been reduced to a state of cultural anarchy. We pray that India may never be reduced to the same state as Europe' (*CW* 8: 374).

52 The Gujarati term for 'object of life' is the philosophically loaded term *purushartha*. *Purushartha* is the first element of Gandhi's definition of civilization. The second element (that which points to the path of duty) is mentioned on p. 65 below.

they are supposed to have become civilised out of savagery. Formerly, in Europe, people ploughed their lands mainly by manual labour. Now, one man can plough a vast tract by means of steam-engines, and can thus amass great wealth. This is called a sign of civilisation. Formerly, the fewest men wrote books that were most valuable. Now, anybody writes and prints anything he likes and poisons people's minds. Formerly, men travelled in wagons; now they fly through the air in trains at the rate of four hundred and more miles per day. This is considered the height of civilisation. It has been stated that, as men progress, they shall be able to travel in airships and reach any part of the world in a few hours. Men will not need the use of their hands and feet. They will press a button and they will have their clothing by their side. They will press another button and they will have their newspaper. A third, and a motorcar will be in waiting for them. They will have a variety of delicately dished-up food. Everything will be done by machinery. Formerly, when people wanted to fight with one another, they measured between them their bodily strength; now it is possible to take away thousands of lives by one man working behind a gun from a hill. This is civilisation. Formerly, men worked in the open air only so much as they liked. Now, thousands of workmen meet together and for the sake of maintenance work in factories or mines. Their condition is worse than that of beasts. They are obliged to work, at the risk of their lives, at most dangerous occupations, for the sake of millionaires. Formerly, men were made slaves under physical compulsion, now[53] they are enslaved by temptation of money and of the luxuries that money can buy. There are now diseases of which people never dreamt before, and an army of doctors is engaged in finding out their cures, and so hospitals have increased. This is a test of civilisation. Formerly, special messengers were required and much expense was incurred in order to send letters; today, anyone can abuse his fellow by means of a

---

53 Tolstoy's *The Slavery of Our Times*, and Taylor's *White Slaves of England* (both listed in the Appendix to *HS*) speak of the 'slavery' created by the new industrial civilisation.

letter for one penny. True, at the same cost, one can send one's thanks also. Formerly, people had two or three meals consisting of homemade bread and vegetables; now, they require something to eat every two hours, so that they have hardly leisure for anything else. What more need I say? All this you can ascertain from several authoritative books. These are all true tests of civilisation. And, if anyone speaks to the contrary, know that he is ignorant. This civilisation takes note neither of morality nor of religion.[54] Its votaries calmly state that their business is not to teach religion. Some even consider it to be a superstitious growth. Others put on the cloak of religion, and prate about morality. But, after twenty years' experience, I have come to the conclusion that immorality is often taught in the name of morality. Even a child can understand that in all I have described above there can be no inducement to morality. Civilisation seeks to increase bodily comforts, and it fails miserably even in doing so.

This civilisation is irreligion,[55] and it has taken such a hold on the people in Europe that those who are in it appear to be half mad. They lack real physical strength or courage. They keep up their energy by intoxication. They can hardly be happy in solitude. Women, who should be the queens of households, wander in the streets, or they slave away in factories. For the sake of a pittance, half a million women in England alone are labouring under trying circumstances in factories or similar institutions. This awful fact is one of the causes of the daily growing suffragette movement.[56]

---

54 'neither of morality nor of religion': morality = *niti*; religion = *dharma*.

55 'irreligion': *adharma*, contrary to dharma.

56 During his 1906 and 1909 visits to London Gandhi established direct contact with the British suffragette movement. *Indian Opinion* carried reports on the arrests of Miss Cobden and Emmeline Pankhurst: while he was very sympathetic to their cause he disapproved of their violent tactics – the attack on the residence of Asquith, disruption of meetings addressed by Balfour and Winston Churchill, harassment of prison officials, hunger strike in jail, destruction of prison property, etc. (*CW* 9: 303, 324–5).

This civilisation is such that one has only to be patient and it will be self-destroyed. According to the teaching of Mahomed this would be considered a Satanic civilisation. Hinduism calls it the Black Age.[57] I cannot give you an adequate conception of it. It is eating into the vitals of the English nation.[58] It must be shunned.[59] Parliaments are really emblems of slavery. If you will sufficiently think over this, you will entertain the same opinion, and cease to blame the English. They rather deserve our sympathy. They are a shrewd nation and I, therefore, believe that they will cast off the evil. They are enterprising and industrious, and their mode of thought is not inherently immoral. Neither are they bad at heart. I, therefore, respect them. Civilisation is not an incurable disease,[60] but it should never be forgotten that the English people are at present afflicted by it.

57 'the Black Age': *kali juga*. According to Hindu mythology, the cycle of time is divided into *kalpa*, *mahayuga* and *yuga*. The four yugas – *krita*, *treta*, *dvapara* and *kali* – constitute one *mahayuga* (supposedly 4,320,000 years); and 1,000 mahajugas constitute one *kalpa*. At the end of each *kalpa* the cycle starts again. Humankind at present lives in the *kali yuga*, the worst segment in the entire cycle of time. It is supposed to have started in 3102 BC and is supposed to last a total of 432,000 years. During the *kali yuga* the sway of dharma is the weakest, compared to the other three yugas, and humans are normally led by violence and egoism (Zimmer 1963, 13–19).
58 The Gujarati text adds: 'This civilisation is destructive, and it is itself bound to perish.'
59 The Gujarati text adds: 'That is why the British Parliament and other parliaments are ineffective against this civilisation.'
60 'Civilisation is not an incurable disease': the Gujarati text reads 'For them [the British] this civilisation is not an incurable disease.' The metaphor of disease occurs again in chs. VII and IX.

CHAPTER VII

*

Why was India lost?

READER: You have said much about civilisation – enough to make me ponder over it. I do not now know what I should adopt and what I should avoid from the nations of Europe, but one question comes to my lips immediately. If civilisation is a disease, and if it has attacked the English nation, why has she been able to take India, and why is she able to retain it?

EDITOR: Your question is not very difficult to answer, and we shall presently be able to examine the true nature of Swaraj; for I am aware that I have still to answer that question. I will, however, take up your previous question. The English have not taken India; we have given it to them. They are not in India because of their strength, but because we keep them.[61] Let us now see whether these propositions can be sustained. They came to our country originally for purposes of trade. Recall the Company Bahadur.[62] Who made it Bahadur? They had not the slightest intention at the time of establishing a kingdom. Who assisted

61 'but because we keep them': one of the underlying assumptions of HS. It was first expressed in 1908, in the paraphrase of Unto This Last: 'The reason why they [the British] rule over us is to be found in ourselves' (CW 8: 373); the idea recurs in chs. XIV and XX as well. See also Seeley [1883] 1909, 197–216. Gandhi had read Seeley at least by 1903 (CW 3: 462).

62 'the Company Bahadur': an honorific title by which the East India Company was known among Indians. 'Bahadur' means brave, powerful, sovereign. The Company received its first charter from Queen Elizabeth I on 31 December 1600. In 1613, Jahangir, the Mogul emperor, issued a firman, permitting the English to establish a trading outpost at Surat, Gujarat. The real foundation of British political dominion over India is said to date from the battle of Plassey in 1757.

the Company's officers? Who was tempted at the sight of their silver? Who bought their goods? History testifies that we did all this. In order to become rich all at once, we welcomed the Company's officers with open arms. We assisted them. If I am in the habit of drinking Bhang, and a seller thereof sells it to me, am I to blame him or myself? By blaming the seller shall I be able to avoid the habit? And, if a particular retailer is driven away, will not another take his place? A true servant of India will have to go to the root of the matter. If an excess of food has caused me indigestion, I will certainly not avoid it by blaming water. He is a true physician who probes the cause of disease, and, if you pose as a physician for the disease of India, you will have to find out its true cause.

READER: You are right. Now, I think you will not have to argue much with me to drive your conclusions home. I am impatient to know your further views. We are now on a most interesting topic. I shall, therefore, endeavour to follow your thought, and stop you when I am in doubt.

EDITOR: I am afraid that, in spite of your enthusiasm, as we proceed further we shall have differences of opinion. Nevertheless, I shall argue only when you still stop me. We have already seen that the English merchants were able to get a footing in India because we encouraged them. When our princes fought among themselves,[63] they sought the assistance of Company Bahadur. That corporation was versed alike in commerce and war. It was unhampered by questions of morality. Its object was to increase its commerce and to make money. It accepted our assistance, and increased the number of its warehouses. To protect the latter it employed an army which was utilised by us also. Is it not then useless to blame the English for what we did at that time? The Hindus and the Mahomedans were at daggers drawn. This, too, gave the Company its opportunity, and thus we created the circumstances that gave the Company its control over India. Hence it is truer to say that we gave India to the English than that India was lost.

---

63 The eighteenth-century internecine wars among Indians (the Moghuls, the Mahrattas and the Sikhs) are being identified as major contributing factors to the rise of British power in India.

READER: Will you now tell me how they are able to retain India?

EDITOR: The causes that gave them India enable them to retain it. Some Englishmen state that they took, and they hold, India by the sword. Both these statements are wrong. The sword is entirely useless for holding India. We alone keep them. Napoleon is said to have described the English as a nation of shopkeepers. It is a fitting description. They hold whatever dominions they have for the sake of their commerce. Their army and their navy are intended to protect it. When the Transvaal offered no such attractions, the late Mr Gladstone discovered that it was not right for the English to hold it. When it became a paying proposition, resistance led to war. Mr Chamberlain soon discovered that England enjoyed a suzerainty over the Transvaal. It is related that someone asked the late President Kruger whether there was gold in the moon? He replied that it was highly unlikely, because, if there were, the English would have annexed it. Many problems can be solved by remembering that money is their God. Then it follows that we keep the English in India for our base self-interest. We like their commerce, they please us by their subtle methods, and get what they want from us. To blame them for this is to perpetuate their power. We further strengthen their hold by quarrelling amongst ourselves. If you accept the above statements, it is proved that the English entered India for the purposes of trade. They remain in it for the same purpose, and we help them to do so. Their arms and ammunition are perfectly useless. In this connection, I remind you that it is the British flag which is waving in Japan, and not the Japanese.[64] The English have a treaty with Japan for the sake of their commerce, and you will see that, if they can manage it, their commerce will greatly expand in that country. They wish to convert the whole world into a vast market for their goods. That they cannot do so is true, but the blame will not be theirs. They will leave no stone unturned to reach the goal.

---

64 The metaphor of the 'flag' is used here to indicate how Japan achieved modernisation: she followed the British example (*CW* 5: 41).

CHAPTER VIII

*

The condition of India

READER: I now understand why the English hold India. I should like to know your views about the condition of our country.

EDITOR: It is a sad condition. In thinking of it, my eyes water and my throat gets parched. I have grave doubts whether I shall be able sufficiently to explain what is in my heart. It is my deliberate opinion that India is being ground down not under the English heel but under that of modern civilisation. It is groaning under the monster's terrible weight. There is yet time to escape it, but every day makes it more and more difficult. Religion is dear to me, and my first complaint is that India is becoming irreligious.[65] Here I am not thinking of the Hindu, the Mahomedan, or the Zoroastrian religion, but of that religion which underlies all religions.[66] We are turning away from God.

READER: How so?

EDITOR: There is a charge laid against us that we are a lazy people, and that the Europeans are industrious and enterprising. We have accepted the charge and we, therefore, wish to change our condition. Hinduism, Islamism, Zoroastrianism, Christianity and all other religions teach that we should remain passive about worldly pursuits and active about godly pursuits, that we should set a limit to our worldly

---

65 'irreligious': *dharma-bhrasht*, a people without dharma.
66 'religion which underlies all religions': a very important concept in Gandhi's political philosophy. Throughout *HS* religion is understood in two different senses: as sect or organised religion, and as ethic, albeit one grounded in some metaphysic.

ambition, and that our religious ambition should be illimitable. Our activity should be directed into the latter channel.

READER: You seem to be encouraging religious charlatanism. Many a cheat has by talking in a similar strain led the people astray.

EDITOR: You are bringing an unlawful charge against religion. Humbug there undoubtedly is about all religions. Where there is light, there is also shadow. I am prepared to maintain that humbugs in worldly matters are far worse than the humbugs in religion. The humbug of civilisation[67] that I endeavour to show to you is not to be found in religion.

READER: How can you say that? In the name of religion Hindus and Mahomedans fought against one another. For the same cause Christians fought Christians. Thousands of innocent men have been murdered, thousands have been burned and tortured in its name. Surely, this is much worse than any civilisation.

EDITOR: I certainly submit that the above hardships are far more bearable than those of civilisation. Everybody understands that the cruelties you have named are not part of religion, although they have been practised in its name; therefore, there is no aftermath to these cruelties. They will always happen so long as there are to be found ignorant and credulous people. But there is no end to the victims destroyed in the fire of civilisation. Its deadly effect is that people come under its scorching flames believing it to be all good. They become utterly irreligious and, in reality, derive little advantage from the world. Civilisation is like a mouse gnawing while it is soothing us. When its full effect is realised, we will see that religious superstition is harmless compared to that of modern civilisation.[68] I am not pleading for a continuance of religious superstitions. We will certainly fight them

---

67 Gandhi takes the offensive now: today the real humbug is the modern secular culture.

68 Gandhi is responding to the nineteenth-century rationalist/secularist prejudice that religion promotes superstition; modernity is the superstition of the secularists.

tooth and nail, but we can never do so by disregarding religion. We can only do so by appreciating and conserving the latter.

READER: Then you will contend that the *Pax Britannica* is a useless encumbrance?

EDITOR: You may see peace if you like; I see none.[69]

READER: You make light of the terror that the Thugs, the Pindaris, the Bhils were to the country.[70]

EDITOR: If you will give the matter some thought, you will see that the terror was by no means such a mighty thing. If it had been a very substantial thing, the other people would have died away before the English advent. Moreover, the present peace is only nominal, for by it we have become emasculated and cowardly. We are not to assume that the English have changed the nature of the Pindaris and the Bhils. It is, therefore, better to suffer the Pindari peril than that someone else should protect us from it, and thus render us effeminate. I should prefer to be killed by the arrow of a Bhil than to seek unmanly protection. India without such protection was an India full of valour. Macaulay betrayed gross ignorance when he libelled Indians as being practically cowards. They never merited the charge. Cowards living in a country inhabited by hardy mountaineers, infested by wolves and tigers must surely find an early grave. Have you ever visited our fields? I assure you that our

---

69 Gandhi here challenges the arguments of Utilitarians such as Fitzjames Stephen that *Pax Britannica* was an unmixed blessing for India (see Stephen 1883, 541–68).

70 'the Thugs': gangs of murderers inhabiting parts of Central India who made their living by plundering and murdering travellers. They practised a corrupt mixture of Islam and Hinduism, their principal deities being Devi, Bhavani, Durga and Kali. They were suppressed by the British between 1830 and 1850. 'the Pindaris': a professional class of free-booters, inhabiting parts of Central India. Good horsemen, they made their living by looting the cattle and property of their victims; what they could not carry, they burned and destroyed. Like the Thugs, they too practised a corrupt mixture of Islam and Hinduism; suppressed by the British in the first half of the nineteenth century. 'the Bhils': an aboriginal tribe, found mostly in Gujarat and Rajasthan, numbering about 600,000 at the turn of the twentieth century. Their religious practices were borrowed from primitive nature worship and certain forms of popular Hinduism.

agriculturists sleep fearlessly on their farms even today, and the English, you and I, would hesitate to sleep where they sleep. Strength lies in absence of fear, not in the quantity of flesh and muscle we may have on our bodies. Moreover, I must remind you who desire Home Rule that, after all, the Bhils, the Pindaris, the Assamese[71] and the Thugs are our own countrymen. To conquer them[72] is your and my work. So long as we fear our own brethren, we are unfit to reach the goal.

71 In 1921 Gandhi apologised to the Assamese for listing them among the 'uncivilised' tribes of India:

> It was certainly on my part a grave injustice done to the great Assamese people, who are every whit as civilised as any other part of India … My stupidity about the Assamese rose, when about 1890 I read an account of the Manipur expedition, when the late Sir John Gorst defended the conduct of the officials towards the late Senapati, saying that governments always liked to lop off tall poppies. Being an indifferent reader of history, I retained with me the impression that the Assamese were jungle [uncivilised] and committed it to writing in 1908 [*sic*]. *(CW 21: 30)*

72 'To conquer them': in the Gujarati text this reads 'To win them over'.

*

The condition of India (cont.): railways[73]

READER: You have deprived me of the consolation I used to have regarding peace in India.[74]

EDITOR: I have merely given you my opinion on the religious aspect, but, when I give you my views as to the poverty[75] of India, you will perhaps begin to dislike me, because what you and I have hitherto considered beneficial for India no longer appears to me to be so.

---

73 The original Gujarati text does not have 'Railways' in the chapter heading; instead it has *Vishesha Vichar* (Additional Thoughts). The railways were first introduced into India in 1853; at the time of the writing of *HS* there were about 26,000 miles of railways in India.

74 The Gujarati text reads: 'You have shattered my illusions about the value of peace in India. You have left me with nothing that I can think of.'

75 Gandhi's criticism of the Indian railways takes place within the context of his views on Indian poverty, derived mainly from Naoroji and R. C. Dutt. The latter had argued that for the reduction of poverty in India, the development of irrigation was more important than that of the railways. But neither British private capital nor the colonial government saw the problem in this way. In the eyes of British investors the railways were more attractive, especially since in the early decades (1850-80) there was a guaranteed profit of 5 per cent charged on Indian revenue. It is true that the railways facilitated the movement of food in times of famine; but it is equally true that the railways did not *produce* food. For the production of more food, irrigation was crucial. Railways without irrigation did not solve the problem of poverty and famines; in a sense it aggravated them in that capital that could have been spent on irrigation was spent instead on the railways, which proved to be both extravagant and wasteful (R. C. Dutt 1904, 166-79, 353-71, 545-55). Naoroji also used the example of the railways to demonstrate his drain theory (Naoroji 1901, 170-3).

READER: What may that be?

EDITOR: Railways, lawyers and doctors have impoverished the country, so much so that, if we do not wake up in time, we shall be ruined.

READER: I do now, indeed, fear that we are not likely to agree at all. You are attacking the very institutions which we have hitherto considered to be good.

EDITOR: It is necessary to exercise patience. The true inwardness of the evils of civilisation you will understand with difficulty. Doctors assure us that a consumptive clings to life even when he is about to die. Consumption does not produce apparent hurt – it even produces a seductive colour about a patient's face, so as to induce the belief that all is well. Civilisation is such a disease,[76] and we have to be very wary.

READER: Very well, then, I shall hear you on the railways.

EDITOR: It must be manifest to you that, but for the railways, the English could not have such a hold on India as they have. The railways, too, have spread the bubonic plague. Without them, masses could not move from place to place. They are the carriers of plague germs. Formerly we had natural segregation. Railways have also increased the frequency of famines, because, owing to facility of means of locomotion, people sell out their grain, and it is sent to the dearest markets. People become careless, and so the pressure of famine increases. They accentuate the evil nature of man. Bad men fulfil their evil designs with greater rapidity. The holy places of India have become unholy. Formerly, people went to these places with very great difficulty. Generally, therefore, only the real devotees visited such places. Nowadays, rogues visit them in order to practise their roguery.

READER: You have given a one-sided account. Good men can visit these places as well as bad men. Why do they not take the fullest advantage of the railways?

EDITOR: Good travels at a snail's pace – it can, therefore, have little to do with the railways. Those who want to do good are not selfish, they are not in a hurry, they know that to impregnate people with good requires a long time. But evil has wings. To build a house takes time. Its

76 'such a disease': modernity is a hidden, but curable, disease.

destruction takes none. So the railways can become a distributing agency for the evil one only. It may be a debatable matter whether railways spread famines, but it is beyond dispute that they propagate evil.

READER: Be that as it may, all the disadvantages of railways are more than counterbalanced by the fact that it is due to them that we see in India the new spirit of nationalism.

EDITOR: I hold this to be a mistake.[77] The English have taught us that we were not one nation before, and that it will require centuries before we become one nation. This is without foundation. We were one nation before they came to India. One thought inspired us. Our mode of life was the same. It was because we were one nation that they were able to establish one kingdom. Subsequently they divided us.

READER: This requires an explanation.

EDITOR: I do not wish to suggest that because we were one nation we had no differences, but it is submitted that our leading men travelled throughout India either on foot or in bullock-carts.[78] They learned one another's languages, and there was no aloofness between them. What do you think could have been the intention of those far-seeing ancestors of ours who established Shevetbindu Rameshwar in the South, Juggernaut in the South-East, and Hardwar in the North as places of pilgrimage?[79] You will admit they were no fools. They knew that worship of God could have

77 Gandhi rejects here an explanation of the rise of Indian nationalism purely in terms of the development of the modern means of communication. He asserts that a sense of Indian identity antedates the introduction of the railways. For Gandhi's notion of nation in *HS*, see Parel 1991, 261–82.

78 By contrasting the railways with the bullock-carts Gandhi drives home the point that speed by itself is not a value to be cherished. Here his ideas were influenced by early twentieth-century critics of the cult of speed, such as Thomas F. Taylor, whose *The Fallacy of Speed* is listed in the Appendix. Gandhi had Maganlal Gandhi of *Indian Opinion* translate this work into Gujarati (*CW* 10: 379).

79 The reference is to the traditional places of pilgrimage said to have been established in the East and West, South and North of India, by Shankaracharya (788–820). Gandhi claims that such places of pilgrimage have contributed greatly towards the forging of a common Indian identity. 'Shevetbindu Rameshwar' is Rameswaram in present-day Tamil Nadu. According to legend, the town is said to have been founded by Rama, the hero of the epic *Ramayana*.

been performed just as well at home. They taught us that those whose hearts were aglow with righteousness had the Ganges in their own homes. But they saw that India was one undivided land so made by nature. They, therefore, argued that it must be one nation. Arguing thus, they established holy places in various parts of India, and fired the people with an idea of nationality in a manner unknown in other parts of the world. Any two Indians are one as no two Englishmen are. Only you and I and others who consider ourselves civilised and superior persons imagine that we are many nations. It was after the advent of railways that we began to believe in distinctions, and you are at liberty now to say that it is through the railways that we are beginning to abolish those distinctions. An opium-eater may argue the advantage of opium-eating from the fact that he began to understand the evil of the opium habit after having eaten it. I would ask you to consider well what I have said on the railways.[80]

READER: I will gladly do so, but one question occurs to me even now. You have described to me the India of the pre-Mahomedan period, but now we have Mahomedans, Parsees and Christians. How can they be one nation? Hindus and Mahomedans are old enemies. Our very proverbs prove it.[81] Mahomedans turn to the West for worship, whilst Hindus turn to the East. The former look down on the Hindus as idolaters.[82] The Hindus worship the cow, the Mahomedans kill her. The Hindus believe in the doctrine of non-killing, the Mahomedans do not. We thus meet with differences at every step. How can India be one nation?[83]

After slaying the wicked Ravana, Rama purified himself here. 'Juggernaut in the South-East' refers to the Temple of Jaganaath ('world-lord') in Jagannath Puri, Orissa, which is in the East, not South-East, as the text has it here – an example of Gandhi's limited knowledge, in 1909, of Indian geography.

80 The Gujarati text adds: 'Doubts will still occur to you. But you will be able to resolve them yourself.'

81 The proverb, cited in the Gujarati text but omitted here, is as follows: 'A Miyan [Muslim] has no use for a Mahadev [Hindu].' Compared to the Gujarati text, the English text is especially careful not to exacerbate Muslim sensibilities.

82 The Gujarati text adds: 'Hindus worship images; Mahomedans are iconoclasts.'

83 The Gujarati text reads: 'How can these differences at every step disappear and how can India be one?'

CHAPTER X

The condition of India (cont.): the Hindus and the Mahomedans

EDITOR: Your last question is a serious one, and yet, on careful consideration, it will be found to be easy of solution. The question arises because of the presence of the railways, of the lawyers, and of the doctors. We shall presently examine the last two. We have already considered the railways. I should, however, like to add that man is so made by nature as to require him to restrict his movements as far as his hands and feet will take him. If we did not rush about from place to place by means of railways and such other maddening conveniences, much of the confusion that arises would be obviated. Our difficulties are of our own creation. God set a limit to a man's locomotive ambition in the construction of his body. Man immediately proceeded to discover means of overriding the limit. God gifted man with intellect that he might know his Maker. Man abused it, so that he might forget his Maker. I am so constructed that I can only serve my immediate neighbours, but, in my conceit, I pretend to have discovered that I must with my body serve every individual in the Universe. In thus attempting the impossible, man comes in contact with different natures, different religions, and is utterly confounded. According to this reasoning, it must be apparent to you that railways are a most dangerous institution. Man has therethrough gone further away from his Maker.

READER: But I am impatient to hear your answer to my question. Has the introduction of Mahomedanism not unmade the nation?[84]

EDITOR: India cannot cease to be one nation because people belonging to different religions[85] live in it. The introduction of foreigners does not necessarily destroy the nation, they merge in it. A country is one nation only when such a condition obtains in it. That country must have a faculty for assimilation.[86] India has ever been such a country. In reality, there are as many religions[87] as there are individuals, but those who are conscious of the spirit of nationality do not interfere with one another's religion.[88] If they do, they are not fit to be considered a nation. If the Hindus believe that India should be peopled only by Hindus, they are living in dreamland.[89] The Hindus, the Mahomedans, the Parsees[90] and

84 The answer to this question forms an important part of his theory of nationalism. The spread of Muslim political power in India took place in three stages:

(1) The conquest of Sind and parts of the Punjab by the close of the tenth century; (2) the Delhi Sultanate from thirteenth to the sixteenth century; (3) the Moghul empire from sixteenth to the middle of the eighteenth century. The battle of Plassey (1757) saw the practical end of the Moghul empire and the formal beginning of British rule. The partition of India in 1947 answers Gandhi's question.

85 'religions': (dharma) used here in the sense of sect, not ethics.

86 'faculty for assimilation': the word used is *samas*. *Samas* is a grammatical technique of forming a new word by integrating two or more pre-existing words. For example the word *mahatma* is formed from *maha* and *atma*. Something of the old identity is retained in the new compound word, but the latter has a new identity of its own. When Gandhi says that the Indian nation has been created by a process of *samas* he means that though the nation is formed out of distinct ethnic, religious and linguistic groups, the new identity that emerges has an identity of its own. India in this sense is a nation. Gandhi is a cultural assimilationist in that all Indians, while retaining their sub-national identities, are supposed to share certain common values and symbols.

87 'religions': (dharma) used in the sense of ethics.

88 'religion': (dharma) used in the sense of sect.

89 The Gujarati text adds: 'The Mohamedans also live in a dreamland if they believe that there should be only Mohamedans here.'

90 'Parsees': descendents of Zoroastrians who, fleeing Muslim persecution in Persia, sought refuge in India in the eighth century. They settled mostly in

the Christians[91] who have made India their country are fellow country-men, and they will have to live in unity if only for their own interest. In no part of the world are one nationality and one religion[92] synonymous terms: nor has it ever been so in India.

READER: But what about the inborn enmity between Hindus and Mahomedans?

EDITOR: That phrase has been invented by our mutual enemy. When the Hindus and Mahomedans fought against one another, they certainly spoke in that strain. They have long since ceased to fight. How, then, can there be any inborn enmity? Pray remember this too, that we did not cease to fight only after British occupation. The Hindus flourished under Moslem sovereigns, and Moslems under the Hindu. Each party recognised that mutual fighting was suicidal, and that neither party would abandon its religion[93] by force of arms. Both parties, therefore, decided to live in peace. With the English advent the quarrels recommenced.

The proverbs you have quoted were coined when both were fighting; to quote them now is obviously harmful. Should we not remember that many Hindus and Mahomedans own the same ancestors, and the same blood runs through their veins?[94] Do people become enemies because they change their religion? Is the God of the Mahomedan different from the God of the Hindu? Religions[95] are different roads converging to the

what is today Bombay and Gujarat. The most distinguished Indian at the turn of the century, Dadabhai Naoroji, 'the Grand Old Man of India', was a Parsee.

91 The introduction of Christianity into India antedates that of Islam, Zoroastrian-ism and Sikhism. According to tradition, Christianity is said to have been introduced into Kerala by St Thomas the Apostle; Indian Christianity received a new impetus in the sixteenth century through the preaching of St Francis Xavier, who arrived in Goa in 1542; and it received an additional impetus in the nineteenth century through the educational and social service activities of both Catholic and Protestant missionaries.

92 'religion': (dharma) used in the sense of sect.

93 'religion': (dharma) used in the sense of sect.

94 In his 1944 talks with Jinnah, the Indian Muslim leader and the future founder of Pakistan, Gandhi returned to the arguments based on the notions of 'same ancestors' and 'same blood'. (See Merriam 1980, 78, 96.)

95 'religions': (dharma) used in the sense of sect.

same point. What does it matter that we take different roads, so long as we reach the same goal? Wherein is the cause for quarrelling?

Moreover, there are deadly proverbs as between the followers of Shiva and those of Vishnu, yet nobody suggests that these two do not belong to the same nation. It is said that the Vedic religion[96] is different from Jainism,[97] but the followers of the respective faiths are not different nations. The fact is that we have become enslaved, and, therefore, quarrel and like to have our quarrels decided by a third party. There are Hindu iconoclasts as there are Mahomedan. The more we advance in true knowledge, the better we shall understand that we need not be at war with those whose religion we may not follow.

READER: Now I would like to know your views about cow protection.[98]

EDITOR: I myself respect the cow, that is, I look upon her with affectionate reverence. The cow is the protector of India, because it, being an agricultural country, is dependent on the cow's progeny. She is a most useful animal in hundreds of ways. Our Mahomedan brethren will admit this.

But, just as I respect the cow, so do I respect my fellow-men. A man is just as useful as a cow, no matter whether he be a Mahomedan or a Hindu. Am I, then, to fight with or kill a Mahomedan in order to save a cow? In doing so, I would become an enemy as well of the cow as of the Mahomedan. Therefore, the only method I know of protecting the cow is that I should approach my Mahomedan brother and urge him for the sake of the country to join me in protecting her. If he would not listen to me, I should let the cow go for the simple reason that the matter is beyond my ability. If I were overfull of pity for the cow, I should sacrifice

---

96 'Vedic religion': the original, pure Hinduism based on the Vedas.

97 'Jainism': a religion founded by Mahavira Vardhamana Jnatiputra, (fl. sixth century BC), a contemporary of Buddha. Rajchandbhai, Gandhi's spiritual adviser in the 1890s, was a Jain.

98 Cow protection societies were established in 1875 by Swami Dayananda. The sacrificial killing of cows by Muslims became a cause of Hindu–Muslim riots (Parel 1969, 179–203).

my life to save her, but not take my brother's. This, I hold, is the law of our religion.[99]

When men become obstinate, it is a difficult thing. If I pull one way, my Moslem brother will pull another. If I put on a superior air, he will return the compliment. If I bow to him gently, he will do it much more so, and, if he does not, I shall not be considered to have done wrong in having bowed. When the Hindus became insistent, the killing of cows increased. In my opinion, cow-protection societies may be considered cow-killing societies. It is a disgrace to us that we should need such societies. When we forgot how to protect cows, I suppose we needed such societies.

What am I to do when a blood-brother is on the point of killing a cow? Am I to kill him, or to fall down at his feet and implore him? If you admit that I should adopt the latter course, I must do the same to my Moslem brother.

Who protects the cow from destruction by Hindus when they cruelly ill-treat her? Who ever reasons with the Hindus when they mercilessly belabour the progeny of the cow with their sticks? But this has not prevented us from remaining one nation.

Lastly, if it be true that the Hindus[100] believe in the doctrine of non-killing and the Mahomedans do not, what, I pray, is the duty of the former? It is not written that a follower of the religion of Ahinsa[101] (non-killing) may kill a fellow-man. For him the way is straight. In order to save one being, he may not kill another. He can only plead – therein lies his sole duty.

But does every Hindu believe in Ahinsa? Going to the root of the matter, not one man really practises such a religion, because we do destroy life. We are said to follow that religion because we want to

99 'the law of our religion': (*dharmic kaida*) religion in the sense of ethics.
100 Gandhi here overstates the case of the Hindus. Neither Tilak nor Savarkar nor Aurobindo Ghose would agree with Gandhi on 'non-killing' as an essential Hindu teaching. See, for example, Aurobindo 1950, 36–42.
101 Although the modern spelling is 'Ahimsa', Gandhi consistently spelt it 'Ahinsa' and this latter spelling has been retained for authenticity.

obtain freedom from liability to kill any kind of life.[102] Generally speaking, we may observe that many Hindus partake of meat and are not, therefore, followers of Ahinsa. It is, therefore, preposterous to suggest that the two cannot live together amicably because the Hindus believe in Ahinsa and the Mahomedans do not.

These thoughts are put into our minds by selfish and false religious teachers.[103] The English put the finishing touch. They have a habit of writing history; they pretend to study the manners and customs of all peoples. God has given us a limited mental capacity, but they usurp the function of the Godhead and indulge in novel experiments. They write about their own researches in most laudatory terms and hypnotise us into believing them. We, in our ignorance, then fall at their feet.[104]

Those who do not wish to misunderstand things may read up the Koran, and will find therein hundreds of passages acceptable to the Hindus; and the Bhagavad-Gita contains passages to which not a Mahomedan can take exception. Am I to dislike a Mahomedan because there are passages in the Koran I do not understand or like? It takes two to make a quarrel. If I do not want to quarrel with a Mahomedan, the latter will be powerless to foist a quarrel on me, and, similarly, I should be powerless if a Mahomedan refuses his assistance to quarrel with me. An arm striking the air will become disjointed. If everyone will try to understand the core of his own religion[105] and adhere to it, and will not allow false teachers[106] to dictate to him, there will be no room left for quarrelling.

READER: But will the English ever allow the two bodies to join hands?

---

102 This is a crucial point in interpreting Gandhi's position on ahimsa: 'religion' (dharma) is used here in the sense of ethics.

103 'selfish and false religious teachers': the Gujarati text adds *shastris* and *mullahs* (respectively Hindu and Muslim religious teachers) to this list.

104 The Gujarati text has: 'We in our credulity believe all that they say.'

105 'the core of his own religion': (*dharmanu swaroop*) the ethical core of religion considered as sect.

106 'false teachers': in the Gujarati text, *shastris* and *mullahs*.

EDITOR: This question arises out of your timidity. It betrays our shallowness. If two brothers want to live in peace, is it possible for a third party to separate them? If they were to listen to evil counsels, we would consider them to be foolish. Similarly, we Hindus and Mahomedans would have to blame our folly rather than the English, if we allowed them to put us asunder. A clay-pot would break through impact; if not with one stone, then with another. The way to save the pot is not to keep it away from the danger point, but to bake it so that no stone would break it. We have then to make our hearts of perfectly baked clay. Then we shall be steeled against all danger. This can be easily done by the Hindus. They are superior in numbers, they pretend that they are more educated, they are, therefore, better able to shield themselves from attack on their amicable relations with the Mahomedans.

There is mutual distrust between the two communities. The Mahomedans, therefore, ask for certain concessions from Lord Morley.[107] Why should the Hindus oppose this? If the Hindus desisted, the English would notice it, the Mahomedans would gradually begin to trust the Hindus, and brotherliness would be the outcome. We should be ashamed to take our quarrels to the English. Everyone can find out for himself that the Hindus can lose nothing by desisting. That man who has inspired confidence in another has never lost anything in this world.

I do not suggest that the Hindus and the Mahomedans will never fight. Two brothers living together often do so. We shall sometimes have our heads broken. Such a thing ought not to be necessary, but all men are not equi-minded. When people are in a rage, they do many foolish things. These we have to put up with. But, when we do quarrel, we certainly do not want to engage counsel and to resort to English or any law courts. Two men fight; both have their heads broken, or one only. How shall a third party distribute justice amongst them? Those who fight may expect to be injured.

---

107 The Minto-Morley Reforms (1909) were introduced by John Morley, the Secretary of State for India, and Lord Minto, the Viceroy. Among other things, they gave Muslims a separate electorate.

CHAPTER XI

*

The condition of India (cont.): lawyers[108]

READER: You tell me that, when two men quarrel, they should not go to a law court. This is astonishing.

EDITOR: Whether you call it astonishing or not, it is the truth. And your question introduces us to the lawyers and the doctors. My firm opinion is that the lawyers have enslaved India, and they have accentuated the Hindu–Mahomedan dissensions, and have confirmed English authority.

READER: It is easy enough to bring these charges, but it will be difficult for you to prove them. But for the lawyers, who would have shown us the road to independence? Who would have protected the poor? Who would have secured justice? For instance, the late Mr Manomohan Ghose defended many a poor man free of charge. The Congress, which you have praised so much, is dependent for its existence and activity upon the work of the lawyers. To denounce such an estimable class of men is to spell justice injustice, and you are abusing the liberty of the press by decrying lawyers.

EDITOR: At one time I used to think exactly like you. I have no desire to convince you that they have never done a single good thing. I honour

---

108 By training Gandhi was a lawyer. He was admitted to the Inner Temple (London) in 1888, and called to the Bar in 1891. After an uncertain start in a legal career in India, he was hired in 1893 as legal counsel to an Indian Muslim trading firm operating in South Africa. From 1894 until 1914 he practised law in South Africa, his income being 'five to six thousand pounds a year' (Fischer 1951, 74). He was disbarred from Inner Temple in 1922, but reinstated posthumously in 1988.

Mr Ghose's memory. It is quite true that he helped the poor. That the Congress owes the lawyers something is believable. Lawyers are also men, and there is something good in every man. Whenever instances of lawyers having done good can be brought forward, it will be found that the good is due to them as men rather than as lawyers. All I am concerned with is to show you that the profession teaches immorality;[109] it is exposed to temptations from which few are saved.

The Hindus and the Mahomedans have quarrelled. An ordinary man will ask them to forget all about it, he will tell them that both must be more or less at fault, and will advise them no longer to quarrel. They go to lawyers. The latter's duty is to side with their clients, and to find out ways and arguments in favour of the clients to which they (the clients) are often strangers. If they do not do so, they will be considered to have degraded their profession. The lawyers, therefore, will as a rule, advance quarrels, instead of repressing them. Moreover, men take up that profession, not in order to help others out of their miseries, but to enrich themselves. It is one of the avenues of becoming wealthy, and their interest exists in multiplying disputes. It is within my knowledge that they are glad when men have disputes. Petty pleaders actually manufacture them. Their touts, like so many leeches, suck the blood of the poor people.[110] Lawyers are men who have little to do. Lazy people, in order to indulge in luxuries, take up such professions. This is a true statement. Any other

109 'immorality': *aniti*. In South Africa he discovered that 'when we go to court of law, some of us are only concerned how to win the case at any cost, and not how truth may prevail. In any case, it never does, so we think, in courts of law. But there are some in the Indian community who just do a little play-acting and make courts swallow any story that they choose. There is no doubt that this happens. It would be a great boon to the community if this habit disappeared' (*CW* 10: 147–8). Again, 'I realised that the true function of a lawyer was to unite parties riven asunder. The lesson was so indelibly burnt into me that a large part of my time during the twenty years of my practice as a lawyer was occupied in bringing about private compromises of hundreds of cases. I lost nothing thereby – not even money, certainly not my soul' (*CW* 39: 111).

110 The Gujarati text adds: 'It is a profession which cannot but result in the encouragement of quarrels.'

argument is a mere pretension. It is the lawyers who have discovered that theirs is an honourable profession. They frame laws as they frame their own praises. They decide what fees they will charge, and they put on so much side that poor people almost consider them to be heaven-born.

Why do they want more fees than common labourers?[111] Why are their requirements greater? In what way are they more profitable to the country than the labourers? Are those who do good entitled to greater payment? And, if they have done anything for the country for the sake of money, how shall it be counted as good?

Those who know anything of the Hindu–Mahomedan quarrels know that they have been often due to the intervention of lawyers.[112] Some families have been ruined through them; they have made brothers enemies. Principalities, having come under lawyers' power, have become loaded with debt. Many have been robbed of their all. Such instances can be multiplied.

But the greatest injury[113] they have done to the country is that they have tightened the English grip. Do you think that it would be possible

111 The inspiration for this idea comes from Ruskin: 'The teachings of *Unto This Last* I understood to be: … That a lawyer's work has the same value as the barber's, inasmuch as all have the same right of earning their livelihood from their work' (*CW* 39: 239). In 1928, replying to a correspondent from Texas, Gandhi stated:

The question of reform of the legal profession is a big one. It does not admit of tinkering. I am strongly of opinion that lawyers and doctors should not be able to charge any fees but that they should be paid a certain fixed sum by the State and the public should receive their services free. They will have paid for them through the taxation that they would have paid for such services rendered to citizens automatically. The poor will be untaxed but the rich and the poor will have then the same amount of attention and skill. Today the best legal talents and the best medical advice are unobtainable by the poor. (*CW* 36: 84)

In 1938, addressing the Bar Association in Peshawar, he reminded his audience of his 'peculiar views' about lawyers and doctors which he had recorded in *HS*. 'A true lawyer', he told them, 'was one who placed truth and service in the first place and the emoluments of the profession in the next place only' (*CW* 68: 97).

112 The introduction of the modern notion of rights-based modern law exacerbated Hindu–Muslim relations.

113 Gandhi's most severe criticism of the modern legal system is that it had become the handmaid of colonial rule.

for the English to carry on their government without law courts? It is wrong to consider that courts are established for the benefit of the people. Those who want to perpetuate their power do so through the courts. If people were to settle their own quarrels, a third party would not be able to exercise any authority over them. Truly, men were less unmanly when they settled their disputes either by fighting or by asking their relatives to decide upon them. They became more unmanly and cowardly when they resorted to the courts of law. It was certainly a sign of savagery when they settled their disputes by fighting. Is it any the less so if I ask a third party to decide between you and me? Surely, the decision of a third party is not always right. The parties alone know who is right. We, in our simplicity and ignorance, imagine that a stranger, by taking our money, gives us justice.

The chief thing, however, to be remembered is that, without lawyers, courts could not have been established or conducted, and without the latter the English could not rule. Supposing that there were only English judges, English pleaders and English police, they could only rule over the English. The English could not do without Indian judges and Indian pleaders. How the pleaders were made in the first instance and how they were favoured you should understand well. Then you will have the same abhorrence for the profession that I have.[114] If pleaders were to abandon their profession and consider it just as degrading as prostitution, English rule would break up in a day. They have been instrumental in having the charge laid against us that we love quarrels and courts, as fish love water. What I have said with reference to the pleaders necessarily applies to the judges; they are first cousins, and the one gives strength to the other.

114 The Gujarati text adds: 'The main key to British power is the law court, and the key to the law court is the lawyer.' For the history of the legal revolution introduced into India by British rule, see Stokes (1959) and Maine (1876).

*

The condition of India (cont.): doctors

READER: I now understand the lawyers; the good they may have done is accidental. I feel that the profession is certainly hateful. You, however, drag in the doctors also, how is that?

EDITOR: The views I submit to you are those I have adopted. They are not original. Western writers have used stronger terms regarding both lawyers and doctors. One writer has likened the whole modern system to the Upas tree.[115] Its branches are represented by parasitical professions, including those of law and medicine, and over the trunk has been raised the axe of true religion. Immorality is the root of the tree. So you will see that the views do not come right out of my mind, but they represent the combined experiences of many. I was at one time a great lover of the medical profession. It was my intention to become a doctor for the sake of the country.[116] I no longer hold that opinion. I now understand why the medicine men (the vaids) among us have not occupied a very honourable status.

---

115 'the Upas tree': *Antiaris toxicaria*: 'a fabulous Javanese tree so poisonous as to destroy life for many miles round ... A baleful power or influence' (*OED*). Madame Blavatsky (1891, 178) mentions the Upas tree, but she does not expand on the meaning of the metaphor as Gandhi does here. *Unto This last* also mentions the Upas tree.

116 This is discussed at some length in the *Autobiography* (*CW* 39: 35).

The English have certainly effectively used the medical profession for holding us. English physicians are known to have used the profession with several Asiatic potentates for political gain.[117]

Doctors have almost unhinged us. Sometimes I think that quacks are better than highly qualified doctors. Let us consider: the business of a doctor is to take care of the body, or, properly speaking, not even that. Their business is really to rid the body of diseases that may afflict it. How do these diseases arise? Surely by our negligence or indulgence. I over-eat, I have indigestion, I go to a doctor, he gives me medicine, I am cured, I over-eat again, and I take his pills again. Had I not taken the pills in the first instance, I would have suffered the punishment deserved by me, and I would not have over-eaten again. The doctor intervened and helped me to indulge myself. My body thereby certainly felt more at ease, but my mind became weakened. A continuance of a course of a medicine must, therefore, result in loss of control over the mind.

I have indulged in vice,[118] I contract a disease, a doctor cures me, the odds are that I shall repeat the vice. Had the doctor not intervened, nature would have done its work, and I would have acquired mastery over myself, would have been freed from vice, and would have become happy.

Hospitals are institutions for propagating sin.[119] Men take less care of their bodies, and immorality increases. European doctors are the worst

---

117 Here the Gujarati text reads differently: 'The pretensions of physicians also know no bounds. It was a British physician who played upon the credulity of the Moghul emperor. He was successful in treating an illness in the emperor's family and was in consequence honoured. It was again a physician who ingratiated himself with the Ameer (of Afghanistan).'

118 'vice': (*vishay*) meaning lust.

119 'Hospitals are institutions for propagating sin': surely one of the most intemperate statements in the entire book. Gandhi later tried to assure critics that he had not written in ignorance of the facts concerning the great positive contributions that modern medicine had made to humanity, and that in writing *HS* he had sought the advice of 'precious medical friends' (among them Dr Pranjivan Mehta). Though he regretted the 'language' with which he chose to express his 'views', he was prepared to change only the language, not the views (*CW* 23: 347–8; *CW* 26: 389). The views in question concerned the tendency of modern medicine to neglect the soul – i.e., the spiritual and moral foundations of bodily health. 'Medicine does often

of all. For the sake of a mistaken care of the human body, they kill annually thousands of animals. They practise vivisection. No religion sanctions this. All say that it is not necessary to take so many lives for the sake of our bodies.

These doctors violate our religious instinct. Most of their medical preparations contain either animal fat or spirituous liquors; both of these are tabooed by Hindus and Mahomedans. We may pretend to be civilised, call religious prohibitions a superstition and wantonly indulge in what we like. The fact remains that the doctors induce us to indulge, and the result is that we have become deprived of self-control and have become effeminate.[120] In these circumstances, we are unfit to serve the country. To study European medicine is to deepen our slavery.

It is worth considering why we take up the profession of medicine. It is certainly not taken up for the purpose of serving humanity. We become doctors so that we may obtain honours and riches.[121] I have

benumb the soul of the patient' (CW 23: 348). 'The advertisements that I see of medicines make me sick. I feel that physicians are rendering no service to humanity whatsoever but the greatest disservice by claiming every medicine as the panacea for all ills of life. I plead for humility, simplicity and truth' (CW 26: 389).

My quarrel with the medical profession in general is that it ignores the soul altogether and strains at nothing in seeking merely to repair such a fragile instrument as the body. Thus ignoring the soul, the profession puts men at its mercy and contributes to the diminution of human dignity and self-control. I note with thankfulness that in the West a school of thought is rising slowly but surely which takes account of the soul in trying to repair a diseased body and which, therefore, relies less on drugs and more on nature as a powerful healing agent. (CW 27: 222)

It should be remembered in this context that (1) Gandhi had undertaken nursing training in South Africa; (2) he had voluntarily entered hospital and undergone surgery in 1924; (3) he took quinine to fight malaria; and (4) his A Guide to Health (1921) was his most widely read work for several decades.

120 The moral basis of this criticism is that modern medicine, taking a purely bodily view of health, ignores need for the health of the soul (the virtue of temperance), which is necessary for the maintenance of even bodily health.

121 Gandhi's criticism is that the modern medical profession was in alliance with modern pharmaceutical industries, and as such was becoming a 'profit'-driven profession. He would like to see it remain an 'honour'- or 'vocation'-driven profession, like that of the soldier.

endeavoured to show that there is no real service of humanity in the profession, and that it is injurious to mankind. Doctors make a show of their knowledge, and charge exorbitant fees. Their preparations, which are intrinsically worth a few pennies, cost shillings. The populace in its credulity and in the hope of ridding itself of some disease, allows itself to be cheated. Are not quacks then, whom we know, better than the doctors who put on an air of humaneness?

CHAPTER XIII

*

What is true civilisation?

READER: You have denounced railways, lawyers and doctors. I can see that you will discard all machinery.[122] What, then, is civilisation?

EDITOR: The answer to that question is not difficult. I believe that the civilisation India has evolved is not to be beaten in the world. Nothing can equal the seeds sown by our ancestors. Rome went, Greece shared the same fate, the might of the Pharaohs was broken, Japan has become westernised, of China nothing can be said, but India is still, somehow or other, sound at the foundation.[123] The people of Europe learn their lessons from the writings of the men of Greece or Rome, which exist no longer in their former glory. In trying to learn from them, the Europeans imagine that they will avoid the mistakes of Greece and Rome. Such is their pitiable condition. In the midst of all this, India remains immovable, and that is her glory. It is a charge against India that her people are so uncivilised, ignorant and stolid, that it is not possible to induce them to adopt any changes. It is a charge really against our merit. What we have tested and found true on the anvil of experience, we dare not change. Many thrust their advice upon India, and she remains steady. This is her beauty; it is the sheet-anchor of our hope.

122 'machinery': ch. xix deals with this topic. By introducing it here Gandhi alerts the reader to the tension that exists between 'true civilisation' and a civilisation based on machinery.

123 'India is still, somehow or other, sound at the foundation': this is the bedrock of Gandhi's defence of Indian civilisation in HS. That foundation is that *artha* and *kama* should be pursued within the framework of dharma. In modern civilisation *artha* and *kama*, according to Gandhi, assert their autonomy from dharma.

Civilisation is that mode of conduct which points out to man the path of duty. Performance of duty and observance of morality are convertible terms. To observe morality is to attain mastery over our mind and our passions. So doing, we know ourselves.[124] The Gujarati equivalent for civilisation means 'good conduct'.[125]

If this definition be correct, then India, as so many writers[126] have shown, has nothing to learn from anybody else,[127] and this is as it should be. We notice that mind is a restless bird; the more it gets the more it

124 In this definition of true civilisation, central to the argument of the book, Gandhi connects the notions of self-knowledge, duty (*farajj*), morality (*niti*), mastery over the mind (*man*) and the senses (*indriyo*).

125 In 1911, in response to a question as to whether it would not have been more accurate to write 'The Gujarati equivalent for civilisation is good conduct (*sudharo*)', Gandhi wrote the following reply:

If 'is' were to be used, the meaning would change. 'Is' is implied in 'equiv-alent' ... the Gujarati word generally used for 'civilisation' means 'a good way of life'. That is what I had meant to say. The sentence 'The Gujarati equivalent for civilisation is *sudharo*' is quite correct. But it is not what I intended to say. Were we to say, "The Gujarati equivalent for civilisation is "good conduct"", according to the rules of grammar, 'good conduct' would have to be taken as a Gujarati phrase ... Please let me know whether it was for this reason or for any other reasons that you concluded that 'means' was the right word. (*CW* 11: 153)

126 'as so many writers': in the Gujarati text this reads: 'as so many British writers'. See *HS*, Appendix ii.

127 'India ... has nothing to learn from anybody else': an obvious hyperbole, to be corrected by his other statements. Thus in 1911 he recommended that Chhaganlal Gandhi, his right-hand man at Phoenix Settlement, should go to London and 'imbibe' its particular atmosphere: 'My own idea was that you should live in London for a year and gather whatever experience and knowledge you could ... if you imbibe the particular kind of atmosphere that obtains there, the voyage to England will have, to my mind, fulfilled its purpose' (*CW* 10: 401-2). In 1929 he wrote: 'The "Western civilisation" which passes for civilisation is disgusting to me. I have given a rough picture of it in *Hind Swaraj*. Time has brought no change in it. It is not my purpose even to imply that everything Western is bad. I have learnt a lot from the West' (*CW* 40: 300). And in 1931 he wrote:

European civilisation is no doubt suited for the Europeans but it will mean ruin for India, if we endeavour to copy it. This is not to say that we may not adopt and assimilate whatever may be good and capable of assimilation by us as it does not also mean that even the Europeans will not have to part with

wants, and still remains unsatisfied. The more we indulge our passions, the more unbridled they become. Our ancestors, therefore, set a limit to our indulgences. They saw that happiness was largely a mental condition.[128] A man is not necessarily happy because he is rich, or unhappy because he is poor. The rich are often seen to be unhappy, the poor to be happy. Millions will always remain poor. Observing all this, our ancestors dissuaded us from luxuries and pleasures. We have managed with the same kind of plough as it existed thousands of years ago. We have retained the same kind of cottages that we had in former times, and our indigenous education remains the same as before. We have had no system of life-corroding competition.[129] Each followed his own occupation or trade,[130] and charged a regulation wage. It was not that we did not know how to invent machinery, but our forefathers knew that, if we

whatever evil might have crept into it. The incessant search for comforts and their multiplication is such an evil, and I make bold to say that the Europeans themselves will have to remodel their outlook, if they are not to perish under the weight of the comforts to which they are becoming slaves. It may be that my reading is wrong, but I know that for India to run after the Golden Fleece is to court certain death. Let us engrave on our hearts the motto of a Western philosopher, 'plain living and high thinking'. (CW 46: 55-6)

As late as 1936, Gandhi thought of London as being 'our Mecca or Kashi [Benares]'. In a letter of recommendation for Kamalnayan Bajaj written to H. S. L. Polak, he stated the following: 'However much we may fight Great Britain, London is increasingly becoming our Mecca or Kashi. Kamalnayan is no exception. I have advised him to take up a course in the London School of Economics. Perhaps you will put him in touch with Professor Laski who may not mind guiding young Bajaj. Muriel [Lester] has undertaken to mother him' (CW 63: 122).

128 The psychology of the mind adumbrated here is basic to Gandhi's moral theory and is derived from *The Bhagavad Gita*. Swaraj, or self-control, means control over the *mind*. On the *Gita's* teachings on the relationship of the mind to the body and the senses, and on how one may attain control over the mind, see Zaehner 1973, 423-5.

129 'life-corroding competition': following Ruskin, Gandhi wants to *moderate* competition by introducing 'social affections' into economic relations.

130 Here Gandhi defends the 'idea' of *varna* and rejects the 'historical' institutions of caste. This quasi-'platonic' approach to *varna* has not convinced critics such as B. R. Ambedkar and the more recent Dalit elite.

set our hearts after such things, we would become slaves and lose our moral fibre. They therefore, after due deliberation, decided that we should only do what we could with our hands and feet. They saw that our real happiness and health consisted in a proper use of our hands[131] and feet. They further reasoned that large cities were a snare and a useless encumbrance,[132] and that people would not be happy in them, that there would be gangs of thieves and robbers, prostitution and vice flourishing in them, and that poor men would be robbed by rich men. They were, therefore, satisfied with small villages. They saw that kings and their swords were inferior to the sword of ethics, and they, therefore, held the sovereigns of the earth to be inferior to the Rishis and the Fakirs.[133] A nation with a constitution like this is fitter to teach others than to learn from others. This nation had courts, lawyers and doctors, but they were all within bounds.[134] Everybody knew that these professions were not particularly superior; moreover, these vakils and vaids[135] did not rob people; they were considered people's dependants, not their masters. Justice was tolerably fair. The ordinary rule was to avoid courts. There were no touts to lure people into them. This evil, too, was noticeable only in and around capitals. The common people lived

131 Manual labour, extolled here, is not a valued activity according to the norms of traditional Indian civilisation. Gandhi came to appreciate it from his reading of Ruskin, Tolstoy and Bondaref. Promotion of manual labour became an integral part of the Gandhian revolution.

132 Gandhi saw in modern Indian cities a real threat to civilised living (*CW* 9: 476); 'Bombay, Calcutta, and the other chief cities of India are the real plague spots' (ibid., 479); 'To me the rise of the cities like Calcutta and Bombay is a matter for sorrow rather than congratulations' (ibid., 509). He idealised and romanticised the Indian village and hoped to reinstate it in a Gandhian India.

133 'Rishis and Fakirs': *rishis* are sages according to Hindu culture; *fakirs*, according to Muslim culture, are religious mendicants of great moral authority.

134 'within bounds': the bounds of dharma. This passage throws light on the real point of his earlier criticism of lawyers and doctors: modernity has 'freed' these professions from the restraints required by traditional morality.

135 'vakils and vaids': lawyers and doctors respectively of pre-modern Indian culture.

independently, and followed their agricultural occupation. They enjoyed true Home Rule.

And where this cursed modern civilisation has not reached, India remains as it was before. The inhabitants of that part of India will very properly laugh at your new-fangled notions. The English do not rule over them, nor will you ever rule over them. Those in whose name we speak we do not know, nor do they know us. I would certainly advise you and those like you who love the motherland to go into the interior that has yet not been polluted by the railways, and to live there for six months;[136] you might then be patriotic and speak of Home Rule.

Now you see what I consider to be real civilisation. Those who want to change conditions such as I have described are enemies of the country and are sinners.

READER: It would be all right if India were exactly as you have described it, but it is also India where there are hundreds of child widows, where two-year-old babies are married, where twelve-year-old girls are mothers and housewives, where women practise polyandry, where the practice of Niyog[137] obtains, where, in the name of religion, girls dedicate themselves to prostitution, and where, in the name of

---

136 '... go into the interior ... for six months': Gandhi believed that home rule would mean something only if it improved the lot of the villagers. This is a belief that the modern Indian elite has not understood or accepted. Writing to Henry Polak from Wardha in 1936, he stated: 'I am trying to become a villager. The place where I am writing this has a population of about 600 – no roads, no post-office, no shop' (*CW* 63: 122).

137 'Niyog': a custom permitting a man to have sexual intercourse with his brother's childless widow, or with the wife of an impotent kinsman, in order to raise children, without committing the sin of incest. Children born out of such unions were regarded as the issue of the woman's husband. Originally intended to provide legitimate heirs for childless relatives, in course of time the custom became corrupted, and became part of the 'privileges' of brahmins. While in some regions brahmins claimed the right to provide the issue upon a childless widow, in others they offered their 'services' even when the woman had other children and the husband was alive. Over the centuries, Niyoga remained a great affront to the dignity of Indian women.

religion, sheep and goats are killed.[138] Do you consider these also symbols of the civilisation that you have described?[139]

EDITOR: You make a mistake. The defects that you have shown are defects. Nobody mistakes them for ancient civilisation. They remain in spite of it. Attempts have always been made, and will be made, to remove them. We may utilise the new spirit that is born in us[140] for purging ourselves of these evils. But what I have described to you as emblems of modern civilisation are accepted as such by its votaries. The Indian civilisation as described by me has been so described by its votaries. In no part of the world, and under no civilisation, have all men attained perfection. The tendency of Indian civilisation is to elevate the moral being, that of the Western civilisation is to propagate immorality. The latter is godless, the former is based on a belief in God. So understanding and so believing, it behoves every lover of India to cling to the old Indian civilisation even as a child clings to its mother's breast.

---

138 Gandhi gives a gruesome account of his 1902 visit to the Kali temple in Calcutta: 'On the way I saw a stream of sheep going to be sacrificed to Kali … We were greeted by rivers of blood. I could not bear to stand there. I was exasperated and restless. I have never forgotten that sight' (*CW* 39: 190).

139 The social evils enumerated in this paragraph constitute the subject matter of Gandhi's critique of Indian civilisation in *HS*.

140 'the new spirit that is born in us': a very important point. Gandhi does recognise the positive contributions made by colonialism. It made Indians self-critical and creative.

CHAPTER XIV

*

How can India become free?

READER: I appreciate your views about civilisation. I will have to think over them. I cannot take in all at once. What, then, holding the views you do, would you suggest for freeing India?

EDITOR: I do not expect my views to be accepted all of a sudden. My duty is to place them before readers like yourself. Time can be trusted to do the rest. We have already examined the conditions for freeing India, but we have done so indirectly; we will now do so directly.[141] It is a world-known maxim that the removal of the cause of a disease results in the removal of the disease itself. Similarly, if the cause of India's slavery be removed, India can become free.

READER: If Indian civilisation is, as you say, the best of all, how do you account for India's slavery?

EDITOR: This civilisation is unquestionably the best, but it is to be observed that all civilisations have been on their trial. That civilisation which is permanent outlives it. Because the sons of India were found wanting, its civilisation has been placed in jeopardy. But its strength is to be seen in its ability to survive the shock. Moreover, the whole of India is not touched. Those alone who have been affected by western civilisation[142] have become enslaved. We measure the universe by our own miserable foot-rule. When we are slaves, we think that the whole

---

141 'indirectly ... directly': an important turning point in the argument of the book. Chs. I-XIII prepare the background for understanding the more positive ideas contained in chs. XIV-XX.

142 'western civilisation': meaning *modern* Western civilisation.

universe is enslaved. Because we are in an abject condition, we think that the whole of India is in that condition. As a matter of fact, it is not so, but it is as well to impute our slavery to the whole of India. But if we bear in mind the above fact, we can see that, if we become free, India is free. And in this thought you have a definition of Swaraj. It is Swaraj when we learn to rule ourselves.[143] It is, therefore, in the palm of our hands. Do not consider this Swaraj to be like a dream.[144] Here there is no idea of sitting still. The Swaraj that I wish to picture before you and me is such that, after we have once realised it, we will endeavour to the end of our lifetime to persuade others to do likewise. But such Swaraj has to be experienced by each one for himself.[145] One drowning man will never save another. Slaves ourselves, it would be a mere pretension to think of freeing others. Now you will have seen that it is not necessary for us to have as our goal the expulsion of the English. If the English become Indianised, we can accommodate them.[146] If they wish to remain in India along with their civilisation, there is no room for them. It lies with us to bring about such a state of things.

READER: It is impossible that Englishmen should ever become Indianised.

143 This is the first time that true swaraj has been defined in the book.

144 Swaraj, in so far as it requires self-rule, is not, and cannot be, a utopia; it is something that can be achieved by the individual here and now.

145 Swaraj for Gandhi is more than an object of research; it is something that has to be experienced internally, giving rise to an internal moral transformation of the individual. Without such an experience, swaraj would remain a mere theory or doctrine; it would never become an internal principle of action in the external political sphere. 'Experience' here has the Tolstoyan meaning, as found in *What is Art*? Compare Gandhi's comment to Joan Bondurant (who was conducting *research* on satyagraha): 'but satyagraha is not a subject for research – you must experience it, use it, live by it' (Bondurant 1965, 146). Inner experience in this context involves an awareness that *artha* and *kama* should be pursued only within the framework of dharma.

146 Here Gandhi answers the question raised in ch. iv: the physical expulsion of the British from India is not of the essence of swaraj; self-transformation is. Gandhi the assimilationist is prepared to welcome 'Indianised' Britons as true Indians.

EDITOR: To say that is equivalent to saying that the English have no humanity in them. And it is really beside the point whether they become so or not. If we keep our own house in order, only those who are fit to live in it will remain, others will leave of their own accord. Such things occur within the experience of all of us.

READER: But it has not occurred in history.

EDITOR: To believe that what has not occurred in history will not occur at all is to argue disbelief in the dignity of man. At any rate, it behoves us to try what appeals to our reason. All countries are not similarly conditioned. The condition of India is unique. Its strength is immeasurable. We need not, therefore, refer to the history of other countries. I have drawn attention to the fact that, when other civilisations have succumbed, the Indian has survived many a shock.

READER: I cannot follow this. There seems little doubt that we shall have to expel the English by force of arms. So long as they are in the country, we cannot rest. One of our poets[147] says that slaves cannot even dream of happiness. We are day by day becoming weakened owing to the presence of the English. Our greatness is gone; our people look like terrified men. The English are in the country like a blight which we must remove by every means.

EDITOR: In your excitement, you have forgotten all we have been considering. We brought the English, and we keep them. Why do you forget that our adoption of their civilisation makes their presence in India at all possible?[148] Your hatred against them ought to be transferred to their civilisation. But let us assume that we have to drive away the English by fighting, how is that to be done?

READER: In the same way as Italy did it. What it was possible for Mazzini and Garibaldi to do, is possible for us. You cannot deny that they were very great men.

147 'One of our poets': there is no reference to poets in the Gujarati text, which only states, 'It appears that slaves cannot even dream of happiness.' The poet in question is Tulsidas; the verse, *paradheen sapnehu sukh nahin*, is taken from his famous *Ramcharitmanas* (Tulsidas 1952, 115).
148 This point was raised earlier in ch. VII.

CHAPTER XV

Italy and India

EDITOR: It is well that you have instanced Italy. Mazzini was a great and good man; Garibaldi was a great warrior. Both are adorable; from their lives we can learn much. But the condition of Italy was different from that of India. In the first instance, the difference between Mazzini and Garibaldi is worth noting. Mazzini's ambition was not, and has not yet been, realised regarding Italy. Mazzini has shown in his writings on the duty of man that every man must learn how to rule himself.[149] This has not happened in Italy. Garibaldi did not hold this view of Mazzini's. Garibaldi gave, and every Italian took, arms. Italy and Austria had the same civilisation; they were cousins in this respect. It was a matter of tit for tat. Garibaldi simply wanted Italy to be free from the Austrian yoke. The machinations of Minister Cavour disgrace that portion of the history of Italy. And what has been the result? If you believe that, because Italians rule Italy, the Italian nation is happy, you are groping in darkness. Mazzini has shown conclusively that Italy did not become free. Victor Emanuel gave one meaning to the expression; Mazzini gave another. According to Emanuel, Cavour, and even Garibaldi, Italy meant the King of Italy and his henchmen. According to Mazzini, it meant the whole of the Italian people, that is, its agriculturists. Emanuel was only its servant. The Italy of Mazzini still remains in a

---

149 In presenting Mazzini as a non-violent moral reformer, Gandhi is responding to Savarkar's interpretation of him as a violent revolutionary. (For Gandhi's short essay on Mazzini, see CW 5: 27-8.) In early 1909 he was reading Mazzini in jail (CW 9: 208).

state of slavery. At the time of the so-called national war, it was a game of chess between two rival kings, with the people of Italy as pawns. The working classes in that land are still unhappy. They, therefore, indulge in assassination, rise in revolt, and rebellion on their part is always expected. What substantial gain did Italy obtain after the withdrawal of the Austrian troops? The gain was only nominal. The reforms for the sake of which the war was supposed to have been undertaken have not yet been granted. The condition of the people in general still remains the same. I am sure you do not wish to reproduce such a condition in India. I believe that you want the millions of India to be happy, not that you want the reins of Government in your hands. If that be so, we have to consider only one thing: how can the millions obtain self-rule? You will admit that people under several Indian princes are being ground down. The latter mercilessly crush them. Their tyranny[150] is greater than that of the English; and, if you want such tyranny in India, then we shall never agree. My patriotism does not teach me that I am to allow

150 'Their tyranny': Gandhi, whose father was a 'prime minister' of an Indian state, remained a life-long critic of the princely order. The point of his criticism was that Indian princes had delegitimised themselves as rulers of India both because of the autocratic nature of their regimes and the wanton manner in which they used public money for private opulence. In 1907 he published with approval an account of the King of Afghanistan's criticism of the dissolute life-style of Indian princes. Such state of affairs, Gandhi commented, was 'a power-ful cause of our miserable plight' (CW 7: 7–8). But his most famous criticism of the princes was made in 1916 in the inaugural lecture he delivered at the opening of Banares Hindu University. He told 'the richly bedecked noblemen' that there was no salvation for India unless they stripped themselves of their jewellery and held it in trust for their people. He reminded them that the public wealth that they so lavishly spent on themselves was created by poor peasants – 'men who grow two blades of grass in the place of one' – and that there could be no swaraj for India 'if we take away or allow others to take away from them almost the whole of the results of their labour'. The lecture so offended the large numbers of princes who were in the audience that the chair had to stop Gandhi and adjourn the meeting abruptly. (For the full text of this speech, see CW 13: 210–16.)

people to be crushed under the heel of Indian princes, if only the English retire. If I have the power, I should resist the tyranny of Indian princes just as much as that of the English. By patriotism I mean the welfare of the whole people, and, if I could secure it at the hands of the English, I should bow down my head to them. If any Englishman dedicated his life to securing the freedom of India, resisting tyranny and serving the land, I should welcome that Englishman as an Indian.

Again, India can fight like Italy only when she has arms. You have not considered this problem at all. The English are splendidly armed; that does not frighten me, but it is clear that, to pit ourselves against them in arms, thousands of Indians must be armed. If such a thing be possible, how many years will it take? Moreover, to arm India on a large scale is to Europeanise it. Then her condition will be just as pitiable as that of Europe. This means, in short, that India must accept European civilisation, and, if that is what we want, the best thing is that we have among us those who are so well trained in that civilisation. We will then fight for a few rights, will get what we can, and so pass our days. But the fact is that the Indian nation will not adopt arms, and it is well that it does not.

READER: You are over-assuming facts. All need not be armed. At first, we will assassinate a few Englishmen and strike terror; then, a few men who will have been armed will fight openly. We may have to lose a quarter of a million[151] men, more or less, but we will regain our land. We will undertake guerrilla warfare, and defeat the English.

EDITOR: That is to say, you want to make the holy land of India unholy. Do you not tremble to think of freeing India by assassination? What we need to do is to kill ourselves. It is a cowardly thought, that of killing others. Whom do you suppose to free by assassination? The millions of India do not desire it. Those who are intoxicated by the wretched modern civilisation think these things. Those who will rise to power by murder will certainly not make the nation happy. Those

151 'a quarter of a million': the Gujarati text reads '20 or 25 lakhs', i.e., 2 or 2.5 million.

who believe that India has gained by Dhingra's act[152] and such other acts in India[153] make a serious mistake. Dhingra was a patriot, but his love was blind. He gave his body in a wrong way; its ultimate result can only be mischievous.

READER: But you will admit that the English have been frightened by these murders, and that Lord Morley's reforms[154] are due to fear.

EDITOR: The English are both a timid and a brave nation. She is, I believe, easily influenced by the use of gunpowder. It is possible that Lord Morley has granted the reforms through fear, but what is granted under fear can be retained only so long as the fear lasts.

---

152 On 1 July 1909, Madan Lal Dhingra, an Indian student, assassinated Sir William Curzon-Wyllie, political aide-de-camp to Lord Morley, the Secretary of State for India, at a reception held by the National Indian Association at the Imperial Institute in South Kensington, London. Gandhi's assessment of the event appeared in *Indian Opinion*. He said, *inter alia*,

I must say that those who believe and argue that such murders may do good for India are ignorant men indeed. No act of treachery can ever profit a nation. Even should the British leave in consequence of such murderous acts, who will rule in their place? The only answer is: the murderers. Who will then be happy? Is the Englishman bad because he is an Englishman? Is it that everyone with an Indian skin is good? If that is so, we can claim no rights in South Africa, nor should there be any angry protest against oppression by Indian princes. India can gain nothing from the rule of murderers – no matter whether they are black or white. (*CW* 9: 302-3, at 303)

153 'and such other acts in India': a clear indication that Gandhi was quite well informed about the activities of secret societies in India. Already in 1908 he had written:

Many people exult at the explosion of bombs. This only shows ignorance and lack of understanding. If all the British were to be killed, those who kill them would become the masters of India, and as a result India would continue in a state of slavery. The bombs with which the British will have been killed will fall on India after the British leave. (*CW* 8: 374)

154 Minto–Morley Reforms, see ch. X (footnote 107).

*

CHAPTER XVI

Brute force[155]

READER: This is a new doctrine: that what is gained through fear is retained only while the fear lasts. Surely, what is given will not be withdrawn?

EDITOR: Not so. The Proclamation of 1857[156] was given at the end of a revolt, and for the purpose of preserving peace. When peace was

155 In the Gujarati text the chapter title is *darugolo*. Earlier in ch. IV the same word was translated as 'arms and ammunition', and in ch. XV, as 'gunpowder'. Gandhi also uses other terms to refer to the same concept: 'body-force' (*sharirbal*), 'gun-force' (*topbal*) and 'force of arms' (*hatyarbal*). What is conveyed by means of these terms is that there is an ethical difference between the use of 'soul-force' and that of 'brute force'.

156 'The Proclamation of 1857': Queen Victoria's Proclamation of 1858. It read in part:

> We hold ourselves bound to the natives of our Indian territories by the same obligations of duty which bind us to all our other subjects; and those obligations, by the blessings of Almighty God, we shall faithfully and conscientiously fulfil ... And it is our further will that, so far as may be, our subjects, of whatever race or creed, be freely and impartially admitted to offices in our service, the duties of which they may be qualified, by their education, ability, and integrity, duly to discharge. (Philips and Pandey 1962, 11)

> There are two points to be noted here. The first is Gandhi's interpretation of the Proclamation as enunciating a principle of political equality between Indians and Britons, an interpretation that colonial administrators in later decades did not accept – to Gandhi's great disillusionment. The second point is Gandhi's appreciation of Queen Victoria's personal involvement in the drafting of the Proclamation. He had reported in *Indian Opinion* that the Queen was not satisfied with the first draft submitted to her, considering it to be 'too tame, and not in keeping with the events that had taken place in India in connection with the Mutiny', and that she had asked Lord Derby, the prime minister, to redraft it,

secured and people became simple-minded, its full effect was toned down. If I ceased stealing for fear of punishment, I would recommence the operation so soon as the fear is withdrawn from me. This is almost a universal experience. We have assumed that we can get men to do things by force and, therefore, we use force.

READER: Will you not admit that you are arguing against yourself? You know that what the English obtained in their own country they have obtained by using brute force. I know you have argued that what they have obtained is useless, but that does not affect my argument. They wanted useless things, and they got them. My point is that their desire was fulfilled. What does it matter what means they adopted? Why should we not obtain our goal, which is good, by any means whatsoever, even by using violence? Shall I think of the means when I have to deal with a thief in the house? My duty is to drive him out anyhow. You seem to admit that we have received nothing, and that we shall receive nothing by petitioning. Why, then, may we not do so by using brute force? And, to retain what we may receive, we shall keep up the fear by using the same force to the extent that it may be necessary. You will not find fault with a continuance of force to prevent a child from thrusting its foot into fire? Somehow or other, we have to gain our end.[157]

EDITOR: Your reasoning is plausible. It has deluded many. I have used similar arguments before now. But I think I know better now, and I shall endeavour to undeceive you. Let us first take the argument that we are justified in gaining our end by using brute force, because the English gained theirs by using similar means.[158] It is perfectly true that they

'laying stress upon the fact that it was a female Sovereign speaking' (CW 3: 432, emphasis added). She had insisted that the document should 'breathe feelings of generosity, benevolence, and religious toleration, and point to the privileges which the Indian will receive in being placed on an equality with the subjects of the British Crown ...' (CW 5: 326).

157 The two metaphors introduced in this paragraph -- those of the thief and the child - are crucial to this argument.

158 The reference is to the Reform Act of 1832. Gandhi is responding to the argument of the Indian revolutionaries that if the British people obtained their rights by using violent means, the Indians also may use similar means to obtain their rights.

used brute force, and that it is possible for us to do likewise, but, by using similar means, we can get only the same thing that they got. You will admit that we do not want that. Your belief that there is no connection between the means and the end is a great mistake.[159] Through that mistake even men who have been considered religious have committed grievous crimes. Your reasoning is the same as saying that we can get a rose through planting a noxious weed.[160] If I want to cross the ocean, I can do so only by means of a vessel; if I were to use a cart for that purpose, both the cart and I would soon find the bottom. 'As is the God, so is the votary' is a maxim worth considering. Its meaning has been distorted, and men have gone astray. The means may be likened to a seed, the end to a tree; and there is just the same inviolable connection between the means and the end as there is between the seed and the tree. I am not likely to obtain the result flowing from the worship of God by laying myself prostrate before Satan. If, therefore, anyone were to say: 'I want to worship God, it does not matter that I do so by means of Satan' it would be set down as ignorant folly. We reap exactly as we sow.[161] The English in 1833[162] obtained greater voting power by violence. Did they by using brute force better appreciate their duty? They wanted the right of voting, which they obtained by using physical force. But real rights are a result of performance of duty;[163] these rights they have not

159 Gandhi's response is based on the supposition that there is an inviolable connection between ends (*sadhya*) and means (*sadhan*).

160 Here Gandhi uses several examples to illustrate his point: those of a rose, a boat, Hindu liturgy, the seed and the tree, and proper worship of God.

161 '... whatever a man sows, that he will also reap' (St Paul's 'Letter to the Galatians', ch. 6, v. 7).

162 'The English in 1833' refers to the Parliamentary Reform Act of 1832. Gandhi has in mind such acts of violence as those associated with this reform, as well as those associated with the 1819 riots of St Peter's Fields, Manchester, the so-called 'Peterloo massacre'.

163 Gandhi explains his theory of rights: *real* rights, in his view, ought to be based on *satya* (truth) and dharma, the sources of duty. Real rights flow from duty. This contrasts with the modern theory of rights which asserts the priority of rights over duties.

obtained. We, therefore, have before us in England the farce of everybody wanting and insisting on his rights, nobody thinking of his duty.
And, where everybody wants rights, who shall give them to whom? I do
not wish to imply that they never perform their duty, but I do wish to
imply that they do not perform the duty to which those rights should
correspond; and, as they do not perform that particular duty, namely,
acquire fitness, their rights have proved a burden to them. In other
words, what they have obtained is an exact result of the means they
adopted. They used the means corresponding to the end. If I want to
deprive you of your watch, I shall certainly have to fight for it; if I want to
buy your watch, I shall have to pay you for it; and, if I want a gift, I shall
have to plead for it; and, according to the means I employ, the watch is
stolen property, my own property, or a donation. Thus we see three
different results from three different means. Will you still say that
means do not matter?

Now we shall take the example given by you of the thief to be driven
out. I do not agree with you that the thief may be driven out by any
means. If it is my father who has come to steal, I shall use one kind of
means. If it is an acquaintance, I shall use another, and, in the case of a
perfect stranger, I shall use a third. If it is a white man, you will perhaps
say, you will use means different from those you will adopt with an
Indian thief. If it is a weakling, the means will be different from those to
be adopted for dealing with an equal in physical strength; and, if the
thief is armed from tip to toe, I small simply remain quiet. Thus we have
a variety of means between the father and the armed man. Again, I fancy
that I should pretend to be sleeping whether the thief was my father or
that strong armed man. The reason for this is that my father would also
be armed, and I should succumb to the strength possessed by either, and
allow my things to be stolen. The strength of my father would make me
weep with pity; the strength of the armed man would rouse in me anger,
and we should become enemies. Such is the curious situation. From
these examples, we may not be able to agree as to the means to be
adopted in each case. I myself seem clearly to see what should be done
in all these cases, but the remedy may frighten you. I, therefore, hesitate

to place it before you. For the time being, I will leave you to guess it, and, if you cannot, it is clear that you will have to adopt different means in each case. You will also have seen that any means will not avail to drive away the thief. You will have to adopt means to fit each case. Hence it follows that your duty is *not* to drive away the thief by any means you like.

Let us proceed a little further. That well-armed man has stolen your property, you have harboured the thought, you are filled with anger; you argue that you want to punish that rogue, not for your own sake, but for the good of your neighbours; you have collected a number of armed men, you want to take his house by assault, he is duly informed of it, he runs away; he, too, is incensed. He collects his brother-robbers, and sends you a defiant message that he will commit robbery in broad day-light. You are strong, you do not fear him, you are prepared to receive him. Meanwhile, the robber pesters your neighbours. They complain before you, you reply that you are doing all for their sake, you do not mind that your own goods have been stolen. Your neighbours reply that the robber never pestered them before, and that he commenced his depredations only after you declared hostilities against him. You are between Scylla and Charybdis. You are full of pity for the poor men. What they say is true. What are you to do? You will be disgraced if you now leave the robber alone. You, therefore, tell the poor men: 'Never mind. Come, my wealth is yours, I will give you arms, I will teach you how to use them; you should belabour the rogue; don't you leave him alone.' And so the battle grows; the robbers increase in numbers; your neighbours have deliberately put themselves to inconvenience. Thus the result of wanting to take revenge upon the robber is that you have disturbed your own peace; you are in perpetual fear of being robbed and assaulted; your courage has given place to cowardice. If you will patiently examine the argument, you will see that I have not overdrawn the picture. This is one of the means. Now let us examine the other.[164] You set this armed robber down as an ignorant brother; you intend to reason with him at a suitable opportunity; you argue that he is, after all,

164 'the other': i.e., the principle of compassion (*daya*).

a fellow-man; you do not know what prompted him to steal. You, therefore, decide that, when you can, you will destroy the man's motive for
stealing. Whilst you are thus reasoning with yourself, the man comes
again to steal. Instead of being angry with him, you take pity on him.
You think that this stealing habit must be a disease with him. Henceforth,
you, therefore, keep your doors and windows open; you change your
sleeping-place, and you keep your things in a manner most accessible
to him. The robber comes again, and is confused, as all this is new to him;
nevertheless, he takes away your things. But his mind is agitated. He
inquires about you in the village, he comes to learn about your broad
and loving heart, he repents, he begs your pardon, returns you your
things, and leaves off the stealing habit.[165] He becomes your servant,
and you find for him honourable employment. This is the second method.
Thus, you see different means have brought about totally different
results. I do not wish to deduce from this that all robbers will act in the
above manner, or that all will have the same pity and love like you, but
I wish only to show that only fair means can produce fair results, and that,
at least in the majority of cases,[166] if not, indeed, in all, the force of love
and pity is infinitely greater than the force of arms. There is harm in the
exercise of brute force, never in that of pity.

Now we will take the question of petitioning.[167] It is a fact beyond
dispute that a petition, without the backing of force, is useless. However,
the late Justice Ranade used to say that petitions served a useful purpose
because they were a means of educating people. They give the latter an

---

165 *Daya* prompts the use of different means – instead of trying to restrain the
thief by violent means, it seeks to restrain him by non-violent means, and if
possible to bring about a change in his character. When only violence was
applied to the thief, his behaviour did not improve; but when *daya* was applied,
it did improve. One of the aims of non-violence is the moral regeneration of the
culprit.

166 'in the majority of cases': this is a very important caveat. The application of the
principle of non-violence allows for exceptions.

167 'petitioning': the method adopted by the Moderates of the Indian National
Congress. Gandhi, following Ranade, endorses it as an effective means of the
political education of the masses.

idea of their condition, and warn the rulers. From this point of view, they are not altogether useless. A petition of an equal is a sign of courtesy; a petition from a slave is a symbol of his slavery. A petition backed by force is a petition from an equal and, when he transmits his demand in the form of a petition, it testifies to his nobility. Two kinds of force can back petitions. 'We will hurt you if you do not give this' is one kind of force; it is the force of arms, whose evil results we have already examined. The second kind of force can thus be stated: 'If you do not concede our demand, we will be no longer your petitioners. You can govern us only so long as we remain the governed; we shall no longer have any dealings with you.' The force implied in this may be described as love-force, soul-force or, more popularly but less accurately, passive resistance.[168] This force is indestructible. He who uses it perfectly understands his position. We have an ancient proverb which literally means: 'One negative cures thirty-six diseases.'[169] The force of arms is powerless when matched against the force of love or the soul.

Now we shall take your last illustration, that of the child thrusting its foot into fire. It will not avail you. What do you really do to the child? Supposing that it can exert so much physical force that it renders you

168 'passive resistance': the Gujarati word used here is *satyagraha*. The account of how Gandhi came to coin this word is given in *CW* 8: 131. *Indian Opinion* called for submission of a suitable word for the new movement Gandhi had intro-duced. Among the words submitted were *pratyupaya* (counter-measure); *kash-tadhin prativartan* (resistance through submission to hardship); *dridha pratipaksha* (firmness in resistance); *sadagraha* (firmness in a good cause). Gandhi preferred the last word, but modified it by changing *sada* into *satya*. Note that *Unto This Last* also speaks of the Soul and its force: 'But he [the worker] being, on the contrary, an engine whose motive power is *a* Soul, the force of this very peculiar agent, as an unknown quantity, enters into all the political economist's equations …' (Ruskin, ed. Yarker, 1978, 30–1). Gandhi takes note of this point in his paraphrase of this work (*CW* 8: 258).

169 The word for 'negative' in the Gujarati text is *nanno*, which carries the meaning of a firm 'no'. The proverb may be interpreted as follows: 'The ability to say a firm "no" will save you from many diseases.' I thank Prof. Bhikhu Parekh for clarifying the meaning of this proverb.

powerless and rushes into fire, then you cannot prevent it. There are only two remedies open to you – either you must kill it in order to prevent it from perishing in the flames, or you must give your own life, because you do not wish to see it perish before your very eyes. You will not kill it. If your heart is not quite full of pity, it is possible that you will not surrender yourself by preceding the child and going into the fire yourself. You, therefore, helplessly allow it to go into the flames. Thus, at any rate, you are not using physical force. I hope you will not consider that it is still physical force, though of a low order, when you would forcibly prevent the child from rushing towards the fire if you could.[170] That force is of a different order, and we have to understand what it is.

Remember that, in thus preventing the child, you are minding entirely its own interest, you are exercising authority for its sole benefit.[171] Your example does not apply to the English. In using brute force against the English, you consult entirely your own, that is, the national

170 Here we find Gandhi attaching an important qualification to the meaning of non-violence. The physical restraining of a child rushing to self-destruction is a non-violent act in Gandhi's sense of non-violence, for the physical restraining here results in the well-being of the child; besides it is not motivated by self-interest. Non-violence requires 'active resistance to evil' (Brock 1972, 468).

171 'sole benefit': This is one instance of the use of physical force being consistent with Gandhi's theory of non-violence. Mrs Graham Polak narrates the case of a young boy being ordered by Gandhi to undergo corporal punishment (Polak 1931, 135–6). He also saw no inconsistency between non-violence and the use of physical force in collective self-defence. Thus in 1918 he actively recruited for the Indian army to fight in World War I, and in 1938 he seemed to defend the use of force against Nazism: 'If there ever could be a justifiable war in the name of and for humanity, a war against Germany, to prevent the wanton persecution of a whole race, would be completely justified. But I do not believe in any war. A discussion of the pros and cons of such a war is therefore outside my horizon or province' (*CW* 68: 138). And in 1947, Gandhi seemed to acquiesce in the Indian use of force in Kashmir (Woodcock 1972, 97). According to Madeleine Slade, one of Gandhi's devoted disciples, he saw no inconsistency between his notion of non-violence and the violence involved in shooting mad dogs and the mercy-killing of badly wounded animals (Slade 1960, 98–9).

interest.[172] There is no question here either of pity or of love. If you say that the actions of the English, being evil, represent fire, and that they proceed to their actions through ignorance, and that, therefore, they occupy the position of a child, and that you want to protect such a child, then you will have to overtake every such evil action by whomsoever committed, and, as in the case of the child, you will have to sacrifice yourself. If you are capable of such immeasurable pity, I wish you well in its exercise.

172 One of the high points of the entire work: here Gandhi rejects the modern principle of reason of state or national interest (*prajano swarth*) as a legitimate principle of international politics. Even against colonial rule, Indians may not invoke that principle, much less employ violence in its application. What he advocates is a non-violent, mutual accommodation between Indians and Britons.

CHAPTER XVII

*

Passive resistance[173]

READER: Is there any historical evidence as to the success of what you have called soul-force or truth-force? No instance seems to have happened of any nation having risen through soul-force. I still think that the evildoers will not cease doing evil without physical punishment.

EDITOR: The poet Tulsidas has said 'Of religion, pity or love is the root, as egotism of the body. Therefore, we should not abandon pity so long as we are alive.'[174] This appears to me to be a scientific

---

173 The Gujarati title of this chapter is *satyagraha-atmabal*.

174 Next to *Bhagavad Gita*, Tulsidas' *Ramayana* had the strongest influence on Gandhi's religio-ethical development. As he states in his *Autobiography*, he regarded it 'as the greatest book in all devotional literature' (*CW* 39: 32). One of the first books published by his International Press, Phoenix, Natal, was an abridged version of this work; in introducing the work to the public he wrote, 'We wish that every Indian goes devoutly through the summary which we are placing before the public, reflect over it, and assimilate the ethical principles so vividly set out in it' (*CW* 9: 98).

The couplet cited here is popularly attributed to Tulsidas. The popular version reads as follows:

> *Daya dharma ka mool hain, pap mool abhiman*
> *Tulsi daya na chandiye, jab lag ghatmen pran*

('Of dharma pity is the root, as egotism is of sin. Therefore, we should not abandon pity so long as we are alive.' [Editor's translation; emphasis added.])

Gandhi here either modifies the first line of the popular version by substituting body for sin, or uses another version of the couplet familiar to him. According to a letter to the present editor from Prof. T. N. Bali, professor of Hindi at Delhi University, this couplet cannot be found in any of Tulsidas' known works.

truth.[175] I believe in it as much as I believe in two and two being four. The force of love is the same as the force of the soul or truth. We have evidence of its working at every step. The universe[176] would disappear without the existence of that force. But you ask for historical evidence. It is, therefore, necessary to know what history means. The Gujarati equivalent means: 'It so happened.' If that is the meaning of history, it is possible to give copious evidence. But, if it means the doings of kings and emperors, there can be no evidence of soul-force or passive resistance in such history. You cannot expect silver-ore in a tin-mine. History, as we know it, is a record of the wars of the world, and so there is a proverb among Englishmen that a nation which has no history, that is, no wars, is a happy nation. How kings played, how they became enemies of one another, and how they murdered one another is found accurately recorded in history, and, if this were all that had happened in the world, it would have been ended long ago. If the story of the universe had commenced with wars, not a man would have been found alive today. Those people who have been warred against have disappeared, as, for instance, the natives of Australia, of whom hardly a man was left alive by the intruders. Mark, please, that these natives did not use soul-force in self-defence, and it does not require much foresight to know that the Australians will share the same fate as their victims. 'Those that wield the sword shall perish by the sword.'[177] With us, the proverb is that professional swimmers will find a watery grave.

The fact that there are so many men still alive in the world shows that it is based not on the force of arms but on the force of truth or love. Therefore, the greatest and most unimpeachable evidence of the success of this force is to be found in the fact that, in spite of the wars of the world, it still lives on.

175 'scientific truth': in Gujarati, *shastra wachan*; scientific according to the science of morals, not according to the modern notion of science.

176 'The universe': i.e., the human universe. Without *daya*, the human universe would become as horrible as *rasatal*, one of the seven 'hells' of Hindu mythology.

177 Gospel of St Matthew, ch. 26, v. 52.

Thousands, indeed tens of thousands, depend for their existence on a very active working of this force. Little quarrels of millions of families in their daily lives disappear before the exercise of this force. Hundreds of nations live in peace. History does not, and cannot, take note of this fact. History is really a record of every interruption of the even working of the force of love or of the soul. Two brothers quarrel; one of them repents and reawakens the love that was lying dormant in him;[178] the two again begin to live in peace; nobody takes note of this. But, if the two brothers, through the intervention of solicitors or some other reason, take up arms or go to law – which is another form of the exhibition of brute force – their doings would be immediately noticed in the press, they would be the talk of their neighbours, and would probably go down to history. And what is true of families and communities is true of nations. There is no reason to believe that there is one law for families and another for nations. History, then, is a record of an interruption of the course of nature. Soul-force, being natural, is not noted in history.

READER: According to what you say, it is plain that instances of this kind of passive resistance are not to be found in history. It is necessary to understand this passive resistance more fully. It will be better, therefore, if you enlarge upon it.

EDITOR: Passive resistance is a method of securing rights by personal suffering; it is the reverse of resistance by arms. When I refuse to do a thing that is repugnant to my conscience, I use soul-force.[179] For instance, the government of the day has passed a law which is applicable to me. I do not like it. If, by using violence, I force the government to repeal the law, I am employing what may be termed body-force. If I do

---

178 The Gujarati text has: 'one of them practises satyagraha against the other'. Omitted from the English text.

179 The Gujarati version of this definition is as follows: 'Satyagraha or soul-force is called passive resistance in English. That word is applicable to a method by which men, enduring pain, secure their rights. Its purpose is the opposite of the purpose of using force of arms (*ladaibal*). When something is not acceptable to me, I do not do that work. In so acting I use satyagraha or soul-force.'

not obey the law, and accept the penalty for its breach, I use soul-force. It involves sacrifice of self.

Everybody admits that sacrifice of self is infinitely superior to sacrifice of others. Moreover, if this kind of force is used in a cause that is unjust, only the person using it suffers. He does not make others suffer for his mistakes. Men have before now done many things which were subsequently found to have been wrong. No man can claim to be absolutely in the right, or that a particular thing is wrong, because he thinks so, but it is wrong for him so long as that is his deliberate judgement. It is, therefore, meet that he should not do that which he knows to be wrong, and suffer the consequence whatever it may be. This is the key to the use of soul-force.

READER: You would then disregard laws – this is rank disloyalty. We have always been considered a law-abiding nation. You seem to be going even beyond the extremists.[180] They say that we must obey the laws that have been passed, but that, if the laws be bad, we must drive out the lawgivers even by force.

EDITOR: Whether I go beyond them or whether I do not is a matter of no consequence to either of us. We simply want to find out what is right, and to act accordingly. The real meaning of the statement that we are a law-abiding nation is that we are passive resisters. When we do not like certain laws, we do not break the heads of lawgivers, but we suffer and do not submit to the laws.[181] That we should obey laws whether good or bad is a new-fangled notion.[182] There was no such thing in former days. The people disregarded those laws they did not like, and suffered the penalties for their breach. It is contrary to our manhood, if we obey laws

---

180 The implication here is that satyagraha, though not a violent form of action, is even more revolutionary than the revolution advocated by the Reader.

181 The Gujarati text here links satyagraha with the ritual of fasting: 'but in order to annul that law we observe fast'. This is the only time that *HS* links satyagraha and fast.

182 'a new-fangled notion'. The reference is to the utilitarian jurisprudence introduced into India in the nineteenth century. Utility replaced dharma as the ethical basis of law. For a full account of this, see Stokes (1959).

repugnant to our conscience. Such teaching is opposed to religion,[183] and means slavery. If the government were to ask us to go about without any clothing, should we do so? If I were a passive resister, I would say to them that I would have nothing to do with their law. But we have so forgotten ourselves and become so compliant, that we do not mind any degrading law.

A man who has realised his manhood, who fears only God, will fear no one else. Man-made laws[184] are not necessarily binding on him. Even the government do not expect any such thing from us. They do not say: 'You must do such and such a thing' but they say: 'If you do not do it, we will punish you.' We are sunk so low, that we fancy that it is our duty and our religion[185] to do what the law lays down. If man will only realise that it is unmanly to obey laws that are unjust, no man's tyranny will enslave him. This is the key to self-rule or home-rule.[186]

It is a superstition and an ungodly thing to believe that an act of a majority binds a minority. Many examples can be given in which acts of majorities will be found to have been wrong, and those of minorities to have been right. All reforms owe their origin to the initiation of minorities in opposition to majorities. If among a band of robbers, a knowledge of robbing is obligatory, is a pious man to accept the obligation? So long as the superstition that men should obey unjust laws exists, so long will their slavery exist. And a passive resister alone can remove such a superstition.

183 'religion': dharma, in the sense of ethics.
184 'Man-made laws': this terminology suggests the distinction between positive law and the higher law of dharma. Note the parallel between Gandhi's legal philosophy and that branch of Western legal philosophy which distinguishes between positive law and natural law.
185 'our duty and our religion': in Gujarati, *farajj* and dharma respectively. Modern legal positivism, according to Gandhi, corrupts the notion of law in that it makes obedience to positive law a political and a moral duty, independently of the question of whether such law is in harmony with dharma or not.
186 There is thus an ethical link between courage, satyagraha and the practice of dharma. Gandhi's swaraj requires that the positive legal system recognises the validity of dharma.

To use brute force, to use gunpowder is contrary to passive resistance, for it means that we want our opponent to do by force that which we desire but he does not. And, if such a use of force is justifiable, surely he is entitled to do likewise by us. And so we should never come to an agreement. We may simply fancy, like the blind horse moving in a circle round a mill, that we are making progress. Those who believe that they are not bound to obey laws which are repugnant to their conscience have only the remedy of passive resistance open to them. Any other must lead to disaster.

READER: From what you say, I deduce that passive resistance is a splendid weapon of the weak,[187] but that, when they are strong, they may take up arms.

EDITOR: This is gross ignorance. Passive resistance, that is, soul-force, is matchless. It is superior to the force of arms. How, then, can it be considered only a weapon of the weak? Physical-force men are strangers to the courage that is requisite in a passive resister. Do you believe that a coward can ever disobey a law that he dislikes? Extremists are considered to be advocates of brute force. Why do they, then, talk about obeying laws? I do not blame them. They can say nothing else. When they succeed in driving out the English, and they themselves become governors, they will want you and me to obey their laws. And that is a fitting thing for their constitution. But a passive resister will say he will not obey a law that is against his conscience, even though he may be blown to pieces at the mouth of a cannon.

What do you think? Wherein is courage required – in blowing others to pieces from behind a cannon or with a smiling face to approach a cannon and to be blown to pieces? Who is the true warrior – he who

187 Gandhi is defending satyagraha against the opinion of some of his South African friends who thought that it was the same as passive resistance practised in England recently by the suffragettes and by the opponents of the Education Act of 1902. Whereas passive resistance was compatible with mild forms of physical violence, satyagraha, Gandhi pointed out, was not. For a full account of Gandhi's distinction between passive resistance and satyagraha, see *Satyagraha in South Africa*, ch. 13 (*CW* 29: 93-7).

keeps death always as a bosom-friend or he who controls the death of others? Believe me that a man devoid of courage and manhood can never be a passive resister.

This, however, I will admit: that even a man weak in body is capable of offering this resistance. One man can offer it just as well as millions. Both men and women can indulge in it. It does not require the training of an army; it needs no Jiu-jitsu. Control over the mind[188] is alone necessary, and, when that is attained, man is free like the king of the forest, and his very glance withers the enemy.

Passive resistance is an all-sided sword; it can be used anyhow; it blesses him who uses it and him against whom it is used. Without drawing a drop of blood, it produces far-reaching results. It never rusts, and cannot be stolen. Competition between passive resisters does not exhaust. The sword of passive resistance does not require a scabbard. It is strange indeed that you should consider such a weapon to be a weapon merely of the weak.

READER: You have said that passive resistance is a speciality of India. Have cannons never been used in India?

EDITOR: Evidently, in your opinion, India means its few princes.[189] To me, it means its teeming millions, on whom depends the existence of its princes and our own.

Kings will always use their kingly weapons. To use force is bred in them. They want to command, but those who have to obey commands, do not want guns; and these are in a majority throughout the world. They have to learn either body-force or soul-force. Where they learn the former, both the rulers and the ruled become like so many mad men, but, where they learn soul-force, the commands of the rulers do not go beyond the point of their swords, for true men disregard unjust commands. Peasants[190] have never been subdued by the sword, and never

---

188 On 'mind', see chs. XIII and XX.
189 For Gandhi's critique of the Indian princes, see ch. XV.
190 Peasants: *khedut* – those who actually cultivated the land. These constituted only a small percentage of the village population, and did not always include the untouchables.

will be. They do not know the use of the sword, and they are not frightened by the use of it by others. That nation is great which rests its head upon death as its pillow. Those who defy death are free from all fear.[191] For those who are labouring under the delusive charms of brute force, this picture is not over-drawn. The fact is that, in India, the nation at large has generally used passive resistance in all departments of life. We cease to co-operate with our rulers when they displease us. This is passive resistance.

I remember an instance when, in a small principality, the villagers were offended by some command issued by the prince. The former immediately began vacating the village. The prince became nervous, apologised to his subjects and withdrew his command. Many such instances can be found in India.[192] Real home rule is possible only

191 Gandhi has terrorists like Dhingra in mind here, terrorists who are willing to die for a cause. But satyagraha, he implies, requires even greater courage than that required of the terrorists.

192 The reference here is to the traditional practice of *dhurna*. Joseph Doke's biography of Gandhi gives the following accounts of *dhurna*. 'The idea of passive resistance as a means of opposing evil is inherent in Indian philosophy. In old time, it was called "to sit dhurna". Sometimes a whole community would adopt this method towards their Prince. It has been so in the history of Porbandar; then trade was dislocated and force helpless before the might of passive resistance.'

Doke cites from Bishop Heber's account of *dhurna*: 'To sit dhurna, or mourning, is to remain motionless in that posture, without food, and exposed to the weather, till the person against whom it is employed consents to the request offered, and the Hindus believe that whoever dies under such a process becomes a tormenting spirit to haunt and afflict his inflexible antagonist.' Heber narrates how on one occasion 'above three hundred thousand persons' around Benares practised mass *dhurna*, 'deserted their houses, shut up their shops, suspended the labour of their farms, forbore to light fires, dress victuals, many of them even to eat, and sat down with folded arms and drooping heads, like so many sheep, on the plain which surrounds Benares' (Doke 1909, 132–3). As practised traditionally, *dhurna* was a form of coercion plain and simple. Under the Indian Penal Code the practice was outlawed by the middle of the nineteenth century (Bose 1962, 80–2; Devanesan 1969, 45).

where passive resistance is the guiding force of the people. Any other rule is foreign rule.[193]

READER: Then you will say that it is not at all necessary for us to train the body?

EDITOR: I will certainly not say any such thing. It is difficult to become a passive resister, unless the body is trained. As a rule, the mind, residing in a body that has become weakened by pampering, is also weak, and, where there is no strength of mind, there can be no strength of soul. We will have to improve our physique by getting rid of infant marriages and luxurious living. If I were to ask a man having a shattered body to face a cannon's mouth, I would make of myself a laughing-stock.

READER: From what you say, then, it would appear that it is not a small thing to become a passive resister, and, if that is so, I would like you to explain how a man may become a passive resister.

EDITOR: To become a passive resister is easy enough, but it is also equally difficult. I have known a lad of fourteen years become a passive resister; I have known also sick people doing likewise; and I have also known physically strong and otherwise happy people being unable to take up passive resistance. After a great deal of experience, it seems to me that those who want to become passive resisters for the service of the country[194] have to observe perfect chastity, adopt poverty, follow truth, and cultivate fearlessness.

In a *Young India* article of 2 February 1922, Gandhi severely condemned the revival of 'sitting *dhurna*' in connection with satyagraha, calling it an 'ancient form of barbarity'. Some students in Calcutta had used this 'crude' and 'cowardly' method to block the passage of their fellow students. Gandhi stated emphatically that *dhurna* had nothing to do with satyagraha.

193 'foreign rule': in Gujarati *ku-raj* (misrule).

194 'for the service of the country': Gandhi converts the four traditional *moral* virtues mentioned here into new *civic* virtues. According to tradition, these virtues were considered to be the means of *individual* self-realisation; Gandhi points out, however, that the practice of the same virtues can also become the means of national regeneration. In a letter written to his son Manilal on 24 November 1909 he explains how the activity of achieving individual self-realisation can contribute to national regeneration as well:

Chastity is one of the greatest disciplines without which the mind cannot attain requisite firmness. A man who is unchaste loses stamina, become emasculated and cowardly. He whose mind is given over to animal passions is not capable of any great effort. This can be proved by innumerable instances. What, then, is a married person to do, is the question that arises naturally; and yet it need not. When a husband and wife gratify the passions, it is no less an animal indulgence on that account. Such an indulgence, except for perpetuating the race, is strictly prohibited. But a passive resister has to avoid even that very limited indulgence, because he can have no desire for progeny. A married man, therefore, can observe perfect chastity. This subject is not capable of being treated at greater length. Several questions arise: How is one to carry one's wife with one? What are her rights, and other such questions? Yet those who wish to take part in a great work are bound to solve these puzzles.[195]

Just as there is necessity for chastity, so is there for poverty.[196] Pecuniary ambition and passive resistance cannot well go together.

First of all, we shall have to consider how we can realise the self and how serve our country … For realising the self, the first essential thing is to cultivate a strong moral sense. Morality means acquisition of virtues such as fearlessness, truth, *brahmacharya* (celibacy) and so on. Service is automatically rendered to the country in this process of cultivating morality. (*CW* 10: 70)

The idea recurs in Gandhi's letter to Maganlal Gandhi (*CW* 10: 206-7).

195 In 1906 Gandhi took the vow of *brahmacharya*. The *heroic* stage of satygraha can be reached only by those who are chaste in word, deed and thought. For Gandhi's thoughts on chastity, see *Autobiography*, III, chs. 7, 8; IV, chs. 25-30 (*CW* 39: 165-71, 252-64). For a critical analysis of Gandhi's approach to *brahmacharya*, see Erikson 1969; Parekh 1989b, 172-206; and Mehta 1977, 179-213. Cf. Tolstoy, who understood chastity in married life to mean abstention from adultery: 'The ideal [proposed by the Sermon on the Mount] is perfect chastity, even in thought. The commandment indicating the level below which it is quite possible not to descend is man's progress towards this ideal, is that of a pure married life, refraining from adultery' (Tolstoy 1935, 121).

196 'poverty': i.e., *voluntary* poverty or simplicity of life or freedom from possessiveness. Gandhi is not at all glorifying involuntary poverty here (*pace* Keer 1973, 782). What he is arguing is that, paradoxical though it may appear to some, the virtue of detachment has a great deal to contribute towards making India economically prosperous.

Those who have money are not expected to throw it away, but they are expected to be indifferent about it. They must be prepared to lose every penny rather than give up passive resistance.

Passive resistance has been described in the course of our discussion as truth-force.[197] Truth, therefore, has necessarily to be followed, and that at any cost. In this connection, academic questions such as whether a man may not lie in order to save a life, etc., arise, but these questions occur only to those who wish to justify lying. Those who want to follow truth every time are not placed in such a quandary, and, if they are, they are still saved from a false position.

Passive resistance cannot proceed a step without fearlessness.[198] Those alone can follow the path of passive resistance who are free from fear, whether as to their possessions, false honour, their relatives, the government, bodily injuries, death.

These observances are not to be abandoned in the belief that they are difficult. Nature has implanted in the human breast ability to cope with any difficulty or suffering that may come to man unprovoked. These qualities are worth having, even for those who do not wish to serve the country. Let there be no mistake as those who want to train themselves in the use of arms are also obliged to have these qualities more or less.[199] Everybody does not become a warrior for the wish. A would-be warrior

---

197 Since satyagraha proceeds from truth-force, it follows that a satyagrahi cannot hide the truth from his or her 'opponent'. Satyagraha requires frankness and openness. This point is stressed in the Gujarati text, where he takes aim at the Indian anarchists and their secret societies. The relevant Gujarati text reads as follows: 'How can anyone demonstrate the power or force of truth unless he dedicates himself to truth? Truth, therefore, is absolutely necessary. It cannot be abandoned, whatever the cost. *Truth has nothing to hide. There is no question, therefore, of satyagrahis maintaining a secret army* (emphasis added).

198 'fearlessness': *abhayata*, lack of cowardice. Compare the virtue of courage needed for the practice of non-violence with the virtue of courage discussed in classical Western political theory.

199 Gandhi's point is that the practice of the four virtues required for satyagraha calls for true heroism; satyagrahis, not anarchists such as Dhingra, are the true heroes.

will have to observe chastity, and to be satisfied with poverty as his lot. A warrior without fearlessness cannot be conceived of. It may be thought that he would not need to be exactly truthful, but that quality follows real fearlessness. When a man abandons truth, he does so owing to fear in some shape or form. The above four attributes, then, need not frighten anyone. It may be as well here to note that a physical-force man has to have many other useless qualities which a passive resister never needs. And you will find that whatever extra effort a swordsman needs is due to lack of fearlessness. If he is an embodiment of the latter, the sword will drop from his hand that very moment. He does not need its support. One who is free from hatred requires no sword. A man with a stick suddenly came face to face with a lion, and instinctively raised his weapon in self-defence. The man saw that he had only prated about fearlessness when there was none in him. That moment he dropped the stick, and found himself free from all fear.

CHAPTER XVIII

*

Education[200]

READER: In the whole of our discussion, you have not demonstrated the necessity for education; we always complain of its absence among us. We notice a movement for compulsory education in our country. The Maharaja Gaekwar has introduced it in his territories.[201] Every eye is directed towards them. We bless the Maharaja for it. Is all this effort, then, of no use?

EDITOR: If we consider our civilisation to be the highest, I have regretfully to say that much of the effort you have described is of no use. The motive of the Maharaja and other great leaders who have been working in this direction is perfectly pure. They, therefore, undoubtedly deserve great praise. But we cannot conceal from ourselves the result that is likely to flow from their effort.

What is the meaning of education?[202] If it simply means a knowledge of letters, it is merely an instrument, and an instrument may be well

200 Prior to writing *HS* Gandhi had experimented with educational reform by establishing the Phoenix School at Phoenix Settlement. It failed due to lack of funds (*CW* 9: 135–9). A second attempt was made on Tolstoy Farm between 1911 and 1913. About 25 boys and girls from different castes and religions were enrolled. The curriculum included arithmetic, languages, Indian history and geography, religious instruction, manual work and sandal-making (*CW* 11: 251–2; 39: 266–73). For information on Gandhi's educational experiments in India, see *CW* 14: 8–36.
201 In 1905, Maharaja Gaekwar of Baroda, Sir Sayaji Rao III, introduced compulsory primary education in Baroda state, the first to do so in India.
202 Education for Gandhi involved the training of mind, will and desires (*CW* 9: 208).

used or abused. The same instrument that may be used to cure a patient may be used to take his life, and so may a knowledge of letters. We daily observe that many men abuse it, and very few make good use of it, and, if this is a correct statement, we have proved that more harm has been done by it than good.

The ordinary meaning of education is a knowledge of letters. To teach boys reading, writing and arithmetic is called primary education. A peasant earns his bread honestly. He has ordinary knowledge of the world. He knows fairly well how he should behave towards his parents, his wife, his children and his fellow-villagers. He understands and observes the rules of morality. But he cannot write his own name. What do you propose to do by giving him a knowledge of letters? Will you add an inch to his happiness? Do you wish to make him discontented with his cottage or his lot? And even if you want to do that, he will not need such an education. Carried away by the flood of Western thought, we came to the conclusion, without weighing pros and cons, that we should give this kind of education to the people.

Now let us take higher education. I have learned Geography, Astronomy, Algebra, Geometry, etc. What of that? In what way have I benefited myself or those around me? Why have I learned these things? Professor Huxley has thus defined education: 'That man I think has had a liberal education who has been so trained in youth that his body is the ready servant of his will and does with ease and pleasure all the work that as a mechanism it is capable of; whose intellect is a clear, cold, logic engine with all its parts of equal strength and in smooth working order ... whose mind is stored with a knowledge of the fundamental truths of nature ... whose passions are trained to come to heel by a vigorous will, the servant of a tender conscience ... who has learnt to hate all vileness and to respect others as himself. Such an one and no other, I conceive, has had a liberal education, for he is in harmony with Nature. He will make the best of her and she of him.'[203]

203 This quotation is taken from an 1869 essay by Thomas Huxley, 'A liberal education: and where to find it' (Huxley 1893, 86).

If this be true education, I must emphatically say that the sciences I have enumerated above I have never been able to use for controlling my senses. Therefore, whether you take elementary education or higher education, it is not required for the main thing. It does not make of us men. It does not enable us to do our duty.

READER: If that is so, I shall have to ask you another question. What enables you to tell all these things to me? If you had not received higher education, how would you have been able to explain to me the things that you have?

EDITOR: You have spoken well. But my answer is simple: I do not for one moment believe that my life would have been wasted, had I not received higher or lower education. Nor do I consider that I necessarily serve because I speak. But I do desire to serve and, in endeavouring to fulfil that desire, I make use of the education I have received. And, if I am making good use of it, even then it is not for the millions, but I can use it only for such as you, and this supports my contention. Both you and I have come under the bane of what is mainly false education. I claim to have become free from its ill effects, and I am trying to give you the benefit of my experience, and, in doing so, I am demonstrating the rottenness of this education.

Moreover, I have not run down a knowledge of letters under all circumstances. All I have shown is that we must not make of it a fetish. It is not our Kamadhuk.[204] In its place it can be of use, and it has its place when we have brought our senses under subjection, and put our ethics on a firm foundation. And then, if we feel inclined to receive that education, we may make good use of it. As an ornament it is likely to sit well on us. It now follows that it is not necessary to make this education compulsory. Our ancient school system is enough.[205] Character-building has the first place in it, and that is primary education. A building erected on that foundation will last.

---

204 'Kamadhuk': the mythical cow that fulfils all one's wishes ('Kamdhuk' in Gandhi's original text).

205 The Phoenix School planned to incorporate certain features of the ancient system: 'Those in Phoenix who live with their families can take in up to eight boarders. It is intended that the boys who may be accepted as boarders will be

READER: Do I then understand that you do not consider English education necessary for obtaining Home Rule?

EDITOR: My answer is yes and no. To give millions a knowledge of English is to enslave them. The foundation that Macaulay laid of education has enslaved us.[206] I do not suggest that he had any such intention, but that has been the result. Is it not a sad commentary that we should have to speak of Home Rule in a foreign tongue?

And it is worthy of note that the systems which the Europeans have discarded are the systems in vogue among us. Their learned men continually make changes. We ignorantly adhere to their cast-off systems. They are trying, each division, to improve its own status. Wales is a small portion of England. Great efforts are being made to revive a knowledge of Welsh among Welshmen. The English Chancellor, Mr Lloyd George is taking a leading part in the movement to make Welsh children speak Welsh.[207] And what is our condition? We write to each other in faulty English, and from this even our MA's are not free; our best thoughts are expressed in English; the proceedings of our Congress are conducted in English; our best newspapers are printed in English. If this state of things continues for a long time, posterity will – it is my firm opinion – condemn and curse us.

treated as one's own children. This practice prevailed in India in olden days, and it should be revived as far as possible' (*CW* 9: 135).

206 'The foundation that Macaulay laid': this refers to Macaulay's 'Minute on Education' of 1835. It laid down, among other things, the policy of providing public funds for education in the English language and of withdrawing public support for education in Arabic and Sanskrit. It was not Macaulay's intention to make English the lingua franca of the Indian masses but only of the Indian elite.

207 During his 1909 stay in London, Gandhi became acquainted with Lloyd George's language policy and drew from it certain conclusions for India:

India will be aroused when we touch all the Indian languages with the spirit of patriotism. Mr. Lloyd George, about whom I have already written, was born in Wales, a principality in Great Britain. It has a dialect of its own and Mr. Lloyd George is taking steps to ensure that Welsh children do not forget their language. How much more need is there for Indians to preserve their languages than for the Welsh to preserve theirs, and how much more keen should we be? (*CW* 9: 492)

It is worth noting that, by receiving English education, we have enslaved the nation. Hypocrisy, tyranny, etc., have increased; English-knowing Indians have not hesitated to cheat and strike terror into the people. Now, if we are doing anything for the people at all, we are paying only a portion of the debt due to them.

Is it not a most painful thing that, if I want to go to a court of justice, I must employ the English language as a medium; that, when I become a barrister, I may not speak my mother-tongue, and that someone else should have to translate to me from my own language? Is not this absolutely absurd? Is it not a sign of slavery? Am I to blame the English for it or myself? It is we, the English-knowing men, that have enslaved India.[208] The curse of the nation will rest not upon the English but upon us.

I have told you that my answer to your last question is both yes and no. I have explained to you why it is yes. I shall now explain why it is no.

We are so much beset by the disease of civilisation, that we cannot altogether do without English education. Those who have already received it may make good use of it wherever necessary. In our dealings with the English people, in our dealings with our own people, when we can only correspond with them through that language, and for the purpose of knowing how much disgusted they (the English) have themselves become with their civilisation, we may use or learn English, as the case may be. Those who have studied English will have to teach morality to their progeny through their mother-tongue,[209] and to teach them another Indian language; but when they have grown up, they may learn

---

208 In 1935, addressing the Annual Meeting of the Hindi Sahitya Sammelan (Hindi Literature Convention) Gandhi stated the following: 'If Hindi could take the place of English I for one should be happy. But we realise full well the importance of the English language. We need the knowledge of English for the study of science and of modern literature, for contact with the rest of the world, for trade and commerce, for keeping in touch with officials and for various other things. We have to learn English whether we wish or not. And this is exactly what is happening. English is an international language' (*CW* 60: 448).

209 Gandhi makes a noteworthy distinction here between using English for the acquisition of secular knowledge and using the mother-tongue for the acquisition of ethical knowledge.

English, the ultimate aim being that we should not need it. The object of making money thereby should be eschewed. Even in learning English to such a limited extent, we will have to consider what we should learn through it and what we should not. It will be necessary to know what sciences we should learn. A little thought should show you that immediately we cease to care for English degrees, the rulers will prick up their ears.

READER: Then what education shall we give?

EDITOR: This has been somewhat considered above, but we will consider it a little more. I think that we have to improve all our languages. What subjects we should learn through them need not be elaborated here. Those English books which are valuable we should translate into the various Indian languages. We should abandon the pretension of learning many sciences. Religious, that is ethical, education[210] will occupy the first place. Every cultured Indian will know in addition to his own provincial language, if a Hindu, Sanskrit; if a Mahomedan, Arabic; if a Parsee, Persian; and all Hindi. Some Hindus should know Arabic and Persian; some Mahomedans and Parsees, Sanskrit. Several Northerners and Westerners should learn Tamil. A universal language for India should be Hindi, with the option of writing it in Persian or Nagri characters.[211] In order that the

---

210 'Religious, that is ethical, education': in Gujarati, 'dharma-based or *niti*-based education'.

211 This is the first time that an Indian leader proposes a language policy for the whole of India. The basic idea expressed here was restated by Gandhi in 1920 and accepted by the Congress as its official policy:

We believe that the present distribution made from time to time to meet the exigencies of a conquering power is unscientific and is calculated to retard the political and social progress of the respective communities speaking a common vernacular and therefore the growth of India as a whole. We therefore feel that so far as the Congress is concerned, we should redivide India into provinces on a linguistic basis ... So far as recognition of Urdu is concerned we have used the common term Hindustani which includes both Hindi and Urdu and we have recognised both scripts, Devanagari and Persian. (*CW* 18: 289–90)

Ironically, his own thoughts were best expressed either in Gujarati or in English, but not in Hindi. For an example, see his letter of 13 November 1945 to Nehru, in which he writes: 'I have had Rajkumari [Amrit Kaur] translate the letter which I wrote to you earlier. I am getting this also translated and will send

Hindus and the Mahomedans may have closer relations, it is necessary to know both the characters. And, if we can do this, we can drive the English language out of the field in a short time. All this is necessary for us slaves. Through our slavery the nation has been enslaved, and it will be free with our freedom.

READER: The question of religious education is very difficult.

EDITOR: Yet we cannot do without it. India will never be godless. Rank atheism cannot flourish in that land. The task is indeed difficult. My head begins to turn as I think of religious education. Our religious teachers are hypocritical and selfish; they will have to be approached. The Mullas, the Dasturs, and the Brahmins[212] hold the key in their hands, but, if they will not have the good sense, the energy that we have derived from English education will have to be devoted to religious education.[213] This is not very difficult. Only the fringe of the ocean has been polluted, and it is those who are within the fringe who alone need cleansing. We who come under this category can even cleanse ourselves, because my remarks do not apply to the millions. In order to restore India to its pristine condition, we have to return to it. In our own civilisation, there will naturally be progress, retrogression, reforms and reactions; but one effort is required, and that is to drive out Western civilisation.[214] All else will follow.

the translation along with this. I serve two purposes by getting the letters translated. First *I can explain to you more clearly in English what I want to say* and secondly I shall be able to know better whether I have understood you fully or not' (*CW* 82: 72; emphasis added).

212 'The Mullas, the Dasturs, and the Brahmins': respectively the traditional teachers of ethics in Islam, Zoroastrianism and Hinduism.

213 'religious education': *nitini kelwani* (ethical education). Gandhi sees the danger inherent in religious education given by 'hypocritical and selfish' religious teachers; he does not propose or endorse such a system of religious education; what he proposes is education in ethics which, though drawn ultimately from religious texts, can still be taught in a non-fundamentalist fashion.

214 'Western civilisation': i.e., *modern* Western civilisation.

CHAPTER XIX

✽

Machinery

READER: When you speak of driving out Western civilisation, I suppose you will also say that we want no machinery.

EDITOR: By raising this question you have opened the wound I had received. When I read Mr Dutt's Economic History of India,[215] I wept; and, as I think of it again, my heart sickens. It is machinery that has impoverished India.[216] It is difficult to measure the harm that Manchester[217] has done to us. It is due to Manchester that Indian handicraft has all but disappeared.

But I make a mistake. How can Manchester be blamed? We wore Manchester cloth, and that is why Manchester wove it. I was delighted when I read about the bravery of Bengal. There are no cloth-mills in that Presidency. They were, therefore, able to restore the original hand-weaving occupation. It is true, Bengal encourages the mill industry of Bombay. If Bengal had proclaimed a boycott of *all* machine-made goods, it would have been much better.[218]

---

215 Listed in Appendix I.

216 In 1940, in reply to a question raised by Dr Ram Manohar Lohia, Gandhi stated the following: 'I do visualise electricity, ship-building, ironworks, machine-making and the like existing side by side with village handicrafts' (CW 71: 130).

217 The cotton industry of Manchester.

218 During the 1905 Swadeshi movement in Bengal only British goods were boycotted.

Machinery has begun to desolate Europe. Ruination is now knocking at the English gates.[219] Machinery is the chief symbol of modern civilisation; it represents a great sin.

The workers in the mills of Bombay have become slaves. The condition of the women working in the mills is shocking. When there were no mills, these women were not starving. If the machinery craze[220] grows in our country, it will become an unhappy land.[221] It may be considered a heresy, but I am bound to say that it were better for us to send money to Manchester and to use flimsy Manchester cloth, than to multiply mills in India.[222] By using Manchester cloth, we would only waste our money, but, by reproducing Manchester in India, we shall keep our money at the price of our blood, because our very moral being will be sapped, and I call in support of my statement the very mill-hands as witnesses. And those who have amassed wealth out of factories are not likely to be better than other rich men. It would be folly to assume that an Indian Rockefeller would be better than the American Rockefeller. Impoverished India can become free, but it will be hard for an India made rich through immorality to regain its freedom. I fear we will have to admit that moneyed men support British rule; their interest is bound up with its stability. Money renders a man helpless. The other thing as harmful is sexual vice. Both are poison. A snake-bite is a lesser poison

219 'the English gates': There is an error in the translation here. There is no mention of England or 'the English gates' in the Gujarati text; instead it mentions that machinery is threatening *India*: 'Machinery has begun to desolate Europe, and that whirlwind is now sweeping over India.' Instead of 'the English gates', the correct translation should read 'the Indian gates'.

220 'craze': in the Gujarati text the word used is *wayaro* (whirlwind).

221 'unhappy hand' in the original.

222 In 1921 in the Preface to the Hindi translation of *HS*, Gandhi significantly modified the position taken here: 'My views in regard to mills have undergone this much change. In view of the present predicament of India, we should produce in our own country all the cloth that we need even by supporting, if necessary, mills in India rather than by cloth made in Manchester' (*CW* 31: 399, n.4). For more on Gandhi's changing attitude towards machinery, see pp. 162–8 below.

than these two, because the former merely destroys the body, but the latter destroy body, mind and soul. We need not, therefore, be pleased with the prospect of the growth of the mill industry.

READER: Are the mills, then, to be closed down?

EDITOR: That is difficult. It is no easy task to do away with a thing that is established. We, therefore, say that the non-beginning of a thing is supreme wisdom. We cannot condemn mill-owners; we can but pity them. It would be too much to expect them to give up the mills, but we may implore them not to increase them. If they would be good, they would gradually contract their business. They can establish in thousands of households the ancient and sacred hand-looms,[223] and they can buy out the cloth that may be thus woven. Whether the mill-owners do this or not, people can cease to use machine-made goods.

READER: You have so far spoken about machine-made cloth, but there are innumerable machine-made things. We have either to import them or to introduce machinery into our country.

EDITOR: Indeed, our gods even are made in Germany. What need, then, to speak of matches, pins and glassware? My answer can be only one. What did India do before these articles were introduced? Precisely

---

223 'the ancient and sacred hand-looms': when he wrote this he did not know the difference between a loom and a spinning-wheel (*charkha*). The idea of the spinning-wheel which was to become such a powerful symbol of the Gandhian revolution came to him in a flash of insight rather than from empirical knowledge of the merits or demerits of the handloom industry. As he stated in 1925: ' ... I had put forward my arguments in its [the spinning-wheel's] favour in *Hind Swaraj* before ever having set my eyes on the spinning-wheel' (*CW* 25: 600). And in 1928: 'It was in London in 1909 that I discovered the wheel. I had gone there leading a deputation from South Africa. It was then that I came in close touch with many earnest Indians – students and others. We had many long conversations about the condition of India and I saw as in a flash that without the spinning-wheel there was no swaraj. I knew at once that everyone had to spin. But I did not then know the distinction between the loom and the wheel and in *Hind Swaraj* used the word loom to mean the wheel' (*CW* 37: 288). 'Even in 1915, when I returned to India from South Africa, I had not actually seen a spinning-wheel' (*CW* 39: 389). It was in Bagasara, Gujarat, that Gandhi first saw a loom (*CW* 26: 458).

the same should be done today. As long as we cannot make pins without machinery, so long will we do without them. The tinsel splendour of glassware we will have nothing to do with, and we will make wicks, as of old, with home-grown cotton, and use hand-made earthen saucers for lamps.[224] So doing, we shall save our eyes and money, and will support Swadeshi, and so shall we attain Home Rule.

It is not to be conceived that all men will do all these things at one time, or that some men will give up all machine-made things at once. But, if the thought is sound, we will always find out what we can give up, and will gradually cease to use this. What a few may do, others will copy, and the movement will grow like the coconut of the mathematical problem.[225] What the leaders do, the populace will gladly follow. The matter is neither complicated nor difficult. You and I shall not wait until we can carry others with us. Those will be the losers who will not do it; and those who will not do it, although they appreciate the truth, will deserve to be called cowards.

READER: What, then, of the tram-cars and electricity?

EDITOR: This question is now too late. It signifies nothing. If we are to do without the railways, we shall have to do without the tram-cars. Machinery is like a snake-hole which may contain from one to a hundred snakes. Where there is machinery there are large cities; and where there are large cities, there are tram-cars and railways; and there only does one see electric light. English villages do not boast any of these things. Honest physicians will tell you that, where means of artificial locomotion have increased, the health of the people has suffered. I remember that, when in a European town there was a scarcity of money, the receipts of the tram-way company, of the lawyers and of the doctors, went down, and the people were less unhealthy. I cannot recall a

---

224 Savarkar selected this passage for special ridicule, when he wrote that under the light of the wick lamps only ignorance and poverty would flourish (Keer 1966, 471).

225 'the coconut of the mathematical problem': the Gujarati text reads as follows: 'First one person will do, then ten, then a hundred, and so on, it will keep increasing, as in the story of the coconut.'

single good point in connection with machinery. Books can be written to demonstrate its evils.

READER: Is it a good point or a bad one that all you are saying will be printed through machinery?

EDITOR: This is one of those instances which demonstrate that sometimes poison is used to kill poison. This, then, will not be a good point regarding machinery. As it expires, the machinery, as it were, says to us: 'Beware and avoid me. You will derive no benefit from me, and the benefit that may accrue from printing will avail only those who are infected with the machinery craze.'[226] Do not, therefore, forget the main thing. It is necessary to realise that machinery is bad. We shall then be able gradually to do away with it. Nature has not provided any way whereby we may reach a desired goal all of a sudden. If, instead of welcoming machinery as a boon, we would look upon it as an evil, it would ultimately go.

226 'machinery craze': the Gujarati text uses a different metaphor: 'the net of machinery' (*sanchani jal*).

CHAPTER XX

*

Conclusion[227]

READER: From your views I gather that you would form a third party. You are neither an extremist nor a moderate.[228]

EDITOR: That is a mistake. I do not think of a third party at all. We do not all think alike. We cannot say that all the moderates hold identical views. And how can those who want to serve only, have a party?[229] I would serve both the moderates and the extremists. Where I should differ from them, I would respectfully place my position before them, and continue my service.

READER: What, then, would you say to both the parties?

EDITOR: I would say to the extremists:[230] – 'I know that you want Home Rule for India; it is not to be had for your asking. Everyone will have to take it for himself. What others get for me is not Home Rule but foreign rule; therefore, it would not be proper for you to say that you have obtained Home Rule, if you expelled the English. I have already described the true nature of Home Rule. This you would never obtain by force of arms. Brute force is not natural to the Indian soil. You will have, therefore, to rely wholly on soul-force. You must not consider that violence is necessary at any stage for reaching our goal.'

---

227 The title of this chapter in Gujarati is *chhutcaro*, 'emancipation'.
228 The reference is to the two factions in the Congress, already referred to in ch. II.
229 'party': *paksh*. Gandhi looks upon politics more as a form of *service* to the community than as a form of struggle for power.
230 What follows constitutes Gandhi's critique of the Extremists.

I would say to the moderates:[231] 'Mere petitioning is derogatory; we thereby confess inferiority. To say that British rule is indispensable is almost a denial of the Godhead. We cannot say that anybody or anything is indispensable except God. Moreover, common sense should tell us that to state that, for the time being, the presence of the English in India is a necessity, is to make them conceited.

'If the English vacated India bag and baggage, it must not be supposed that she would be widowed. It is possible that those who are forced to observe peace under their pressure would fight after their withdrawal. There can be no advantage in suppressing an eruption; it must have its vent. If, therefore, before we can remain at peace, we must fight amongst ourselves, it is better that we do so. There is no occasion for a third party to protect the weak. It is this so-called protection which has unnerved us. Such protection can only make the weak weaker. Unless we realise this, we cannot have Home Rule. I would paraphrase the thought of an English divine and say that anarchy under home rule were better than orderly foreign rule. Only, the meaning that the learned divine attached to home rule is different from Indian Home Rule according to my conception. We have to learn, and to teach others, that we do not want the tyranny of either English rule or Indian rule.'[232]

If this idea were carried out, both the extremists and the moderates could join hands. There is no occasion to fear or distrust one another.

READER: What, then, would you say to the English.[233]

EDITOR: To them I would respectfully say: 'I admit you are my rulers. It is not necessary to debate the question whether you hold India by the sword or by my consent. I have no objection to your remaining in my country, but, although you are the rulers, you will have to remain as servants of the people. It is not we who have to do as you wish, but it is you who have to do as we wish. You may keep the riches that you have

---

231 This constitutes Gandhi's critique of the Moderates.
232 Gandhi does not see any real moral difference between British colonial rule and the sort of home rule proposed by the Reader.
233 What follows constitutes Gandhi's critique of colonial rule in India.

drained away from this land, but you may not drain riches henceforth. Your function will be, if you so wish, to police India; you must abandon the idea of deriving any commercial benefit from us. We hold the civilisation that you support, to be the reverse of civilisation. We consider our civilisation to be far superior to yours. If you realise this truth, it will be to your advantage; and, if you do not, according to your own proverb, you should only live in our country in the same manner as we do. You must not do anything that is contrary to our religions. It is your duty as rulers that, for the sake of the Hindus, you should eschew beef, and for the sake of the Mahomedans, you should avoid bacon and ham. We have hitherto said nothing, because we have been cowed down, but you need not consider that you have not hurt our feelings by your conduct. We are not expressing our sentiments either through base selfishness or fear, but because it is our duty now to speak out boldly. We consider your schools and law courts to be useless. We want our own ancient schools and courts to be restored. The common language of India is not English but Hindi. You should, therefore, learn it. We can hold communication with you only in our national language.

'We cannot tolerate the idea of your spending money on railways and the military. We see no occasion for either. You may fear Russia; we do not. When she comes we will look after her. If you are with us, we will then receive her jointly. We do not need any European cloth. We will manage with articles produced and manufactured at home. You may not keep one eye on Manchester, and the other on India. We can work together only if our interests are identical.

'This has not been said to you in arrogance. You have great military resources. Your naval power is matchless. If we wanted to fight with you on your own ground, we should be unable to do so; but, if the above submissions be not acceptable to you, we cease to play the ruled. You may, if you like, cut us to pieces. You may shatter us at the cannon's mouth. If you act contrary to our will, we will not help you, and, without our help, we know that you cannot move one step forward.

'It is likely that you will laugh at all this in the intoxication of your power. We may not be able to disillusion you at once, but, if there be any manliness in us, you will see shortly that your intoxication is suicidal, and that your laugh at our expense is an aberration of intellect. We believe that, at heart, you belong to a religious nation.[234] We are living in a land which is the source of religions. How we came together need not be considered, but we can make mutual good use of our relations.

'You English who have come to India are not a good specimen of the English nation, nor can we, almost half-Anglicised Indians, be considered a good specimen of the real Indian nation. If the English nation were to know all you have done, it would oppose many of your actions. The mass of the Indians have had few dealings with you. If you will abandon your so-called civilisation, and search into your own scriptures, you will find that our demands are just. Only on condition of our demands being fully satisfied may you remain in India, and if you remain under those conditions, we shall learn several things from you, and you will learn many from us. So doing, we shall benefit each other and the world. But that will happen only when the root of our relationship is sunk in a religious soil.'[235]

READER: What will you say to the nation?

EDITOR: Who is the nation?[236]

READER: For our purposes it is the nation that you and I have been thinking of, that is, those of us who are affected by European civilisation, and who are eager to have Home Rule.

---

234 Perhaps the most important point in Gandhi's critique of colonialism is that it is inconsistent with the teachings of Christianity. The suggestion here is that Great Britain should recover its Christian culture.

235 'in a religious soil': the original Gujarati is *dharmakshetrme* (in the field of dharma), a very evocative term, because it is also the very first word of *Bhagavad Gita*. When the British will integrate their modern culture within the framework of their traditional culture, and when Indians will integrate their modern culture within the framework of their traditional culture, both will be able to contribute significantly to universal culture.

236 In *HS* Gandhi uses the idea of nation (*praja*) in two senses: the first refers to the Indian people as a whole composed of Hindus, Muslims, Christians, Sikhs, Parsees, Buddhists and others. The second refers to the modern educated elite – the lawyers, the doctors, the wealthy, etc.

EDITOR: To these I would say:[237] 'It is only those Indians who are imbued with real love who will be able to speak to the English in the above strain without being frightened, and those only can be said to be so imbued who conscientiously believe that Indian civilisation is the best, and that European is a nine days' wonder. Such ephemeral civilisations have often come and gone, and will continue to do so. Those only can be considered to be so imbued, who, having experienced[238] the force of the soul within themselves, will not cower before brute force, and will not, on any account, desire to use brute force. Those only can be considered to have been so imbued who are intensely dissatisfied with the present pitiable condition, having already drunk the cup of poison.[239]

If there be only one such Indian, he will speak as above to the English, and the English will have to listen to him.[240]

These demands are not demands, but they show our mental state. We will get nothing by asking; we shall have to take what we want, and we need the requisite strength for the effort, and that strength will be available to him only who

1 will only on rare occasions make use of the English language;
2 if a lawyer, will give up his profession, and take up a hand-loom;
3 if a lawyer, will devote his knowledge to enlightening both his people and the English;
4 if a lawyer, will not meddle with the quarrels between parties, but will give up the courts and from his experience induce the people to do likewise;
5 if a lawyer, will refuse to be a judge, as he will give up his profession;

237 The nineteen points that follow are addressed to the modern educated elite. Implementation of these points would make them fit for true home rule.
238 The importance of 'experiencing' soul-force is stressed again. See ch. XIV.
239 The true Indian nationalist would have to become self-critical, especially with respect to his/her attitude towards modernity.
240 Cf: 'The great Thoreau has said that a worthy cause should never be deemed lost, that it is bound to triumph, so long as there is at least one sincere man to fight for it' (*CW* 10: 386).

6 if a doctor, will give up medicine, and understand that, rather than mending bodies, he should mend souls;

7 if a doctor, he will understand that, no matter to what religion he belong, it is better that bodies remain diseased rather than that they are cured through the instrumentality of the diabolical vivisection that is practised in European schools of medicine;

8 although a doctor, will take up a hand-loom, and, if any patients come to him, will tell them the cause of their diseases, and will advise them to remove the cause rather than pamper them by giving useless drugs; he will understand that, if by not taking drugs, perchance the patient dies, the world will not come to grief, and that he will have been really merciful to him;

9 although a wealthy man, regardless of his wealth, will speak out his mind and fear no one;

10 if a wealthy man, will devote his money to establishing hand-looms, and encourage others to use hand-made goods by wearing them himself;

11 like every other Indian, will know that this is a time for repentance, expiation and mourning;

12 like every other Indian, will know that to blame the English is useless, that they came because of us, and remain also for the same reason, and that they will either go or change their nature only when we reform ourselves;[241]

13 like others, will understand that, at a time of mourning, there can be no indulgence, and that, whilst we are in a fallen state, to be in gaol or in banishment is much the best;

14 like others, will know that it is superstition to imagine it necessary that we should guard against being imprisoned in order that we may deal with the people;

15 like others, will know that action is much better than speech; that it is our duty to say exactly what we think and face the consequences, and that it will be only then that we shall be able to impress anybody with our speech;

241 A theme underlying *HS*.

16 like others, will understand that we will become free only through suffering;

17 like others, will understand that deportation for life to the Andamans[242] is not enough expiation for the sin of encouraging European civilisation;

18 like others, will know that no nation has risen without suffering; that, even in physical warfare, the true test is suffering and not the killing of others, much more so in the warfare of passive resistance;

19 like others, will know that it is an idle excuse to say that we will do a thing when the others also do it; that we should do what we know to be right, and that others will do it when they see the way; that, when I fancy a particular delicacy, I do not wait till others taste it; that to make a national effort and to suffer are in the nature of delicacies; and that to suffer under pressure is no suffering.

READER: This is a large order. When will all carry it out?

EDITOR: You make a mistake. You and I have nothing to do with the others. Let each do his duty. If I do my duty, that is, serve myself, I shall be able to serve others. Before I leave you, I will take the liberty of repeating:

1 Real home-rule is self-rule or self-control.[243]

2 The way to it is passive resistance: that is soul-force or love-force.

3 In order to exert this force, Swadeshi in every sense is necessary.

4 What we want to do should be done, not because we object to the English or that we want to retaliate, but because it is our duty to do so. Thus, supposing that the English remove the salt-tax, restore our money, give the highest posts to Indians, withdraw the English troops, we shall certainly not use their machine-made goods, nor use the English language, nor many of their industries. It is worth

242 The Andaman Islands were India's penal colony, and many terrorists, including Ganesh Savarkar, the brother of Vinayak Damodar Savarkar, were in the Andamans at the time of the writing of *HS*.

243 The Gujarati text reads: 'One's rule over one's own mind is real swaraj.' The mind, again, is shown to be the key faculty in Gandhi's ethics.

noting that these things are, in their nature, harmful; hence we do not want them. I bear no enmity towards the English, but I do towards their civilisation.

In my opinion, we have used the term 'Swaraj' without understanding its real significance. I have endeavoured to explain it as I understand it, and my conscience testifies that my life henceforth is dedicated to its attainment.

Appendices

*

I. SOME AUTHORITIES

The following books are recommended for perusal to follow up the study of the foregoing:

'The Kingdom of God Is Within You' - Tolstoy.
'What Is Art?' - Tolstoy.
'The Slavery of Our Times' - Tolstoy.
'The First Step' - Tolstoy.
'How Shall We Escape?' - Tolstoy.
'Letter to a Hindoo' - Tolstoy.
'The White Slaves of England' - Sherard.
'Civilization: Its Cause and Cure' - Carpenter.
'The Fallacy of Speed' - Taylor.
'A New Crusade' - Blount.
'On the Duty of Civil Disobedience' - Thoreau.
'Life Without Principle' - Thoreau.
'Unto This Last' - Ruskin.
'A Joy For Ever' - Ruskin.
'Duties of Man' - Mazzini.
'Defence and Death of Socrates' - From Plato.
'Paradoxes of Civilization' - Max Nordau.
'Poverty and Un-British Rule in India' - Naoroji.
'Economic History of India' - Dutt.
'Village Communities' - Maine.

II. TESTIMONIES BY EMINENT MEN

The following extracts from Mr Alfred Webb's valuable collection, if the testimony given therein be true, show that the ancient Indian civilisation has little to learn from the modern:

118

Victor Cousin (1792–1867)

Founder of systematic eclecticism in philosophy

'On the other hand, when we read with attention the poetical and philosophical movements of the East, above all, those of India, which are beginning to spread in Europe, we discover there so many truths, and truths so profound, and which make such a contrast with the meanness of the results at which the European genius has sometimes stopped, that we are constrained to bend the knee before that of the East, and to see in this cradle of the human race the native land of the highest philosophy.'

J. Seymour Keay, MP

Banker in India and India agent (writing in 1883)

'It cannot be too well understood that our position in India has never been in any degree that of civilians bringing civilisation to savage races. When we landed in India we found there a hoary civilisation, which during the progress of thousands of years had fitted itself into the character and adjusted itself to the wants of highly intellectual races. The civilisation was not perfunctory, but universal and all-pervading – furnishing the country not only with political systems, but with social and domestic institutions of the most ramified description. The beneficent nature of these institutions as a whole may be judged of from their effects on the character of the Hindu race. Perhaps there are no other people in the world who show so much in their characters the advantageous effects of their own civilisation. They are shrewd in business, acute in reasoning, thrifty, religious, sober, charitable, obedient to parents, reverential to old age, amiable, law-abiding, compassionate towards the helpless, and patient under suffering.'

Friedrich Max Mueller, LLD

'If I were to ask myself from what literature we here in Europe, we who have been nurtured almost exclusively on the thoughts of Greeks and

Romans, and of one Semitic race, the Jewish, may draw that corrective which is most wanted in order to make our inner life more perfect, more comprehensive, more universal, in fact more truly human, a life, not for this life only, but a transfigured and eternal life – again I should point to India.'

Michael G. Mulhall, FRSS

Statistics (1899)

Prison population per 100,000 of inhabitants:

Several European States	100 to 230
England and Wales	190
India	38

Dictionary of Statistics, Michael G. Mulhall, FRSS: Routledge and Sons, 1899.

Colonel Thomas Munro

Thirty-two years' service in India

'If a good system of agriculture, unrivalled manufacturing skill, a capacity to produce whatever can contribute to convenience or luxury; schools established in every village, for teaching reading, writing, and arithmetic; the general practice of hospitality and charity among each other; and above all a treatment of the female sex, full of confidence, respect and delicacy, are among the signs which denote a civilised people, then the Hindus are not inferior to the nations of Europe; and if civilisation is to become an article of trade between the two countries, I am convinced that this country [England] will gain by the import cargo.'

Frederick von Schlegel

'It cannot be denied that the early Indians possessed a knowledge of the true God; all their writings are replete with sentiments and expressions, noble, clear, and severely grand, as deeply conceived and reverently expressed as in any human language in which men have spoken of their God ... Among nations possessing indigenous philosophy and metaphysics, together with an innate relish for these pursuits, such as at present characterises Germany, and, in olden times, was the proud distinction of Greece, Hindustan holds the first rank in point of time.'

Sir William Wedderburn, Bart.

'The Indian village has thus for centuries remained a bulwark against political disorder, and the home of the simple domestic and social virtues. No wonder, therefore, that philosophers and historians have always dwelt lovingly on this ancient institution which is the natural social unit and the best type of rural life; self-contained, industrious, peace-loving, conservative in the best sense of the word ... I think you will agree with me that there is much that is both picturesque and attractive in this glimpse of social and domestic life in an Indian village. It is a harmless and happy form of human existence. Moreover, it is not without good practical outcome.'

I. Young

Secretary, Sassoon Mechanics' Institutes (within recent years)
'Those races [the Indian], viewed from a moral aspect, are perhaps the most remarkable people in the world. They breathe an atmosphere of moral purity, which cannot but excite admiration, and this is especially the case with the poorer classes, who, notwithstanding the privations of their humble lot, appear to be happy and contented. True children of nature, they live on from day to day, taking no thought of tomorrow, and thankful for the simple fare which Providence has provided for them. It is curious to witness the spectacle of coolies of both sexes returning home at night-fall after a hard day's work often lasting from sunrise to sunset. In spite of fatigue from the effects of the unremitting toil, they are for the most part gay and animated, conversing cheerfully

together and occasionally breaking into snatches of light-hearted song. Yet what awaits them on their return to the hovels which they call home? A dish of rice for food, and the floor for a bed. Domestic felicity appears to be the rule among the Natives, and this is the more strange when the customs of marriage are taken into account, parents arranging all such matters. Many Indian households afford examples of the married state in its highest degree of perfection. This may be due to the teachings of the Shastras, and to the strict injunctions which they inculcate with regard to marital obligations; but it is no exaggeration to say that husbands are generally devotedly attached to their wives, and in many instances the latter have the most exalted conception of their duties towards their husbands.'

Abbé J. A. Dubois

Missionary in Mysore (extracts from letter dated Seringapatam
15th December, 1820)

'The authority of married women within their houses is chiefly exerted in preserving good order and peace among the persons who compose their families; and a great many among them discharge this important duty with a prudence and a discretion which have scarcely a parallel in Europe. I have known families composed of between thirty and forty persons, or more, consisting of grown sons and daughters, all married and all having children, living together under the superintendence of an old matron – their mother or mother-in-law. The latter, by good management, and by accommodating herself to the temper of the daughters-in-law, by using, according to circumstances, firmness or forbearance, succeeded in preserving peace and harmony during many years amongst so many females, who had all jarring interests, and still more jarring tempers. I ask you whether it would be possible to attain the same end, in the same circumstances, in our countries, where it is scarcely possible to make two women living under the same roof to agree together.

In fact, there is perhaps no kind of honest employment in a civilised country in which the Hindu females have not a due share. Besides the management of the household, and the care of the family, which (as already noticed) is under their control, the wives and daughters of husbandmen attend and assist their husbands and fathers in the labours of agriculture. Those of tradesmen assist theirs in carrying on their trade. Merchants are attended and assisted by theirs in their shops. Many females are shopkeepers on their own account; and *without a knowledge of the alphabet* or of the decimal scale, they keep by other means their accounts in excellent order, and are considered as still shrewder than the males themselves in their commercial dealings.'

Supplementary writings

*

GANDHI'S LETTER TO H. S. L. POLAK

In 1909 Henry Polak, one of Gandhi's close friends, was on a visit to India to lobby for South African Indians. In this letter Gandhi gives him a preview of *HS*. [Ed.]

London   October 14, 1909

My dear Henry,

... As you will be seeing practically the whole of India – a privilege I have myself not yet been able to enjoy – I think I should jot down the definite conclusions to which I have almost arrived after more matured observations made here.

The thing was brewing in my mind, but there was no certain clear light. The heart and brain became more active after I accepted the invitation of the Peace and Arbitration Society to speak to them on 'East and West'. It came off last night. I think this meeting was a splendid success; they were earnest folk, but some insolent questions were put on the South African situation. You will not be surprised to learn that even in Hampstead there were men enough to stand up for the tragedy in South Africa, and to talk all the claptrap about the Indian trader being a canker, and what not. A dear old lady got up and said that I had uttered disloyal sentiments and, just as we have to deal with idolaters in South Africa who would think of and cling to form and superficiality as in the case of finger-impressions, so had I last night in the Friends' Meeting House. My main purpose was, in all the questions that were addressed to me, forgotten, and details were warmly taken up and discussed. The following are the conclusions:

1 There is no impassable barrier between East and West.

2 There is no such thing as Western or European civilisation, but there is a modern civilisation, which is purely material.

3 The people of Europe, before they were touched by modern civilisation, had much in common with the people of the East; anyhow, the people of India, and even today, Europeans who are not touched by modern civilisation are far better able to mix with the Indians than the offspring of that civilisation.

4 It is not the British people who are ruling India, but it is modern civilisation, through its railways, telegraphs, telephones, and almost every invention which has been claimed to be a triumph of civilisation.

5 Bombay, Calcutta, and other chief cities of India are the real plague spots.

6 If British rule was replaced tomorrow by Indian rule based on modern methods, India would be no better, except that she would be able then to retain some of the money that is drained away to England; but, then, Indians would only become a second or fifth edition of Europe or America.

7 East and West can only and really meet when the West has thrown overboard modern civilisation, almost in its entirety. They can also seemingly meet when the East has also adopted modern civilisation. But that meeting would be an armed truce, even as it is between, say, Germany and England, both of which nations are living in the Hall of Death in order to avoid being devoured, the one by the other.

8 It is simply impertinence for any man or any body of men to begin or contemplate reform of the whole world. To attempt to do so by means of highly artificial and speedy locomotion is to attempt the impossible.

9 Increase of material comforts, it may be generally be laid down, does not in any way whatsoever conduce to moral growth.

10 Medical science is the concentrated essence of Black Magic. Quackery is infinitely preferable to what passes for high medical skill.

11 Hospitals are the instruments that the Devil has been using for his own purpose, in order to keep his hold on his kingdom. They perpetuate vice, misery and degradation, and real slavery.

12 I was entirely off the track when I considered that I should receive a medical training. It would be sinful for me in any way whatsoever to take part in the abominations that go on in the hospitals.

   If there were no hospitals for venereal disease, or even for consumptives, we should have less consumption, and less sexual vice amongst us.

13 India's salvation consists in unlearning what she has learnt during the past fifty years.

   The railways, telegraphs, hospitals, lawyers, doctors, and such like have all to go, and the so-called upper classes have to learn to live conscientiously and religiously and deliberately the simple peasant life, knowing it to be a life giving true happiness.

14 Indians should wear no machine-made clothing, whether it comes out of European mills or Indian mills.

15 England can help India to do this, and then she will have justified her hold of India. There seem to be many in England today who think likewise.

16 There was true wisdom in the sages of old having so regulated society as to limit the material condition of the people: the rude plough of perhaps five thousand years ago is the plough of the husbandman today. Therein lies salvation. People live long, under such conditions, in comparative peace much greater than Europe has enjoyed after having taken up modern activity, and I feel that every enlightened man, certainly every Englishman, may, if he chooses, learn this truth and act according to it.

There is much more than I can write upon today, but the above is enough food for reflection. You will be able to check me when you find me to be wrong. You will notice, too, that it is the true spirit of passive resistance that has brought me to the above almost definite conclusions. As a passive resister, I am unconcerned whether such a gigantic reformation, shall I call it, can be brought about among people who derive their satisfaction from the present mad rush. If I realise the truth of it, I should rejoice in following it, and, therefore, I could not wait until the whole body of people had commenced. All of us who think likewise have to take the necessary step; and the rest, if we are in the right, must follow. The theory is there: our practice will have to approach it as much as possible. Living in the midst of the rush, we may not be able to shake ourselves free from all taint. Every time I get into a railway car, use a motor-bus, I know I am doing violence to my sense of what is right. I do not fear the logical result on that basis. The visiting of England is bad, and any communication between South Africa and India by means of the Ocean's grey-hounds is also bad, and so on. You and I can, and may, outgrow those things in our present bodies, but the chief thing is to put our theory right. You will be seeing there (India) all sorts of conditions of men. I, therefore, feel that I should no longer withhold from you what I call the progressive step I have taken mentally. If you agree with me, it will be your duty to tell the revolutionaries and everybody else that the freedom they want, or they think they want, is not to be obtained by killing people or doing violence, but by setting themselves right, and by becoming and remaining truly Indian. Then the British rulers will be servants and not masters. They will be trustees and not tyrants, and they will live in perfect peace with the whole inhabitants of India. The future, therefore, lies not with the British race, but with the Indians themselves, and if they have sufficient self-abnegation and abstemiousness, they can make themselves free this very moment, and when we have arrived in India at the simplicity which is still ours largely and which was ours entirely until a few years ago, it will still be possible for the best Indians and the best Europeans to see one another throughout the length and breadth of India and act as the leaven. When there was no rapid locomotion, traders and preachers went on foot, from one end of the country to the other, braving all the dangers, not for pleasure, not for recreating their health, (though all that followed from their tramps), but for the sake of humanity. Then were Benares and other places of pilgrimage holy cities, whereas today they are an abomination ...

Now I think I have given you a terrible dose, I hope you will be able to digest it. It is very likely that you with your great imagination and sound common sense have perhaps, in your varied experience there, probably come to the conclusions independently of me. After all, they are not new but they have only now assumed such a concrete form and taken a violent possession of me ...

(Source: *CW* 9: 478–81)

*

GANDHI'S LETTER TO LORD AMPTHILL

In this letter, Gandhi gave Lord Ampthill also a preview of *HS*. Upon
receipt of the letter Lord and Lady Ampthill invited Gandhi for a
private lunch and to discuss its contents. Unfortunately, the lunch
had to be cancelled due to the sudden illness of their son. No new date
was set for a lunch as Gandhi had to leave London for South Africa on
13 November 1909. (For the text of Ampthill's lunch invitation see his
letters of 4.11.1909 and 7.11.1909 to Gandhi in the Sabarmati Ashram
Grantalaya Collection, SN 5152 and 5165.) [Ed.]

London   October 30, 1909

My Lord,

I have for some time past been wishing to place before Your Lordship
the result of my observations made here during my brief stay on the
nationalist movement among my countrymen.

If you will permit me to say so, I would like to say that I have been
much struck by Your Lordship's candour, sincerity and honesty of which
one notices nowadays such an absence among our great public men. I
have noticed too that your imperialism does not blind you to matters of
obvious justice and that your love of India is genuine and great. All this
coupled with my desire to withhold nothing from Your Lordship regarding my own activity about Indian matters as they may have a direct or an
indirect bearing on the struggle in the Transvaal, emboldens if it does
not require me to inform you of what I have seen.

I have made it a point to see Indians here of every shade of opinion.
Opposed as I am to violence in any shape or form, I have endeavoured

specially to come into contact with the so-called extremists who may be better described as the party of violence. This I have done in order if possible to convince them of the error of their ways. I have noticed that some of the members of this party are earnest spirits, possessing a high degree of morality, great intellectual ability and lofty self-sacrifice. They wield an undoubted influence on the young Indians here. They are certainly unsparing in their efforts to impress upon the latter their convictions. One of them came to me with a view to convince me that I was wrong in my methods and that nothing but the use of violence, covert or open or both, was likely to bring about redress of the wrongs they consider they suffer.

An awakening of the national consciousness is unmistakable. But among the majority it is in a crude shape and there is not a corresponding spirit of self-sacrifice. Everywhere I have noticed impatience of British rule. In some cases the hatred of the whole race is virulent. In almost all cases distrust of British statesman is writ large on their minds. They (the statesmen) are supposed to do nothing unselfishly. Those who are against violence are so only for the time being. They do not disapprove of it. But they are too cowardly or too selfish to avow their opinions publicly. Some consider that the time for violence is not yet. I have practically met no one who believes that India can ever become free without resort to violence.

I believe that repression will be unavailing. At the same time, I feel that the British rulers will not give liberally and in time. The British people appear to me to be obsessed by commercial selfishness. The fault is not of men but of the system and the system is represented by the present civilisation which has produced its blasting effect as well on the people here as on India. India suffers additionally only in so far as it is exploited in the interest of foreign capitalists. The true remedy lies, in my humble opinion, in England discarding modern civilisation which is ensouled by this spirit of selfishness and materialism, is vain and purposeless and is a negation of the spirit of Christianity. But this is a large order. It may then be just possible that the British rulers in India may at least do as the Indians do and not impose upon them the modern civilisation. Railways, machinery and corresponding increase of indulgent habits are the true badges of slavery of the Indian people as they are of Europeans. I, therefore, have no quarrel with the rulers. I have every quarrel with their methods. I no longer believe as I used to in Lord Macaulay as a benefactor through his minute on education. I think a great deal too much is being made of *pax Britannica*. To me the rise of the cities like Calcutta and Bombay is a matter for sorrow rather than congratulation. India has lost in having broken up a part of her village system. Holding these views, I share the national spirit but I totally dissent from the methods whether of the extremists or of the moderates. For either party relies ultimately on violence. Violent methods must mean acceptance of modern civilisation and therefore of the same ruinous competition we notice here and consequent destruction of true morality. I should be uninterested in the fact as to who rules. I should expect rulers to rule according to my wish otherwise I cease to help them to rule me. I become a passive resister against them. Passive resistance is soul-force exerted against physical force. In other words love conquering hatred.

I do not know how far I have made myself understood and I do not know how far I carry you with me in my reasoning. But I have put the case in the above manner before my countrymen. My purpose in writing to Your Lordship is twofold. The first is to tell Your Lordship that, whenever I can get the time, I would like to take my humble share in national regeneration and the second is either to secure Your Lordship's cooperation in the larger work if it ever comes to me or to invite your criticism.

The information I have given Your Lordship is quite confidential and not to be made use of prejudicially to my countrymen. I feel that no useful purpose will be served unless the truth is known and proclaimed.

If you will pursue the inquiry further, I shall be pleased to answer any questions you may wish to put. Mr. Ritch has full knowledge of the contents of this letter. If a discussion is considered necessary, I am at your service.

In conclusion, I hope I have not unduly or unwarrantably trespassed upon your courtesy and attention.

I remain etc ...

(Source: *CW* 9: 508–10)

*

PREFACE TO GANDHI'S EDITION OF THE ENGLISH

TRANSLATION OF LEO TOLSTOY'S *LETTER TO A HINDOO*

Gandhi wrote this Preface and translated the *Letter to a Hindoo* into
Gujarati during the same week that he composed *Hind Swaraj*. [Ed.]

S. S. Kildonan Castle   November 19, 1909

The letter that is printed below is a translation prepared by one of
Tolstoy's translators of his letter written in Russian in reply to a letter
from the Editor of the *Free Hindustan*. The letter, after having passed from
hand to hand, at last came into my possession through a friend who
asked me, as one much interested in Tolstoy's writings, whether I
thought it to be worth publishing. I at once replied in the affirmative
and told him I should translate it myself into Gujarati and induce others
to translate and publish it into various Indian vernaculars.

The letter as received by me was a typewritten copy. It was, therefore,
referred to the author who confirmed it as his and kindly granted me
permission to print it.

To me, as a humble follower of that great teacher whom I have long
looked upon as one of my guides, it is a matter of honour to be connected with the publication of his letter, such, especially, as the one
which is now being given to the world.

It is a mere statement of fact to say that every Indian, whether he own
up to it or not, has national aspirations. But there are as many opinions
as there are Indian nationalists, as to the exact meaning of that aspiration and more especially as to the methods to be used to attain the end.

135

One of the accepted and 'time-honoured' methods to attain the end is that of violence. The assassination of Sir [William] Curzon Wylie was an illustration in its worst and [most] detestable form of that method. Tolstoy's life has been devoted to replacing the method of violence for removing tyranny or securing reform by the method of non-resistance to evil. He would meet hatred expressed in violence by love expressed in self-suffering. He admits of no exception to whittle down this great and divine law of Love. He applies it to all the problems that worry mankind.

When a man like Tolstoy, one of the clearest thinkers in the Western world, one of the greatest writers, one who, as a soldier, has known what violence is and what it can do, condemns Japan for having blindly followed the law of modern science, falsely so-called, and fears for that country 'the greatest calamities', it is for us to pause and consider whether, in our impatience of English rule, we do not want to replace one evil by another and a worse. India, which is the nursery of the great faiths of the world, will cease to be nationalist India, whatever else it may become, when it goes through the process of civilisation in the shape of reproduction on that sacred soil of gun factories and hateful industrialism, which has reduced the people of Europe to a state of slavery and all but stifled among them the best instincts, which are the heritage of the human family.

If we do not want the English in India, we must pay the price. Tolstoy indicates it:

> Do not resist evil, but also yourselves participate not in evil, in the violent deeds of the administration of the law courts, the collection of taxes and, what is more important, of the soldiers, and no one in the world will enslave you,

passionately declares the sage of Yasnaya Polyana. Who can question the truth of what he says in the following:

> A commercial company enslaved a nation comprising 200 million. Tell this to a man free from superstition and he will fail to grasp what these words mean. What does it mean that thirty thousand people, not athletes but rather weak and ill-looking, have enslaved

200 million of vigorous, clever, strong, freedom-loving people? Do not the figures make it clear that not the English but the Indians have enslaved themselves?

One need not accept all that Tolstoy says – some of his facts are not accurately stated – to realise the central truth of his indictment of the present system which is to understand and act upon the irresistible power of the soul over the body, of love, which is an attribute of the soul, over the brute or body force generated by the stirring up in us of evil passions.

There is no doubt that there is nothing new in what Tolstoy preaches. But his presentation of the old truth is refreshingly forceful. His logic is unassailable. And, above all, he endeavours to practise what he preaches. He preaches to convince. He is sincere and in earnest. He commands attention.

M. K. Gandhi

(Source: *CW* 10: 3–5)

*

GANDHI–TOLSTOY LETTERS

GANDHI TO TOLSTOY

Johannesburg   4 April 1910
Dear Sir,

You will recollect my having carried on correspondence with you
whilst I was temporarily in London. As a humble follower of yours, I
send you herewith a booklet which I have written. It is my own translation of a Gujarati writing. Curiously enough, the original writing has
been confiscated by the Government of India. I, therefore, hastened the
above publication of the translation. I am most anxious not to worry
you, but, if your health permits it and if you can find the time to go
through the booklet, needless to say I shall value very highly your
criticism of the writing. I am sending also a few copies of your *Letter to
a Hindoo*, which you authorised me to publish. It has been translated into
one of the Indian languages also.

I am,

Your obedient servant,

M. K. Gandhi.

(Source: *CW* 10: 210)

TOLSTOY TO GANDHI

Yasnaya Polyana   8 May 1910
Dear Friend,

I just received your letter and your book *Indian Home Rule*.

I read your book with great interest because I think that the question you treat in it – the passive resistance – is a question of the greatest importance not only for India but for the whole humanity.

I could not find your former letters, but came across your biography by J. Doss [Doke] which too interested me much deeply and gave me the possibility to know and understand you better.

I am at present not quite well and therefore abstain from writing to you all what I have to say about your book and all your work which I appreciate very much, but I will do it as soon as I will feel better.

Your friend and brother.

[Leo Tolstoy]

(Source: *CW* 10: 505)

GANDHI AND THE 'FOUR CANONICAL AIMS OF LIFE' (*PURUSHARTHAS*)

An updated theory of the 'canonical aims of life' (*Purusharthas*) is the general framework of Gandhi's philosophy. The good life consists in the co-ordinated pursuit of dharma (ethical integrity), artha (wealth and power, or economics and politics), kama (pleasure) and moksha (spiritual transcendence). Supporting evidence is presented below. [Ed.]

From Gandhi's *Foreword* to *Gokhale's Speeches*

Gandhi regarded Gokhale as his 'political guru'. In the *Foreword* he states that the secret of Gokhale's achievements was the co-ordinated pursuit of artha, dharma and moksha. [Ed.]

In these difficult and degenerate times [*kali-kal*], the pure spirit of dharma is hardly in evidence anywhere. Men who go about the world calling themselves *rishis*, *munis* and *sadhus* rarely show this spirit in themselves. Obviously, they have no great treasure of dharma to guard …

I have not the least doubt that Gokhale was wise in the truth of the Self. He never made a show of ritual practices but his life was full of the true spirit of dharma. Every age is known to have its predominant mode of spiritual effort [*pravartti*] best suited for the attainment of moksha. Whenever the spirit of dharma is on the decline, it is revived through such an effort [*pravartti*] in tune with the times. In this age, our degradation reveals itself through our political condition. Not taking a comprehensive view of things, we run away with the belief that, if but our political conditions improved, we would rise from this fallen state. This is only partially true. To be sure, we cannot rise again till our political conditions changes for the better; but it is not true that we shall necessarily progress if our political condition undergoes a change, irrespective of the manner in which it is brought about. If the means employed are impure, the change will be not in the direction of progress but very likely the opposite. Only a change brought about in our political condition by pure means can lead to real progress. Gokhale not only perceived this right at the beginning of his public life but also followed the principle in action. Everyone had realised that popular awakening could be brought about only through political activity. If such activity was spiritualised it could show the path to moksha. He placed this great ideal before his Servants of India Society and before the whole nation. He firmly declared that, unless our political movement was informed with the spirit of dharma, it would be barren. The writer who took notice of his death in *The Times of India* drew particular attention to this aspect of Gokhale's mission and, doubting if his efforts to create political *sannyasis* would bear fruit, warned the Servants of India Society, which he left as his legacy, to be vigilant. In this age, only political *sannyasis* can fulfil and adorn the idea of *sannyasa*, others will more likely than not disgrace the *sannyasis*'s saffron garb. No Indian who aspires to follow the way of true dharma can afford to remain aloof from politics. In other words, one who aspires to a truly dharmic life cannot fail to undertake public service [*lok seva*] as his mission, and we are today so much caught up in the political machine that service of the people is impossible without taking part in politics. In olden days, our peasants, though ignorant of who ruled them, led their simple lives free from fear; they can no longer afford to be so unconcerned. In the circumstances that obtain today, in following the path of dharma they must take into account the political conditions. If our *sadhus, rishis, munis, maulvis* and priest realised the truth of this, we would have a Servants of India Society in every village, the spirit of dharma would come to prevail all over India, the political system which has become odious would reform itself, India would regain the spiritual empire which, we know, it enjoyed in the days gone by, the bonds which hold India under subjection would be severed in an instant, and the ideal state which an ancient seer [the prophet Isaiah] described in his immortal words would come into being: 'And they shall beat swords into ploughshares and their spears into pruning hooks'[Isaiah 2, 4] and 'The wolf and the lamb shall feed together and the lion shall eat straw like the bullock'[Isaiah 65, 25]. Gokhale's ideal in life was to labour to bring about this state of affairs. That, indeed, is his message and I believe that whoever reads his writings with an open mind will recognise this message in every word of his. (Source: *CW* 14: 200–2)

From the Introduction to Gandhi's *Autobiography*

What I want to achieve – what I have been striving and pining to achieve these thirty years – is self-realisation [*atma darshan*], to see God face to face [*ishwarno-sakshatkar*], to attain moksha. I live and move and have my being in pursuit of this goal. All that I do by way of speaking and writing, and all my ventures in the political field, are directed to this same end. (Source: *CW* 39: 3).

From the Farewell to Gandhi's *Autobiography*

To see the universal and all-pervading Spirit of Truth face to face [*satya-narayanana-pratyaksha darshan*] one must be able to love the meanest of creation as oneself. And a man who aspires after that cannot afford to keep out of any field of life. That is why my devotion to Truth has drawn me into the field of politics; and I can say without the slightest hesitation, and yet in all humility, that those who say that religion [dharma] has nothing to do with politics do not know what religion [dharma] means. (Source: *CW* 39: 401).

From the Introduction to Gandhi's Translation
of the *Bhagavad Gita*

The common belief is that dharma and artha are mutually antagonistic to each other. 'In worldly activities such as trade and commerce, dharma has no place. Let dharma operate in the field of dharma, and artha in that of artha' – we hear many secular [*laukik*] people say. In my opinion, the author of the *Gita* has dispelled this delusion. He has drawn no line of demarcation between moksha and worldly pursuits.

(Editor's translation from the Gujarati text of Gandhi's *Anasakti Yoga* (Ahmedabad: Navajivan, 1975), p. 23)

*

GANDHI–NEHRU DIALOGUE

Gandhi and Nehru are the pre-eminent founders of modern India. As their famous 1945 correspondence, given below, reveals, Nehru had difficulty with some of the issues raised in *Hind Swaraj*. However, towards the end of his career as prime minister, he saw himself as striving to implement the basic teachings of Gandhi's public philosophy, especially those relating to the sanctity of the means and the need to maintain a balance between the political, ethical and spiritual pursuits in national life. Supporting evidence is taken from the little known *The Mind of Mr Nehru*, a long interview that Nehru gave in 1959, in his seventieth year, to R.K. Karanjia, and published with a Foreword by the philosopher Sarvepalli Radhakrishnan. [Ed.]

GANDHI TO NEHRU

October 5, 1945

My dear Jawaharlal,

I have been desirous of writing to you for many days but have not been able to do so before today. The question of whether I should write to you in English or Hindustani was also in my mind. I have at length preferred to write to you in Hindustani.

The first thing I want to write about is the difference of outlook between us. If the difference is fundamental then I feel the public should also be made aware of it. It would be detrimental to our work for Swaraj to keep them in the dark. I have said that I still stand by the system of

Government envisaged in *Hind Swaraj*. These are not mere words. All the experience gained by me since 1908 [*sic*] when I wrote the booklet has confirmed the truth of my belief. Therefore if I am left alone in it I shall not mind, for I can only bear witness to the truth as I see it. I have not *Hind Swaraj* before me as I write. It is really better for me to draw the picture anew in my own words. And whether it is the same as I drew in *Hind Swaraj* or not is immaterial for both you and me. It is not necessary to prove the rightness of what I said then. It is essential only to know what I feel today. I am convinced that if India is to attain true freedom and through India the world also, then sooner or later the fact must be recognised that people will have to live in villages, not in towns, in huts, not in palaces. Crores of people will never be able to live at peace with each other in towns and palaces. They will then have no recourse but to resort to both violence and untruth. I hold that without truth and non-violence there can be nothing but destruction for humanity. We can realise truth and non-violence only in the simplicity of village life and this simplicity can best be found in the Charkha and all that the Charkha connotes. I must not fear if the world today is going the wrong way. It may be that India too will go that way and like the proverbial moth burn itself eventually in the flame round which it dances more and more furiously. But it is my bounden duty up to my last breath to try to protect India and through India the entire world from such a doom. The essence of what I have said is that man should rest content with what are his real needs and become self-sufficient. If he does not have this control he cannot save himself. After all the world is made up of individuals just as it is the drops that constitute the ocean. I have said nothing new. This is a well known truth.

But I do not think I have stated this in *Hind Swaraj*. While I admire modern science, I find that it is the old looked at in the true light of modern science which should be reclothed and refashioned aright. You must not imagine that I am envisaging our village life as it is today. The village of my dreams is still in my mind. After all every man lives in the world of his dreams. My ideal village will contain intelligent human beings. They will not live in dirt and darkness as animals.

Men and women will be free and able to hold their own against any one in the world. There will be neither plague, nor cholera nor small-pox; no one will be idle, no one will wallow in luxury. Everyone will have to contribute his quota of manual labour. I do not want to draw a large scale picture in detail. It is possible to envisage railways, post and telegraph offices etc. For me it is material to obtain the real article and the rest will fit into the picture afterwards. If I let go the real thing, all else goes.

On the last day of the Working Committee it was decided that this matter should be fully discussed and the position clarified after a two or three days session. I should like this. But whether the Working Committee sits or not I want our position vis-à-vis each other to be clearly understood by us for two reasons. Firstly, the bond that unites us is not only political work. It is immeasurably deeper and quite unbreakable. Therefore it is that I earnestly desire that in the political field also we should understand each other clearly. Secondly neither of us thinks himself useless. We both live for the cause of India's freedom and we would both gladly die for it. We are not in need of the world's praise. Whether we get praise or blame is immaterial to us. There is no room for praise in service. I want to live to 125 for the service of India but I must admit that I am now an old man. You are much younger in comparison and I have therefore named you as my heir. I must, how-ever, understand my heir and my heir should understand me. Then alone shall I be content.

If you feel you should meet me to talk over what I have written we must arrange a meeting.

You are working hard. I hope you are well. I trust Indu [Indira Gandhi] too is fit.

Blessings from

BAPU

(Source: Nehru 1958, 505–7)

CW 81: 319–21 gives a different translation of the same letter. I have preferred the above translation since that is the one to which Nehru actually responded. [Ed.]

NEHRU'S REPLY TO GANDHI

Anand Bhawan, Allahabad   October 9, 1945
My dear Bapu,

I have received today, on return from Lucknow, your letter of the 5th October. I am glad you have written to me fully and I shall try to reply at some length but I hope you will forgive me if there is some delay in this, as I am at present tied up with close-fitting engagements. I am only here now for a day and a half. It is really better to have informal talks but just at present I do not know when to fit this in. I shall try.

Briefly put, my view is that the question before us is not one of truth versus untruth or non-violence versus violence. One assumes as one must that true cooperation and peaceful methods must be aimed at, and a society which encourages these must be our objective. The whole question is how to achieve this society and what its content should be. I do not understand why a village should necessarily embody truth and non-violence. A village, normally speaking, is backward intellectually and culturally and no progress can be made from a backward environment. Narrow-minded people are much more likely to be untruthful and violent.

Then again we have to put down certain objectives like a sufficiency of food, clothing, housing, education, sanitation etc. which should be the minimum requirements for the country and for everyone. It is with these objectives in view that we must find out specifically how to attain them speedily. Again it seems to me inevitable that modern means of transport as well as many other modern developments must continue and be developed. There is no way out of it except to have them. If that is so, inevitably a measure of heavy industry exists. How far will that fit in with a purely village society? Personally I hope that heavy or light industries should all be decentralised as far as possible and this is feasible now because of the development of electric power. If two types of economy exist in the country there should be either conflict between the two or one will overwhelm the other.

The question of independence and protection from foreign aggression, both political and economic, has also to be considered in this context. I do not think it is possible for India to be really independent unless she is a technically advanced country. I am not thinking for the moment in terms of just armies but rather of scientific growth. In the present context of the world we cannot even advance culturally without a strong background of scientific research in every department. There is today in the world a tremendous acquisitive tendency both in individuals and groups and nations, which leads to conflicts and wars. Our entire society is based on this more or less. That basis must go and be transformed into one of cooperation, not of isolation which is impossible. If this is admitted and is found feasible then attempts should be made to realise it not in terms of an economy, which is cut off from the rest of the world, but rather one which cooperates. From the economic or political point of view an isolated India may well be a kind of vacuum which increases the acquisitive tendencies of others and thus creates conflicts.

There is no question of palaces for millions of people. But there seems to be no reason why millions should not have comfortable up-to-date homes where they can lead a cultured existence. Many of the present overgrown cities have developed evils which are deplorable. Probably we have to discourage this overgrowth and at the same time encourage the village to approximate more to the culture of the town.

It is many years ago since I read *Hind Swaraj* and I have only a vague picture in my mind. But even when I read it 20 or more years ago it seemed to me completely unreal. In your writings and speeches since then I have found much that seemed to me an advance on that old position and an appreciation of modern trends. I was therefore surprised when you told us that the old picture still remains intact in your mind. As you know, the Congress has never considered that picture, much less adopted it. You yourself have never asked it to adopt it except for certain relatively minor aspects of it. How far it is desirable for the Congress to consider these fundamental questions, involving varying philosophies of life, it is for you to judge. I should imagine that a body like the Congress should not lose itself in arguments over such matters which can only produce great confusion in people's minds resulting in inability to act in the present. This may also result in creating barriers between the

Congress and others in the country. Ultimately of course this and other questions will have to be decided by representatives of free India. I have a feeling that most of these questions are thought of and discussed in terms of long ago, ignoring the vast changes that have taken place all over the world during the last generation or more. It is 38 years since *Hind Swaraj* was written. The world has completely changed since then, possibly in a wrong direction. In any event any consideration of these questions must keep present facts, forces and the human material we have today in view, otherwise it will be divorced from reality. You are right in saying that the world, or a large part of it, appears to be bent on committing suicide. That may be an inevitable development of an evil seed in civilisation that has grown. I think it is so. How to get rid of this evil, and yet how to keep the good in the present as in the past is our problem. Obviously there is good too in the present.

These are some random thoughts hurriedly written down and I fear they do injustice to the grave import of the questions raised. You will forgive me, I hope, for this jumbled presentation. Later I shall try to write more clearly on the subject.

I hope you are keeping well and have completely recovered from the attack of influenza.

Yours affectionately,

JAWAHARLAL

(Source: Nehru 1958: 507–10)

GANDHI TO NEHRU

Poona   November 13, 1945

My dear Jawaharlal,

Our talk of yesterday made me glad. I am sorry it could not be longer. I feel it cannot be finished in a single sitting, but will necessitate frequent meetings between us. I am so constituted that, if only I were physically fit to run about, I would myself overtake you, wherever you might be, and return after a couple of days' heart-to-heart talk with you. I have done so before. It is necesary that we understand each other well and that others also should clearly understand where we stand. It would not matter if ultimately we might have to agree to differ so long as we remained one at heart as we are today. The impression that I have gathered from our yesterday's talk is that there is not much difference in our outlook. To test this I put down below the gist of what I have understood. Please correct me if there is any discrepancy.

1 The real question, according to you, is how to bring about man's highest intellectual, economic, political and moral development. I agree entirely.
2 In this there should be an equal right and opportunity for all.
3 In other words, there should be equality between the town-dwellers and the villagers in the standard of food and drink, clothing and other living conditions. In order to achieve this equality today people should be able to produce for themselves the necessaries of life, i.e. clothing, foodstuffs, dwellings and lighting and water.
4 Man is not born to live in isolation but is essentially a social animal independent and interdependent. No one can or should ride on another's back. If we try to work out the necessary conditions for such a life, we are forced to the conclusion that the unit of society should be a village, or call it a small and manageable group of people who would, in the ideal, be self-sufficient (in the matter of their vital requirements) as a unit and bound together in bonds of mutual cooperation and inter-dependence.

If I find that so far I have understood you correctly, I shall take up consideration of the second part of the question in my next.

I had got Rajkumari [Amrit Kaur] to translate into English my first letter to you. It is still lying with me. I am enclosing for you an English translation of this. It will serve a double purpose. An English translation might enable me to explain myself more fully and clearly to you. Further, it will enable me to find out precisely if I have fully and correctly understood you.

Blessings to Indu [Indira Gandhi].

Blessings from

BAPU

(Source: Nehru 1958, 511–12)

NEHRU'S 1959 INTERVIEW

Karanjia asked Nehru whether 1947 marked the end of the Gandhian epoch and the beginning of the Nehru epoch. [Ed.]

NEHRU: You are wrong in using words like the Nehru epoch or the Nehru policy. I would call ours the authentic Gandhian era and the policies and philosophy which we seek to implement are the policies and philosophy taught to us by Gandhiji. There has been no break in the continuity of our thoughts before and after 1947, though, of course, new technological and scientific advances since have made us rethink in some ways and adapt our policies to the new times. But here also Gandhiji was in many ways prophetic. His thoughts and approaches and solutions helped us to cover the chasm between the Industrial Revolution and the Nuclear Era. (Source: R. K. Karanjia, *The Mind of Mr Nehru: An Interview by R. K. Karanjia*, Foreword by S. Radhakrishnan, London: Ruskin House, George Allen and Unwin, 1960, p. 23)

Nehru was asked whether Gandhi 'broke and emasculated' his 'earlier faith in scientific Socialism with his sentimental and spiritual solutions'.

NEHRU: Some of Gandhiji's approaches were old-fashioned and I disputed them, even combated them, as you know very well. But on the whole it is wrong to say that he broke or emasculated me or anybody else. Any such thing would be against his way of doing things. The most important thing he insisted upon was the importance of means: ends were shaped by the means that led to them, and therefore the means had to be good, pure, and truthful. That is what we learnt from him and it is well we did so.

On the other hand, what you say about sentimental and spiritual solutions may be true. I take it that by sentiment you mean humanity – that is, the deep human approach which has always been as much part of my thinking as it was Gandhiji's. The spiritual approach, too, is necessary and good, and I have always shared it with Gandhiji, probably more so today when we see the need of finding some answers to the spiritual emptiness facing our technological civilisation than I did yesterday. (Source: Ibid., p. 25)

Nehru was asked whether it was not unlike the Nehru of yesterday 'to talk in terms of ethical and spiritual solutions? What you say raises visions of Mr Nehru in search of God in the evening of his life!'

NEHRU: If you put it that way, my answer is: Yes, I have changed. The emphasis on ethical and spiritual solutions is not unconscious. It is deliberate, quite deliberate. There are good reasons for it. First of all, apart from material development that is imperative, I believe that the human mind is hungry for something deeper in terms of moral and spiritual development, without which all the material advance may not be worth while ...

The old Hindu idea that there is a divine essence in the world and every individual possesses something of it and can develop it, appeals to me in terms of a life force. I do not happen to be a religious man, but I do believe in something – call it religion or anything you like, which raises man above his normal level and gives human personality a new dimension of spiritual quality and moral depth. Now whatever helps to raise man above himself, be it some god or even a stone image, is good, obviously it is a good thing and must not be discouraged. Speaking for myself, my religion is tolerance of all religions, creeds and philosophies. (Source: Ibid., 32–3)

Nehru was asked whether the cultivation of leisure required something more than what a 'purely scientific or Marxist approach' had to offer.

NEHRU: Yes it is really the problem of creating *a fully integrated human being* – that is, with what might be called the spiritual and ethical counterpart of the purely material machinery of planning and development being brought into the making of man. Planning and development have now become an almost scientific and mathematical formula. Given a sound basis, they are bound to produce desired results in what is known as the welfare state with a self-developing economy. But is that enough really? I don't think so. Even in states with highly developed economies material progress by itself appears to have failed to provide people with a fully integrated life. There is a vacuum. There is maladjustment. Once you solve the problem of unemployment, for example, the

next and bigger problem becomes one of the employment of leisure itself. For as soon as man gets the material comfort he desires, something deeper inside him hungers for – well something deeper, something spiritual and ethical.
(Source: Ibid., p. 34. Italics in the original.)

Nehru was asked how he reacted to the new possibilities opening up in the space age.

NEHRU: ...*What the world is groping for today seems to be a new dimension in human existence, a new balance. Only a fully integrated man with spiritual depth and moral strength will be able to meet the challenges of the new times.* Material advance without spiritual balance can be disastrous.
(Source: Ibid., p. 103. Italics in the original.)

*

ECONOMIC DEVELOPMENT AND MORAL
DEVELOPMENT (1916)

This lecture, entitled 'Does economic progress clash with real pro-gress?', was delivered on 22 December 1916 to a meeting of the Muir Central College Economic Society, Allahabad. It contains Gandhi's basic ideas on economic development. Note its wide intellectual cul-ture, quoting as it were in one breath the New Testament, Shakespeare and A. R. Wallace, the co-discoverer with Darwin of the principle of natural selection. [Ed.]

When I accepted Mr. Kapildeva Malaviya's invitation to speak to you upon the subject of this evening, I was painfully conscious of my limi-tations. You are an economic society. You have chosen distinguished specialists for the subjects included in your syllabus for this year and the next. I seem to be the only speaker ill-fitted for the task set before him. Frankly and truly, I know very little of economics, as you naturally understand them. Only the other day, sitting at an evening meal, a civilian friend deluged me with a series of questions on my crankisms. As he proceeded in his cross-examination, I being a willing victim, he found no difficulty in discovering my gross ignorance of the matters I appeared to him to be handling with a cocksureness worthy only of a man who knows not that he knows not. To his horror and even indig-nation, I suppose, he found that I had not even read books on economics by such well-known authorities as Mill, Marshall, Adam Smith and a host of such other authors. In despair, he ended by advising me to read these works before experimenting in matters economic at the expense of the public. He little knew that I was a sinner past redemption.

153

My experiments continue at the expense of trusting friends. For, there come to us moments in life when about some things we need no proof from without. A little voice within us tells us, 'You are on the right track, move neither to your left nor right, but keep to the straight and narrow way.' With such help we march forward slowly indeed, but surely and steadily. That is my position. It may be satisfactory enough for me, but it can in no way answer the requirements of a society such as yours. Still it was no use my struggling against Mr. Kapildeva Malaviya. I knew that he was intent upon having me to engage your attention for one of your evenings. Perhaps you will treat my intrusion as a welcome diversion from the trodden path. An occasional fast after a series of sumptuous feasts is often a necessity. And as with the body, so, I imagine, is the case with the reason. And if your reason this evening is found fasting instead of feasting, I am sure it will enjoy with the greater avidity the feast that Rao Bahadur Pandit Chandrika Prasad has in store for you for the 12th of January.

Before I take you to the field of my experiences and experiments, it is perhaps best to have a mutual understanding about the title of this evening's address: *Does economic progress clash with real progress?* By economic progress, I take it, we mean material advancement without limit and by real progress we mean moral progress, which again is the same thing as progress of the permanent element in us. The subject may therefore be stated thus: 'Does not moral progress increase in the same proportion as material progress?' I know that this is a wider proposition than the one before us. But I venture to think that we always mean the larger one even when we lay down the smaller. For we know enough of science to realise that there is no such thing as perfect rest or repose in this visible universe of ours. If therefore material progress does not clash with moral progress, it must necessarily advance the latter. Nor can we be satisfied with the clumsy way in which sometimes those who cannot defend the larger proposition put their case. They seem to be obsessed with the concrete case of thirty millions of India stated by the late Sir William Wilson Hunter to be living on one meal a day. They say that before we can think or talk of their moral welfare, we must satisfy their daily wants. With these, they say, material progress spells moral progress. And then is taken a sudden jump: what is true of thirty millions is true of the universe. They forget that hard cases make bad law. I need hardly say to you how ludicrously absurd this deduction would be. No one has ever suggested that grinding pauperism can lead to anything else than moral degradation. Every human being has a right to live and therefore to find the wherewithal to feed himself and where necessary to clothe and house himself. But, for this very simple performance, we need no assistance from economists or their laws.

'Take no thought for the morrow' [St Matthew, ch. 6, v. 34] is an injunction which finds an echo in almost all the religious scriptures of the world. In well-ordered society, the securing of one's livelihood should be and is found to be the easiest thing in the world. Indeed, the test of orderliness in a country is not the number of millionaires it owns, but the absence of starvation among its masses. The only statement that has to be examined is whether it can be laid down as a law of universal application that material advancement means moral progress.

Now let us take a few illustrations. Rome suffered a moral fall when it attained high material affluence. So did Egypt and so perhaps most countries of which we have any historic record. The descendants, kinsmen of the royal and divine Krishna, too, fell when they were rolling in riches. We do not deny to the Rockefellers and the Carnegies possession of an ordinary measure of morality but we gladly judge them indulgently. I mean that we do not even expect them to satisfy the highest standard of morality. With them material gain has not necessarily meant moral gain. In South Africa, where I had the privilege of associating with thousands of our countrymen on most intimate terms, I observed almost invariably that the greater the possession of riches, the greater was their moral turpitude. Our rich men, to say the least, did not advance the moral struggle of passive resistance as did the poor. The rich men's sense of self-respect was not so much injured as that of the poorest. If I were not afraid of treading on dangerous ground, I would even come nearer home and show you that possession of riches has been a hindrance to real growth. I venture to think that the scriptures of the world are far safer and sounder treatises on laws of economics than many of the modern text-books.

The question we are asking ourselves this evening is not a new one. It was addressed to Jesus two thousand years ago. St. Mark [ch. 10, vv. 17–31] has vividly described the scene. Jesus is in his solemn mood; he is earnest. He talks of eternity. He knows the world about him. He is himself the greatest economist of his time. He succeeded in economising time and space – he transcended them. It is to him at his best that one comes running, kneels down, and asks: '"Good Master, what shall I do that I may inherit eternal life?" And Jesus said unto him: "Why callest thou me good? There is none good but one, that is God. Thou knowest the commandments. Do not commit adultery, Do not kill, Do not steal, Do not bear false witness, Defraud not, Honour thy father and mother." And he answered and said unto him: "Master, all these have I observed from my youth." Then Jesus beholding him, loved him and said unto him: "One thing thou lackest. Go thy way, sell whatever thou hast and give to the poor, and thou shalt have treasure in heaven – come take up the cross and follow me." And he was sad at that saying and went away grieved – for he had great possessions. And Jesus looked around about and said unto his disciples: "How hardly shall they that have riches enter into the kingdom of God." And the disciples were astonished at his words. But Jesus answereth again and saith unto them: "Children, how hard it is for them that trust in riches to enter into the kingdom of God. It is easier for a camel to go through the eye of a needle than for a rich man to enter into the kingdom of God!"'

Here you have an eternal rule of life stated in the noblest words the English language is capable of producing. But the disciples nodded unbelief as we do even to this day. To him they said as we say today: 'But look how the law fails in practice. If we sell all and have nothing, we shall have nothing to eat. We must have money or we cannot even be reasonably moral.' So they state their case thus. 'And they were astonished out of measure saying among themselves: "Who then can be saved?" And Jesus looking upon them saith: "With men it is impossible but not with God, for with God all things are possible." Then Peter began to say unto him: "Lo, we have left all, and have followed thee." And Jesus answered and said: "Verily I say unto you there is no man that has left house or brethren or sisters, or father or mother, or wife or children or lands for my sake and the Gospels, but he shall receive one hundred fold, now in this time houses and brethren and sisters and mothers and children and lands with persecutions and in the world to come eternal life. But many that are first shall be last and the last first."' You have here the result or reward, if you prefer the term, of following the law.

I have not taken the trouble of copying similar passages from the other non-Hindu scriptures and I will not insult you by quoting in support of the law stated by Jesus passages from the writings and sayings of our own sages, passages even stronger if possible than the Biblical extracts I have drawn your attention to. Perhaps the strongest of all the testimonies in favour of the affirmative answer to the question before us are the lives of the greatest teachers of the world. Jesus, Mahomed, Buddha, Nanak, Kabir, Chaitanya, Shankara, Dayanand, Ramkrishna were men who exercised an immense influence over and moulded the character of thousands of men. The world is the richer for their having lived in it. And they were all men who deliberately embraced poverty as their lot.

I should not have laboured my point as I have done, if I did not believe that, insofar as we have made the modern materialistic craze our goal, insofar are we going downhill in the path of progress. I hold that economic progress in the sense I have put it is antagonistic to real progress. Hence the ancient ideal has been the limitation of activities promoting wealth. This does not put an end to all material ambition. We should still have, as we have always had, in our midst people who make the pursuit of wealth their aim in life. But we have always recognised that it is a fall from the ideal. It is a beautiful thing to know that the wealthiest among us have often felt that to have remained voluntarily poor would have been a higher state for them. That you cannot serve God and Mammon is an economic truth of the highest value. We have to make our choice. Western nations today are groaning under the heel of the monster-god of materialism. Their moral growth has become stunted. They measure their progress in £.s.d. American wealth has become the standard. She is the envy of the other nations. I have heard many of our countrymen say that we will gain American wealth but avoid its methods. I venture to suggest that such an attempt if it were made is foredoomed to failure.

We cannot be 'wise, temperate and furious' in a moment 'Who can be wise, amazed, temperate and furious, /Loyal and neutral, in a moment? / No man,' [*Macbeth*, II. iii]. I would have our leaders to teach us to be morally supreme in the world. This land of ours was once, we are told, the abode of the gods. It is not possible to conceive gods inhabiting a land which is made hideous by the smoke and the din of mill chimneys and factories and whose roadways are traversed by rushing engines dragging numerous cars crowded with men mostly who know not what they are after, who are often absent-minded, and whose tempers do not improve by being uncomfortably packed like sardines in boxes and finding themselves in the midst of utter strangers who would oust them if they could and whom they would in their turn oust similarly. I refer to these things because they are held to be symbolical of material progress. But they add not an atom to our happiness. This is what [Alfred Russel] Wallace [1823–1913], the great scientist, has said as his deliberate judgement:

> In the earliest records which have come down to us from the past, we find ample indications that general ethical considerations and conceptions, the accepted standard of morality, and the conduct resulting from these were in no degree inferior to those which prevail today.

In a series of chapters, he then proceeds to examine the position of the English nation under the advance in wealth it has made. He says:

> This rapid growth of wealth and increase of our power over nature put too great a strain upon our crude civilisation, on our superficial Christianity, and it was accompanied by various forms of social immorality almost as amazing and unprecedented.

He then shows how factories have risen on the corpses of men, women and children, how as the country has rapidly advanced in riches, it has gone down in morality. He shows this by dealing with insanitation, life-destroying trades, adulteration, bribery and gambling. He shows how, with the advance of wealth, justice has become immoral, deaths from alcoholism and suicide have increased, the average of premature births and congenital defects has increased, and prostitution has become an institution. He concludes his examination by these pregnant remarks:

> The proceedings of the divorce courts show other aspects of the result of wealth and leisure, while a friend who had been a good deal in London society assured me that both in country houses and in London various kinds of orgies were occasionally to be met with which would hardly have been surpassed in the period of the most dissolute empe-rors. Of war, too, I need say nothing. It has always been more or less chronic since the rise of the Roman Empire; but there is now undoubt-edly a disinclination for war among all civilised peoples. Yet the vast burden of armaments, taken together with the most pious declara-tions in favour of peace, must be held to show an almost total absence of morality as a guiding principle among the governing classes.

Under the British aegis, we have learnt much, but it is my firm belief that there is little to gain from Britain in intrinsic morality, that if we are not careful, we shall introduce all the vices that she has been a prey to, owing to the disease of materialism. We can profit by that connection only if we keep our civilisation, and our morals, straight, i.e., if instead of boasting of the glorious past, we express the ancient moral glory in our own lives and let our lives bear witness to our past. Then we shall benefit her and ourselves. If we copy her because she provides us with rulers, both they and we shall suffer degradation. We need not be afraid of ideals or of reducing them to practice even to the uttermost. Ours will only then be a truly spiritual nation when we shall show more truth than gold, greater fearlessness than pomp of power and wealth, greater charity than love of self. If we will but clean our houses, our palaces and temples of the attributes of wealth and show in them the attributes of morality, we can offer battle to any combinations of hostile forces with-out having to carry the burden of a heavy militia. Let us seek first the kingdom of God and His righteousness and the irrevocable promise is that everything will be added unto us. These are real economics. May you and I treasure them and enforce them in our daily life.

An interesting discussion followed in the course of which several students put questions to the lecturer.

Professor [Stanley] Jevons: '... It was necessary for economists to exist. It was not their business to lay down what the end should be. That was the business of philosophers ...'

Professor Gidwani, president of the society, thanked the lecturer for his address.

Professor Higginbottom said that there was no economic problem which could be separated from the moral problem.

Mr. Gandhi in the course of his remarks referred to Mr. Jevons' remark about the need for economists and said that it was said that dirt was matter misplaced. So also when an economist was misplaced, he was hurtful. He certainly thought that the economist had a place in the economy of nature when he occupied the humble sphere for which he was created. If an economist did not investigate the laws of God and show them how to distribute wealth so that there might not be poverty, he was a most unwelcome intrusion on the Indian soil. He would also suggest for the reflection of their economic students and professors that what might be good for England and America need not necessarily be good for India. He thought that most of the economic laws which were consistent with moral laws were of universal application, but there might be in their restricted application some distinction and difference. So he would utter the note of warning that Indian conditions being in some respects so essentially different from the English and American conditions, it was necessary to bring to bear on the matters that presented themselves to the economists a fresh mind. If they did so, both Indians and the economists would derive benefit. Mr. Higginbottom, he said, was studying the real economics that were so necessary for India and reducing his studies inch by inch to practice and that was the safest guide to follow, whether they were students or professors. Referring to a question by a student, he said that a man should not hoard money for selfish ends, but if he wished to hoard money as a trustee for the millions of India, he would say that he might have as much riches as he could. Ordinarily, economists prescribed laws for the rich people. It was against those economists that he would always cry out.

As regards another question, whether factories should not be replaced by cottage industries, Mr. Gandhi spoke approvingly of the suggestion but said that the economists should first of all examine with patience their indigenous institutions. If they were rotten, they must be wiped out and if there were remedies which could be suggested for their betterment, they should improve them.

(Source: *CW* 13: 310–17)

GANDHI ON MACHINERY (1919−47)

No other question treated in *Hind Swaraj*, not even that of the lawyers, doctors and hospitals, has provoked as much controversy as has the question of machinery – in the current idiom, 'technology'. Gandhi's thinking on machinery underwent gradual development, the main features of which are traced below. [Ed.]

1919

'There is thus room in the country for both the mill industry and the handloom weaving. So let mills increase as also spinning-wheels and handlooms. And I should think that these latter are no doubt machines. The handloom is a miniature weaving mill. The spinning-wheel is a miniature spinning-mill. I would wish to see such beautiful little mills in every home. But the country is fully in need of the hand-spinning and hand-weaving industry. Agriculturists in no country can live without some industry to supplement agriculture ... Even if we have sufficient mills in the country to produce cloth enough for the whole country, we are bound to provide our peasantry, daily being more and more impoverished, with some supplementary industry, and that which can be suitable to crores of people is hand-spinning and hand-weaving. Opposition to mills or machinery is not the point. What suits our country is the point. I am not opposed to the movement of manufacturing machines in the country, nor to making improvements in machinery. I am only concerned with what these machines are meant for. I may ask, in the words of Ruskin, whether these machines will be such as would blow off a million

162

men in a minute or they will be such as would turn waste lands into arable and fertile land. And if legislation were in my hands, I would penalise the manufacture of [labour-saving] machines and protect the industry which manufactures nice ploughs which can be handled by every man.'
(*CW* 16: 134–5)

1922

'India does not need to be industrialised in the modern sense of the term. It has 750,000 villages scattered over a vast area ... The people are rooted to the soil, and the vast majority are living a hand-to-mouth life ... pauperism is growing. There is no doubt also that the millions are living in enforced idleness for at least four months in the year. Agriculture does not need revolutionary changes. The Indian peasant requires a supplementary industry. The most natural is the introduction of the spinning-wheel, not the handloom. The latter cannot be introduced in every home, whereas the former can, and it used to be so even a century ago. It was driven out not by economic pressure, but by force deliberately used as can be proved from authentic records. The restoration, therefore, of the spinning-wheel solves the economic problem of India at a stroke ... I hope you will not allow yourself to be prejudiced by anything you might have heard about my strange views about machinery. I have nothing to say against the development of any other industry in India by means of machinery, but I do say that to supply India with cloth manufactured either outside or inside through gigantic mills is an economic blunder of the first magnitude, just as it would be to supply cheap bread though huge bakeries established in the chief centres in India and to destroy the family stove.'
(*CW* 22: 401–2)

1924

'What I object to, is the *craze* for machinery, not machinery as such. The craze is for what they call labour-saving machinery. Men go on "saving labour" till thousands are without work and thrown on the open streets to die of starvation. I want to save time and labour, not for a fraction of mankind, but for all. I want the concentration of wealth, not in the hands of the few, but in the hands of all. Today machinery merely helps a few to ride on the backs of millions. The impetus behind it all is not the philanthropy to save labour, but greed. It is against this constitution of things that I am fighting with all my might.

... scientific truths and discoveries should first of all cease to be the mere instruments of greed. Then labourers will not be over-worked and machinery instead of becoming a hindrance will be a help. I am aiming, not at eradication of all machinery, but limitations ...

The supreme consideration is man. The machine should not tend to make atrophied the limbs of man. For instance, I would make intelligent exceptions. Take the case of the Singer Sewing Machine. It is one of the few useful things ever invented, and there is a romance about the device itself. Singer saw his wife labouring over the tedious process of sewing and seaming with her own hands, and simply out of his love for her he devised the sewing machine, in order to save her from unnecessary labour ...

It is an alteration in the condition of labour that I want. This mad rush for wealth must cease, and the labourer must be assured, not only of a living wage, but a daily task that is not a mere drudgery. The machine will, under these conditions, be as much a help to the man working it as to the State, or the man who owns it. The present mad rush will cease, and the labourer will work ... under attractive and ideal conditions ... Therefore, replace greed by love and everything will come right.'
(*CW* 25: 251–2)

1931

'I hold that the machinery method is harmful when the same thing can be done easily by millions of hands not otherwise occupied ... Western observers hastily argue from Western conditions that what may be true of them must be true of India where conditions are different in so many material respects. Applications of the laws of economics vary with varying conditions.

The machinery method is no doubt easy. But it is not necessarily a blessing on that account ... If the craze for the machinery method continues, it is highly likely that a time will come when we shall be so incapacitated and weak that we shall begin to curse ourselves for having forgotten the use of the living machines given to us by God.'
(*CW* 47: 89–90)

'Machinery is a grand yet awful invention. It is possible to visualise a stage at which the machines invented by man may finally engulf civilisation. If man controls the machines, then they will not; but should man lose his control over the machines and allow them to control him, then they will certainly engulf civilisation and everything.'
(*CW* 48: 353)

1934

'When as a nation we adopt the spinning-wheel, we not only solve the question of unemployment but we declare that we have no intention of exploiting any nation, and we also end exploitation of the poor by the rich ... When I say I want independence for the millions, I mean to say not only that the millions may have something to eat and to cover themselves with, but that they will be free from the exploitation of people here and outside. We can never industrialise India, unless, of course, we reduce our population from 350 millions to 35 millions or hit upon markets wider than our own and dependent on us. It is time we realised that, where there is unlimited human power, complicated machinery on a large scale has no place ... We cannot industrialise ourselves, unless we make up our mind to enslave humanity.'
(*CW* 58: 400)

1935

'Machinery well used has to help and ease human effort. The present use of machinery tends more and more to concentrate wealth in the hands

of a few in total disregard of millions of men and women whose bread is
snatched by it out of their mouths.'
(*CW* 61: 416)

1936

[Responding to a Japanese correspondent who asked whether Gandhi
was against this machine age]:

'To say that is to caricature my views. I am not against machinery as
such, but I am totally opposed to it when it masters us ...

Q. "You would not industrialise India?"

A. "I would indeed, in my sense of the term. The village communities
should be revived. Indian villages produced and supplied to the Indian
towns and cities all their wants. India became impoverished when our
cities became foreign markets and began to drain the villages dry by
dumping cheap and shoddy goods from foreign lands."'
(*CW* 64: 118)

1940

'We should not use machinery for producing things which we can
produce without its aid and have got the capacity to do so. As machinery
makes you its slave, we want to be independent and self-supporting; so
we should not take the help of machinery when we can do without it.
We want to make our villages free and self-sufficient and through them
achieve our goal – liberty – and also protect it. I have no interest in the
machine nor [do] I oppose it. If I can produce my things myself, I become
my master and so need no machinery.'
(*CW* 71: 383)

1945

Here Gandhi makes the connection between machinery and
violence. [Ed.]

'Another danger in making more and more use of machinery is that we have to make great efforts for the protection of it, that is to say, we shall have to keep an army as is being done today elsewhere in the world. The fact is that even if there is no danger of aggression from outside we shall be slaves to those who will be in control of the big machinery. Take the case of the atom bomb. Those nations who have atom bombs are feared even by their friends. If we take a wise view, we shall be saved from the working of machinery.'
(*CW* 82: 132–3)

1946

Gandhi's definition of a machine, as given in his address to the Indian Industries Ministers' Conference, Poona. The text of the address is not available. The following is taken from a report on it published in *CW* 85: 95. [Ed.]

'Ours has been described as the machine age, because the machine dominates our economy. Now, what is a machine? – one may ask. In a sense, man is the most wonderful machine in creation. It can be neither duplicated nor copied.

He [Gandhi] had, however, used the word not in its wider sense but in the sense of an appliance that tended to displace human or animal labour instead of supplementing it or merely increasing its efficiency. That was the first differentiating characteristic of the machine. The second characteristic was that there was no limit to its growth or evolution. That could not be said of human labour. There was no limit beyond which its capacity or mechanical efficiency could not go. Out of this circumstance arose the third characteristic of the machine. It seems to be possessed of a will or genius of its own. It was antagonistic to man's labour. Thus it tended more to displace man, one machine doing the work of a hundred, if not a thousand, who went to swell the army of the unemployed and the under-employed, not because it was desirable but because that was its law.'

Gandhi was asked if he would oppose adoption of the flush system as one way of eradicating untouchability. He replied as follows. [Ed.]

'Where there is ample supply of water and [where] modern sanitation can be introduced without any hardship on the poor, I have no objection to it [the flush system]. In fact, it should be welcomed as a means of improving the health of the city concerned. At the moment, it can only be introduced in towns. My opposition to machinery is much misunderstood. I am not opposed to machinery as such. I am opposed to machinery which displaces labour and leaves it idle.'
(*CW* 85: 239–40)

1947

'Machine-power can make a valuable contribution towards economic progress. But a few capitalists have employed machine-power regardless of the interests of the common man and that is why our condition has deteriorated today.'
(*CW* 87: 249)

*

CONSTRUCTIVE PROGRAMME: ITS MEANING
AND PLACE (1941, REV. 1945)

While *Hind Swaraj* gives the general outline of Gandhi's political philosophy, the 'Constructive programme', originally addressed to the members of the Indian National Congress, discusses some of the concrete steps by which that philosophy may be implemented. The value of this document lies in the fact that it illustrates the point that according to Gandhi every sound political philosophy ought to have its corresponding constructive programme – one that contributes to the betterment of the lives of members of civil society. [Ed.]

INTRODUCTORY

The constructive programme may otherwise and more fittingly be called construction of *poorna* swaraj or complete independence by truthful and non-violent means.

Effort for construction of independence so called through violent and, therefore, necessarily untruthful means we know only too painfully. Look at the daily destruction of property, life and truth in the present war.

Complete independence through truth and non-violence means the independence of every unit, be it the humblest of the nation, without distinction of race, colour or creed. This independence is never exclusive. It is, therefore, wholly compatible with interdependence within or without. Practice will always fall short of the theory, even as the drawn line falls short of the theoretical line of Euclid. Therefore, complete independence will be complete only to the extent of our approach in practice to truth and non-violence.

Let the reader mentally plan out the whole of the constructive programme, and he will agree with me that, if it could be successfully worked out, the end of it would be the independence we want ...

[T]here is no such thing as an imaginary or even perfect definition of independence through violence. For it presupposes only ascendency of that party of the nation which makes the most effective use of violence. In it perfect equality, economic or otherwise, is inconceivable.

But for my purpose, which is to convince the reader of the necessity of following out the constructive programme in the non-violent effort, the acceptance of my argument about the ineffectiveness of violence for the attainment of independence is not required. The reader is welcome to the belief that independence of this humblest unit is possible under the scheme of violence, if this effort enables him also to admit that it is a certainty through the complete execution of the programme by the nation.

Let us now examine the items:

i. Communal unity

Everybody is agreed about the necessity of this unity. But everybody does not know that unity does not mean political unity, which may be imposed. It means an unbreakable heart unity. The first thing essential for achieving such unity is for every Congressman, whatever his religion may be, to represent in his own person Hindu, Muslim, Christian, Zoroastrian, Jew, etc., shortly, every Hindu and non-Hindu. He has to feel his identity with every one of the millions of the inhabitants of Hindustan. In order to realise this, every Congressman will cultivate personal friendship with persons representing faiths other than his own. He should have the same regard for the other faiths as he has for his own ...

ii. Removal of untouchability

At this time of the day it is unnecessary to dilate upon the necessity of the removal of this blot and curse upon Hinduism. Congressmen have certainly done much in this matter. But I am sorry to have to say that many Congressmen have looked upon this item as a mere political necessity and not something indispensable, so far as Hindus are concerned, for the very existence of Hinduism. If Hindu Congressmen take up the cause for its own sake, they will influence the so-called *sanatanis* (traditionalists) far more extensively than they have hitherto done. They should approach them not in a militant spirit but, as befits their nonviolence, in a spirit of friendliness. And so far as Harijans are concerned, every Hindu should make common cause with them and befriend them in their awful isolation – such isolation as perhaps the world has never seen in the monstrous immensity one witnesses in India. I know from experience how difficult the task is. But it is part of the task of building the edifice of swaraj. And the road to swaraj is steep and narrow. There are many slippery ascents and many deep chasms. They have all to be negotiated with unfaltering step before we can reach the summit and breathe the fresh air of freedom.

iii. Prohibition

Although like communal unity and removal of untouchability prohibition has been on the Congress programme since 1920, Congressmen have not taken the interest they might have taken in this very vital social and moral reform. If we are to reach our goal through non-violent effort, we may not leave to the future government the fate of lakhs of men and women who are labouring under the curse of intoxicants and narcotics.

Medical men can make a most effective contribution towards the removal of this evil. They have to discover ways of weaning the drunkard and the opium addict from the curse.

Women and students have a special opportunity in advancing this reform. By many acts of loving service they can acquire on addicts a hold which will compel them to listen to the appeal to give up the evil habit ...

iv. Khadi

Khadi is a controversial subject. Many people think that in advocating khadi I am sailing against a headwind and am sure to sink the ship of swaraj and that I am taking the country to the dark ages. I do not propose to argue the case for khadi in this brief survey. I have argued it sufficiently elsewhere. Here I want to show what every Congressman, and for that matter every Indian, can do to advance the cause of khadi. It connotes the beginning of economic freedom and equality of all in the country. The proof of the pudding is in the eating. Let everyone try, and he or she will find out for himself or herself the truth of what I am saying. Khadi must be taken with all its implications. It means a whole-sale swadeshi mentality, a determination to find all the necessaries of life in India and that too through the labour and intellect of the villagers. That means the reversal of the existing process. That is to say that, instead of half a dozen cities of India and Great Britain living on the exploitation and the ruin of the 700,000 villages of India, the latter will be largely self-contained, and will voluntarily serve the cities of India and even the outside world in so far as it benefits both the parties.

This needs a revolutionary change in the mentality and tastes of many. Easy though the non-violent way is in many respects, it is very difficult in many others. It vitally touches the life of every single Indian, makes him feel aglow with the possession of power that has lain hidden within himself, and makes him proud of his identity with every drop of the ocean of Indian humanity. This non-violence is not the inanity for which we have mistaken it through all these long ages; it is the most potent force as yet known to mankind and on which its very existence is dependent. It is that force which I have tried to present to the Congress and through it to the world. Khadi to me is the symbol of unity of Indian humanity, of its economic freedom and equality and, therefore, ultimately, in the poetic expression of Jawaharlal Nehru, 'the livery of India's freedom'.

Moreover, khadi mentality means decentralisation of production and distribution of the necessaries of life …

v. Other village industries

These stand on a different footing from khadi. There is not much scope for voluntary labour in them. Each industry will take the labour of only a certain number of hands. These industries come in as a handmaid to khadi. They cannot exist without khadi, and khadi will be robbed of its dignity without them. Village economy cannot be complete without the essential village industries such as hand-grinding, hand-pounding, soap-making, paper-making, match-making, tanning, oil-pressing, etc ... When we have become village-minded, we will not want imitations of the West or machine-made products, but we will develop a true national taste in keeping with the vision of a new India in which pauperism, starvation and idleness will be unknown.

vi. Village sanitation

Divorce between intelligence and labour has resulted in criminal negligence of the villages. And so, instead of having graceful hamlets dotting the land, we have dung-heaps. The approach to many villages is not a refreshing experience. Often one would like to shut one's eyes and stuff one's nose; such is the surrounding dirt and offending smell. If the majority of Congressmen were derived from our villages, as they should be, they should be able to make our villages models of cleanliness in every sense of the word. But they have never considered it their duty to identify themselves with the villagers in their daily lives. A sense of national or social sanitation is not a virtue among us. We may take a kind of a bath, but we do not mind dirtying the well or the tank or river by whose side or in which we perform ablutions. I regard this defect as a great vice which is responsible for the disgraceful state of our villages and the sacred banks of the sacred rivers and for diseases that spring from insanitation.

vii. New or basic education

... This education is meant to transform village children into model villagers. It is principally designed for them. The inspiration for it has come from the villages ... Primary education is a farce designed without regard to the wants of the India of the villages and for that matter even of the cities. Basic education links the children, whether of the cities or the villages, to all that is best and lasting in India. It develops both the body and the mind, keeps the child rooted to the soil with a glorious vision of the future, in the realisation of which he or she begins to take his or her share from the very commencement of his or her career in school ...

viii. Adult education

This has been woefully neglected by Congressmen. Where they have not neglected it, they have been satisfied with teaching illiterates to read and write. If I had charge of adult education, I should begin with opening the minds of the adult pupils to the greatness and vastness of their country ...

ix. Women

I have included service of women in the constructive programme, for though satyagraha has automatically brought India's women out from their darkness as nothing else could have in such an incredibly short space of time, Congressmen have not felt the call to see that women become equal partners in the fight for swaraj. They have not realised that woman must be the true helpmate of man in the mission of service. Woman has been suppressed under custom and law for which man was responsible and in the shaping of which she had no hand. In a plan of life based on non-violence, woman has as much right to shape her own destiny as man has to shape his. But as every right in a non-violent society proceeds from the previous performance of a duty, it follows that rules of social conduct must be framed by mutual co-operation and consultation. They can never be imposed from outside. Men have not realised this truth in its fullness in their behaviour towards women. They have considered themselves to be lords and masters of women instead of considering them as their friends and co-workers. It is the privilege of Congressmen to give women of India a lifting hand. Women are in the position somewhat of the slave of old who did not know that he could or ever had to be free. And when freedom came, for the moment he felt helpless. Women have been taught to regard themselves as slaves of men. It is up to Congressmen to see that they enable them to realise their full status and play their part as equals of men.

This revolution is easy, if the mind is made up. Let Congressmen begin with their own homes. Wives should not be dolls and objects of indulgence, but should be treated as honoured comrades in common service. To this end those who have not received a liberal education should receive such instruction as is possible from their husbands. The same observation applies, with the necessary changes, to mothers and daughters.

It is hardly necessary to point out that I have given a one-sided picture of the helpless state of India's women. I am quite conscious of the fact that in the villages generally they hold their own with their men-folk and in some respects even rule them. But to the impartial outsider the legal and customary status of woman is bad enough throughout and demands radical alteration.

x. Education in health and hygiene

… The art of keeping one's health and the knowledge of hygiene is by itself a separate subject of study and corresponding practice. In a well-ordered society the citizens know and observe the laws of health and hygiene. It is established beyond doubt that ignorance and neglect of the laws of health and hygiene are responsible for the majority of diseases to which mankind is heir …

Mens *sana in corpore sano* is perhaps the first law for humanity. A healthy mind in a healthy body is a self-evident truth. There is an inevitable connection between mind and body. If we were in possession of healthy minds, we would shed all violence and, naturally obeying the laws of health, we would have healthy bodies without an effort. I hope, therefore, that no Congressman will disregard this item of the constructive programme …

xi. Provincial languages

In this section Gandhi points out the importance of India's provincial languages for the cultural regeneration of the country as a whole. [Ed.]

xii. National language

In this section Gandhi supports the case of Hindi as India's national langauge. [Ed.]

xiii. Economic equality

This last is the master-key to non-violent independence. Working for economic equality means abolishing the eternal conflict between capital and labour. It means the levelling down of the few rich in whose hands is concentrated the bulk of the nation's wealth on the one hand, and levelling up of the semi-starved naked millions on the other. A nonviolent system of government is clearly an impossibility so long as the wide gulf between the rich and the hungry millions persists ...

I adhere to my doctrine of trusteeship in spite of the ridicule that has been poured upon it. It is true that it is difficult to reach. So is non-violence. But we made up our minds in 1920 to negotiate that steep ascent. We have found it worth the effort. It involves a daily growing appreciation of the working of non-violence ...

This non-violent experiment is still in the making. We have nothing much yet to show by way of demonstration. It is certain, however, that the method has begun to work though ever so slowly in the direction of equality ... Those who think that major reforms will come after the advent of swaraj are deceiving themselves as to the elementary working of non-violent swaraj. It will not drop from heaven all of a sudden one fine morning. But it has to be built up brick by brick by corporate self-effort. We have travelled a fair way in that direction. But a much longer and weary distance has to be covered before we can behold swaraj in its glorious majesty ...

xiv. Kisans (peasantry)

The programme is not exhaustive. Swaraj is a mighty structure ...

Those who would know my method of organising *kisans* may profitably study the movement in Champaran when satyagraha was tried for the first time in India with the result all India knows. It became a mass movement which remained wholly non-violent from start to finish. It affected over twenty lakhs of *kisans*. The struggle centred round one specific grievance which was a century old. There had been several violent revolts to get rid of the grievance. The *kisans* were suppressed. The non-violent remedy succeeded in full in six months. The *kisans* of Champaran became politically conscious without any direct effort ...

The reader may also profitably study the *kisan* movements in Kheda, Bardoli and Borsad. The secret of success lies in a refusal to exploit the *kisans* for political purposes outside their own personal and felt grievances. Organisation round a specific wrong they understand. They need no sermons on non-violence. Let them learn to apply non-violence as an effective remedy which they can understand, and later when they are told that the method they were applying was non-violent, they readily recognise it as such ...

xv. Labour

Ahmedabad Labour Union is a model for all India to copy. Its basis is nonviolence, pure and simple. It has never had a set-back in its career. It has gone on from strength to strength without fuss and without show. It has its hospital, its school for the children of mill-hands, its classes for adults, its own printing press and khadi depot, and its own residential quarters. Almost all the hands are voters and decide the fate of elections. They came on the voters' list at the instance of the Provincial Congress Committee. The organisation has never taken part in party politics of the Congress. It influences the municipal policy of the city. It has to its credit very successful strikes which were wholly non-violent. Mill-owners and labour have governed their relations largely through voluntary arbitration. If I had my way, I would regulate all the labour organisations of India after the Ahmedabad model ...

xvi. Adivasis (aboriginals)

In this section Gandhi advocates working with Adivasis in order to promote in them the spirit of self-help and national consciousness. [Ed.]

xvii. Lepers

In this section Gandhi pays special attention to the plight of those afflicted by leprosy, and thanks the missionaries for their pioneering work in this regard. [Ed.]

xviii. Students

In this section Gandhi advises students to abstain from party politics and to integrate the theory of non-violence with their academic studies. [Ed.]

xix. Place of civil disobedience

I have said in these pages that civil disobedience is not absolutely necessary to win freedom through purely non-violent effort, if the co-operation of the whole nation is secured in the constructive programme. But such good luck rarely favours nations or individuals. Therefore, it is necessary to know the place of civil disobedience in a nationwide non-violent effort.

It has three definite functions:

1 It can be effectively offered for the redress of a local wrong.
2 It can be offered without regard to effect, though aimed at a particular wrong or evil, by way of self-immolation in order to rouse local consciousness or conscience. Such was the case in Champaran when I offered civil disobedience without any regard to the effect and well

knowing that even the people might remain apathetic. That it proved otherwise may be taken, according to taste, as God's grace or a stroke of good luck.

3 In the place of full response to constructive effort, it can be offered as it was in 1941. Though it was a contribution to and part of the battle for freedom, it was purposely centred round a particular issue, i.e., free speech. Civil disobedience can never be directed for a general cause such as for independence. The issue must be definite and capable of being clearly understood and within the power of the opponent to yield. This method properly applied must lead to the final goal.

I have not examined here the full scope and possibilities of civil disobedience. I have touched enough of it to enable the reader to understand the connection between constructive programme and civil disobedience. In the first two cases, no elaborate constructive programme was or could be necessary. But when civil disobedience is itself devised for the attainment of independence, previous preparation is necessary, and it has to be backed by the visible and conscious effort of those who are engaged in the battle. Civil disobedience is thus a stimulation for the fighters and a challenge to the opponent. It should be clear to the reader that civil disobedience in terms of independence without the co-operation of the millions by way of constructive effort is mere bravado and worse than useless.

CONCLUSION

This is not a thesis written on behalf of the Congress or at the instance of the Central Office. It is the outcome of conversations I had with some co-workers in Sevagram. They had felt the want of something from my pen showing the connection between constructive programme and civil disobedience and how the former might be worked. I have endeavoured to supply the want in this pamphlet. It does not purport to be exhaustive, but it is sufficiently indicative of the way the programme should be worked.

Let not the reader make the mistake of laughing at any of the items as being part of the movement for independence. Many people do many things, big and small, without connecting them with non-violence or independence. They have then their limited value as expected. The same man appearing as a civilian may be of no consequence, but appearing in his capacity as General he is a big personage, holding the lives of millions at his mercy. Similarly, the charkha [the spinning-wheel] in the hands of the poor widow brings a paltry pice to her, in the hands of a Jawaharlal [Nehru] it is an instrument of India's freedom. It is the office which gives the charkha its dignity. It is the office assigned to the constructive programme which gives it an irresistible prestige and power.

Such at least is my view. It may be that of a mad man. If it makes no appeal to the Congressman, I must be rejected. For my handling of civil disobedience without the constructive programme will be like a para-lysed hand attempting to lift a spoon.

(Source: *CW* 75: 146–66)

*

GANDHI'S POLITICAL VISION: THE PYRAMID
VS THE OCEANIC CIRCLE (1946)

Gandhi's vision of the relationship between the individual, the state and the world community is articulated in an interview he granted on 28 July 1946. [Ed.]

Question: You have said in your article in the *Harijan* of July 15, under the caption 'The Real Danger' that Congressmen in general certainly do not know the kind of independence they want. Would you kindly give them a broad but comprehensive picture of the Independent India of your own conception?

Answer: I do not know that I have not, from time to time, given my idea of Indian independence. Since, however, this question is part of a series, it is better to answer it even at the risk of repetition.

Independence of India should mean independence of the whole of India, including what is called India of the States and the other foreign powers, French and Portuguese, who are there, I presume, by British sufferance. Independence must mean that of the people of India, not of those who are today ruling over them. The rulers should depend on the will of those who are under their heels. Thus, they have to be servants of the people, ready to do their will.

Independence must begin at the bottom. Thus, every village will be a republic or *panchayat* having full powers. It follows, therefore, that every village has to be self-sustained and capable of managing its affairs even to the extent of defending itself against the whole world. It will be trained and prepared to perish in the attempt to defend itself against any onslaught from without. Thus, ultimately, it is the individual who is the unit. This does not exclude dependence on and willing help from neighbours or from the world. It will be a free and voluntary play of mutual forces. Such a society is necessarily highly cultured in which every man and woman knows what he or she wants and, what is more, knows that no one should want anything that others cannot have with equal labour.

This society must naturally be based on truth and non-violence which, in my opinion, are not possible without a living belief in God, meaning a self-existent, all-knowing living Force which inheres in every other force known to the world and which depends on none and which will live when all other forces may conceivably perish or cease to act. I am unable to account for my life without belief in this all-embracing living Light.

In this structure composed of innumerable villages, there will be ever-widening, never-ascending circles. Life will not be a pyramid with the apex sustained by the bottom. But it will be an oceanic circle whose centre will be the individual always ready to perish for the village, the latter ready to perish for the circle of villages, till at last the whole becomes one life composed of individuals, never aggressive in their arrogance but ever humble, sharing the majesty of the oceanic circle of which they are integral units.

Therefore the outermost circumference will not wield power to crush the inner circle but will give strength to all within and derive its own strength from it. I may be taunted with the retort that this is all Utopian and, therefore, not worth a single thought. If Euclid's point, though incapable of being drawn by human agency, has an imperishable value, my picture has its own for mankind to live. Let India live for this true picture, though never realisable in its completeness. We must have a proper picture of what we want, before we can have something approaching it. If there ever is to be a republic of every village in India, then I claim verity for my picture in which the last is equal to the first or, in other words, no one is to be the first and none the last.

In this picture every religion has its full and equal place. We are all leaves of a majestic tree whose trunk cannot be shaken off its roots which are deep down in the bowels of the earth. The mightiest wind cannot move it.

In this there is no room for machines that would displace human labour and that would concentrate power in a few hands. Labour has its unique place in a cultured human family. Every machine that helps every individual has a place. But I must confess that I have never sat down to think out what that machine can be. I have thought of Singer's sewing machine. But even that is perfunctory. I do not need it to fill in my picture.

Question: Do you believe that the proposed Constituent Assembly could be used for the realisation of your picture?

Answer: The Constituent Assembly has all the possibilities for the realisation of my picture. Yet I cannot hope for much, not because the State Paper holds no such possibilities but because the document, being wholly of a voluntary nature, requires the common consent of the many parties to it. These have no common goal. Congressmen themselves are not of one mind even on the contents of Independence. I do not know how many swear by non-violence or the charkha or, believing in decentralisation, regard the village as the nucleus. I know on the contrary that many would have India become a first-class military power and wish for India to have a strong centre and build the whole structure round it. In the medley of these conflicts I know that if India is to be leader in clean action based on clean thought, God will confound the wisdom of these big men and will provide the villages with the power to express themselves as they should.

Question: If the Constituent Assembly fizzles out because of the 'danger from within', as you have remarked in the above-mentioned article, would you advise the Congress to accept the alternative of general country-wide strike and capture of power, either non-violently or with the use of necessary force? What is your alternative in that eventuality if the above is not approved by you?

Answer: I must not contemplate darkness before it stares me in the face. And in no case can I be party, irrespective of non-violence, to a universal strike and capture of power. Though, therefore, I do not know what I should do in the case of a breakdown, I know that the actuality will find me ready with an alternative. My sole reliance being on the living Power which we call God, He will put the alternative in my hands when the time has come, not a minute sooner.

(Source: *CW* 85: 32–4)

*

DRAFT CONSTITUTION OF CONGRESS (1948)

Written on the day before his assassination, the following document is popularly known as Gandhi's 'Last Will and Testament'. Watching the behaviour of India's political intelligentsia after independence Gandhi became convinced that they were more interested in making personal gains than in serving the people. It confirmed his fear, already expressed in *Hind Swaraj*, ch. IV, that home rule without *swaraj* would only mean the replacement of the British 'tiger' by the Indian 'tiger'. To the last Gandhi believed that political, social and economic development could become a reality only when *swaraj* as political self-government was accompanied by *swaraj* as moral self-rule. Gandhi's last political message is that in a free society political parties must be inspired by the ideal that politics is a form of *public service* rather than a means of *dominating* fellow citizens. [Ed.]

New Delhi   January 29, 1948

Though split into two, India having attained political independence through means devised by the Indian National Congress, the Congress in its present shape and form, i.e., as a propaganda vehicle and parliamentary machine, has outlived its use. India has still to attain social, moral and economic independence in terms of its seven hundred thousand villages as distinguished from its cities and towns. The struggle for the ascendancy of civil over military power is bound to take place in India's progress towards its democratic goal. It must be kept out of unhealthy competition with political parties and communal bodies. For these and other similar reasons, the A.I.C.C. resolves to disband the existing Congress organisation

184

and flower into a Lok Sevak Sangh [Society to Serve the People] under the following rules with power to alter them as occasion may demand.

Every panchayat of five adult men or women being villagers or village-minded shall form a unit.

Two such contiguous panchayats shall form a working party under a leader elected from among themselves.

When there are one hundred such panchayats, the fifty first-grade leaders shall elect from among themselves a second-grade leader and so on, the first-grade leaders meanwhile working under the second-grade leader. Parallel groups of two hundred panchayats shall continue to be formed till they cover the whole of India, each succeeding group of panchayats electing a second-grade leader after the manner of the first. All second-grade leaders shall serve jointly for the whole of India and severally for their respective areas. The second-grade leaders may elect, whenever they deem necessary, from among themselves a chief who will, during pleasure, regulate and command all the groups.

(As the final formation of provinces or districts is still in a state of flux, no attempt has been made to divide this group of servants into provincial or district councils and jurisdiction over the whole of India has been vested in the group or groups that may have been formed at any given time. It should be noted that this body of servants derive their authority or power from service ungrudgingly and wisely done to their master, the whole of India.)

1 Every worker shall be a habitual wearer of khadi made from self-spun yarn or certified by the A.I.S.A. and must be a teetotaller. If a Hindu, he must have abjured untouchability in any shape or form in his own person or in his family and must be a believer in the ideal of inter-communal unity, equal respect and regard for all religions and equal-ity of opportunity and status for all irrespective of race, creed or sex.

2 He shall come in personal contact with every villager within his jurisdiction.

3 He shall enrol and train workers from amongst the villagers and keep a register of all these.

4 He shall keep a record of his work from day to day.

5 He shall organise the villages so as to make them self-contained and self-supporting through their agriculture and handicrafts.

6 He shall educate the village folk in sanitation and hygiene and take all measures for prevention of ill health and disease among them.

7 He shall organise the education of the village folk from birth to death along the lines of Nayee Talim, in accordance with the policy laid down by the Hindustani Talimi Sangh.

8 He shall see that those whose names are missing on the statutory voters' roll are duly entered therein.

9 He shall encourage those who have not yet acquired the legal qualification, to acquire it for getting the right of franchise.

10 For the above purposes and others to be added from time to time, he shall train and fit himself in accordance with the rules laid down by the Sangh for the due performance of duty.

The Sangh shall affiliate the following autonomous bodies:

A.I.S.A.
A.I.V.I.A.
Hindustani Talimi Sangh
Harijan Sevak Sangh
Goseva Sangh

FINANCE

The Sangh shall raise finances for the fulfilment of its mission from among the villagers and others, special stress being laid on collection of poor man's pice.

M. K. G.

(Source: *CW* 90: 526–8)

Bibliography

*

Anthony, P. D., 1983. *John Ruskin's Labour: A Study of Ruskin's Social Theory*, Cambridge.

Aurobindo, Sri, 1972. *Bande Mataram: Early Writngs I*, Pondicherry.

1950. *Essays on the Gita*, New York.

Balfour, Lady Betty, 1899. *The History of Lord Lytton's Indian Administration, 1876–1880*, London.

Barker, Ernest, 1949. 'Gandhi, a bridge and reconciler', in *Mahatma Gandhi*, S. Radhakrishnan (ed.), London.

Berg, Maxine, 1980. *The Machinery Question and the Making of Political Economy 1815–1848*, Cambridge.

Birla, G. D., 1953. *In the Shadow of the Mahatma*, Bombay.

Blavatsky, H. P., 1891. 'Civilization, the death of art and beauty', *Lucifer*, ii, pp. 177–86.

Blount, Godfrey, 1903. *A New Crusade: An Appeal*, London.

Bondurant, Joan, 1965. *Conquest of Violence: The Gandhian Philosophy of Conflict*, Berkeley, CA.

Bose, Nirmal Kumar, 1962. *Studies in Gandhism*, Calcutta.

1974. *My Days With Gandhi*, Calcutta.

Brock, Peter, 1972. *Pacifism in Europe to 1914*, Princeton, NJ.

Brown, Judith, 1972. *Gandhi's Rise to Power: Indian Politics 1915–1922*, Cambridge.

1977. *Gandhi and Civil Disobedience: The Mahatma In Indian Politics 1928–34*, Cambridge.

1989. *Gandhi: Prisoner of Hope*, New Haven, CT.

Buber, Martin, 1939. *Two Letters to Gandhi*, Jerusalem.

Carlyle, Thomas, 1907. *On Heroes, Hero-Worship and the Heroic in History*, Boston.

Carpenter, Edward, 1897. *Civilization: Its Cause and Cure and Other Essays*, London.

Carter, April, 1995. *Mahatma Gandhi: A Selected Bibliography* (Bibliographies of World Leaders, no. 2), Westport, CT.

Catlin, George, 1950. *In the Path of Mahatma Gandhi*, Chicago.

Chatfield, Charles, 1976. *The Americanization of Gandhi: Images of the Mahatma*, New York.

Chatterjee, Margaret, 1983. *Gandhi's Religious Thought*, London.

1992. *Gandhi and His Jewish Friends*, London.

Chatterjee, Partha, 1986. *Nationalist Thought and the Colonial World*, London.

Copley, A., 1987. *Gandhi: Against the Tide*, Oxford.

Dalton, Dennis, 1993. *Mahatma Gandhi: Non-Violent Power in Action*, New York.

Desai, Mahadev, 1968–76. *Day to Day With Gandhi*, 9 vols., Varanasi.

Devanesan, C. D. S., 1969. *The Making of the Mahatma*, New Delhi.

Doke, Joseph, 1909. *An Indian Patriot in South Africa*, London.

Dutt, R. C, 1902. *The Economic History of India under Early British Rule, from the Rise of the British Power in 1757 to the Accession of Queen Victoria in 1837*, vol. I, London.

    1904. *The Economic History of India in the Victorian Age, from the Accession of Queen Victoria in 1837 to the Commencement of the Twentieth Century*, vol. II, London.

Erikson, Erik, 1969. *Gandhi's Truth: On the Origins of Militant Nonviolence*, New York.

Fischer, Louis, 1951. *The Life of Mahatma Gandhi*, London.

Forster, E. M., 1949. 'Mahatma Gandhi', in *Mahatma Gandhi*, S. Radhakrishnan (ed.), London.

Fox, Richard G. 1989. *Gandhian Utopia: Experiments with Culture*, Boston.

Frank, G., 1925. 'Industrial counter-revolution: Gandhi or Ford its prophets?', *Century*, 109, pp. 568–72, New York.

Gandhi, M. K., 1909–46. *Gandhi-Kallenbach Correspondence, 1909–1946*, 4 vols., Nehru Memorial Museum and Library, New Delhi.

    1958–94. *The Collected Works of Mahatma Gandhi*, 100 vols., New Delhi.

Gandhi, Prabhudas, 1957. *My Childhood with Gandhi*, Ahmedabad.

Gandhi, Rajmohan, 1995. *The Good Boatman: A Portrait of Gandhi*, New Delhi.

Ganguli, B. N., 1973. *Gandhi's Social Philosophy: Perspective and Relevance*, New York.

Ghosh, Sudhir, 1967. *Gandhi's Emissary*, London.

Gokhale, G. K., 1908. *The Speeches of the Honourable Mr. G. K. Gokhale, CLE.*, Madras.

Green, Martin, 1979. *The Challenge of the Mahatmas*, New York.

    1983. *Tolstoy and Gandhi: Men of Peace*, New York.

    1986. *The Origins of Nonviolence: Tolstoy and Gandhi in Their Historical Setting*, University Park, MD.

    1993. *Gandhi: Voice of a New Age Revolution*, New York.

Hay, Stephen N., 1969. 'Jain influences on Gandhi's early thought', in *South Asia Series*, University of California, Berkeley, CA.

Heard, Gerald, 1938. 'A great natural phenomenon: the vision of a new order', *The Aryan Path*, IX, pp. 450–2.

    1949. 'The hour and the man', in *Mahatma Gandhi*, S. Radhakrishnan (ed.), London.

Hobbes, Thomas, 1952. *Hobbe's Leviathan*, Oxford.

Hunt, James, 1978. *Gandhi in London*, New Delhi.

1986. *Gandhi and the Nonconformists: Encounters in South Africa*, New Delhi.

Huttenback, Robert Arthur, 1971. *Gandhi in South Africa*, Ithaca, NY.

Huxley, Thomas, 1893. *Science and Education*, London.

Iyer, Raghavan, 1983. *The Moral and Political Thought of Mahatma Gandhi*, London.

(ed.), 1986-7. *The Moral and Political Writings of Mahatma Gandhi*, 3 vols., Oxford.

Kapur, Sudarshan, 1992. *Raising Up a Prophet: The African-American Encounter with Gandhi*, Boston.

Karanjia, R. K., 1960. *The Mind of Mr Nehru*, London.

Keer, Dhananjay, 1966. *Veer Savarkar*, 2nd edn, Bombay.

1973. *Mahatma Gandhi: Political Saint and Unarmed Prophet*, Bombay.

Ker, James Campbell, 1917. *Political Trouble in India: 1907-1917*, Calcutta.

Khanna, Suman, 1985. *Gandhi and the Good Life*, New Delhi.

Kingsford, Anna, 1881. *The Perfect Way in Diet*, London.

Lanza del Vasto, Joseph Jean, 1972. *Return to the Sources*, Jean Sidgwick (tr.), New York.

1974. *Gandhi to Vioba: The New Pilgrimage*, Philip Leon (tr.), New York.

Maine, Henry Sumner, 1876. *Village Communities in the East and West*, London.

Maitland, Edward and Kingsford, Anna, 1881. *The Perfect Way or The Finding of Christ*, London.

Majumdar, R. C. 1975. *History of the Freedom Movement in India*, vol. 2, Calcutta.

Mashruwala, K. G., 1951. *Gandhi and Marx*, Ahmedabad.

1971. *Towards a Sarvodaya Order*, Ahmedabad.

1983. *In Quest of Truth and Humanity*, Ahmedabad.

Maude, Aylmer, 1930. 'Gandhi and Tolstoy', *Contemporary Review*, 137, pp. 701-5.

Maududi, Sayyid Abul Ala, 1977. *Jihad in Islam*, Damascus.

1976. *Political Theory of Islam*, Lahore.

Mazzini, Giuseppe, 1907. *Mazzini's Essays*, London.

Mehta, P. J., 1911. *M. K. Gandhi and the South African Question*, Madras.

Mehta, Ved, 1977. *Mahatma Gandhi and His Disciples*, New York.

Merriam, Allen Hayes, 1980. *Gandhi and Jinnah*, Calcutta.

Merton, Thomas (ed.), 1965. *Gandhi on Non-Violence*, New York.

(ed.). 1971. *The Nonviolent Alternative*, New York.

Moon, Penderel (ed.), 1973. *Wavel: The Viceroy's Journal*, London.

1989. *The British Conquest and Dominion of India*, London.

Moulton, Edward, 1985. 'Allan Octavian Hume and the Indian National Congress, a reassessment', *South Asia*, VIII, pp. 5-24.

Murry, John Middleton, 1949. 'The challenge of Gandhi', in *Mahatma Gandhi*, S. Radhakrishnan (ed.), London.

Murthy, Srinivasa (ed.), 1987. *Mahatma Gandhi and Tolstoy: letters*, Long Beach, CA.

Nadwi, Abul Hasan Ali (Ali Miyan), 1982. *Islam and the World*, Lucknow.

Naess, Arne, 1974. *Gandhi and Group Conflict: An Exploration of Satyagraha – Theoretical Background*, Oslo.

Naipaul, V. S., 2008. *A Writer's People: Ways of Looking and Feeling*, New York.

Nair, Sankaran, 1922. *Gandhi and Anarchy*, Madras.

Nanda, B. R., 1958. *Mahatma Gandhi: A Biography*, Delhi.

1974. *Gokhale, Gandhi and the Nehrus*, London.

1977. *Gokhale*, Princeton, New Jersey.

1985. *Gandhi and His Critics*, Delhi.

1989. *Gandhi and Pan-Islamism*, Delhi.

Nandy, Ashis, 1987. *Traditions, Tyranny, and Utopias*, Delhi.

Naoroji, Dadabhai, 1901. *Poverty and Un-British Rule in India*, London.

Nehru, Jawaharlal, 1958. *A Bunch of Old Letters*, London.

Nordau, Max, 1895. *Conventional Lies of Our Civilization* (tr. from the seventh German edn), London.

1906. *Paradoxes* (tr. from the fifth German edn), London.

Panter-Brick, Simone, 1966. *Gandhi Against Machiavelli*, Bombay.

Pantham, Thomas, 1988. 'On modernity, rationality and morality: Habermas and Gandhi', *Indian Journal of Social Science* I, pp. 187–208.

Parekh, Bhikhu, 1989a. *Gandhi's Political Philosophy*, London.

1989b. *Colonialism, Tradition and Reform: An Analysis of Gandhi's Political Discourse*, New Delhi.

Parel, Anthony J., 1969. 'The political symbolism of the cow in India', *Journal of Commonwealth Political Studies*, VII, pp. 179–203.

1991. 'Gandhi's idea of nation in *Hind Swaraj*', *Gandhi Marg*, 13, pp. 261–82.

1993. 'Documentation', *Gandhi Marg*, 15, pp. 240–54.

2006. *Gandhi's Philosophy and the Quest for Harmony*, Cambridge.

2008. 'Gandhi and the emergence of the modern Indian political canon', *The Review of Politics* 70 (2008), 40–63.

Patel, C. N., 1981. *Mahatma Gandhi in His Gujarati Writings*, New Delhi.

Pearson, Drew, 1924. 'Are Gandhi and Ford on the same road?', *Asia*, 24, pp. 948–9.

Penty, Arthur, 1925. 'Gandhi or Ford?', *G. K.'s Weekly*, p. 79.

Philips, C. H., and Pandey, B. N. (eds.), 1962. *The Evolution of India and Pakistan 1858 to 1947: Select Documents*, London.

Polak, Millie Graham, 1931. *Mr. Gandhi: The Man*, London.

Power, Paul (ed.), 1971. *The Meanings of Gandhi*, Hawaii.

Prasad, Nageshwar (ed.), 1985. *Hind Swaraj: A Fresh Look*, New Delhi.

Pyarelal, 1965. *Mahatma Gandhi: The Early Phase*, Ahmedabad.

Radhakrishnan, S. (ed.), 1949. *Mahatma Gandhi: Essays and Reflections on His Life and Work*, London.

Rolland, Romain, 1976. *Romain Rolland and Gandhi Correspondence*, New Delhi.

Rothermund, Dietmar, 1991. *Mahatma Gandhi*, New Delhi.

Rudolph, Lloyd I., 1990. 'Gandhi in the mind of America', in *Conflicting Images*, Nathan Glazer and Sulochana Raghavan Glazer (eds.), Glen Dale, MD.

Rudolph, S. H., and Lloyd I., 1983. *Gandhi: The Traditional Roots of Charisma*, Chicago.

Ruskin, John, 1911. 'A joy for ever', in *The Works of John Ruskin*, London.

  1978. *Unto This Last*, P. M. Yarker (ed.), London and Glasgow.

Savarkar, V. D., 1909. *The Indian War of Independence 1857*, London.

  1923. *Hindutva: Who is a Hindu?*, Delhi.

Seeley, J. R., [1883] 1909. *The Expansion of England*, Boston.

Seshachari, C, 1969. *Gandhi and the American Scene: An Intellectual History and Inquiry*, Bombay.

Sethi, J. D., 1979. *Gandhi Today*, New Delhi.

Sherard, Robert H., 1897. *The White Slaves of England*, London.

Shirer, William L., 1979. *Gandhi: A Memoir*, New York.

Slade, Madeleine (Mira Behn), 1960. *The Spirit's Pilgrimage*, New York.

Spencer, Herbert, 1878. *The Study of Sociology*, London and New York.

  1893. *Principles of Ethics*, vol. 2, London and New York.

Stephen, James Fitzjames, 1883. 'Foundations of the government of India', *The Nineteenth Century*, pp. 541–68.

Stokes, Eric, 1959. *The English Utilitarians and India*, Oxford.

Swann, Maureen, 1985. *Gandhi: The South African Experience*, Johannesburg.

Taylor, Thomas F. 1909. *The Fallacy of Speed*, London.

Tendulkar, D. G., 1951–4. *Mahatma: Life of Mohandas Karamchand Gandhi*, 8 vols., New Delhi.

Thoreau, David Henry, 1982. 'Civil disobedience' [1849], 'Life without principle' [1873], in *The Portable Thoreau*, New York.

Tolstoy, Leo, 1901. *How Shall We Escape?*, Christchurch, Hants.

  1924. *What Is Art?*, Aylmer Maude (tr.), Oxford.

  1935. *The Kingdom of God Is Within You*, Aylmer Maude (tr.), Oxford.

  1952. 'The first step', in *Recollections and Essays*, Aylmer Maude (tr.), Oxford.

  1985. *Diaries*, vol. 2, 1895–1910, R. F. Christian (tr.), New York.

  1987. 'Letter to a Hindoo', in *Mahatma Gandhi and Leo Tolstoy: Letters*, B. Srinivasa Murthy (ed.), Long Beach, CA.

  1990. 'The slavery of our times', in *Government is Violence*, David Stephen (ed.), London.

Tulsidas, 1952. *Ramcharita Manas*, Hanuman Prasad Poddar (ed.), Gorakhpur.

Unnithan, T. K. N., 1956. *Gandhi and Free India*, Groningen.

Varma, Ravindra, 1985. *Gandhi's Theory of Trusteeship: An Essay in Understanding*, Bombay.

Wallace, A. R., 1913. *Social Environment and Moral Progress*, London.

Watson, Francis, 1969. *The Trial of Mr. Gandhi*, London.

Williams, Howard, 1881. *The Ethics of Diet*, London.

Woodcock, George, 1972. *Gandhi*, London.

Yagnik, Indulal, 1943. *Gandhi As I Know Him*, Delhi.

Zaehner, R. C., 1973. *The Bhagavad Gita*, Oxford.

Zimmer, Heinrich, 1963. *Myths and Symbols in Indian Art and Civilisation*, New York.

Index

*

Page numbers in italics indicate notes

193

15301021R00163

Printed in Great Britain
by Amazon